THE SCIENCE OF POLITICS

An Introduction to Hypothesis Formation and Testing

William H. Coogan
Oliver H. Woshinsky
The University of Southern Maine

UNIVERSITY
PRESS OF
AMERICA

LANHAM • NEW YORK • LONDON

Copyright © 1982 by

University Press of America, Inc.

P.O. Box 19101, Washington, D.C. 20036

Library of Congress Cataloging in
Publication Data

Coogan, William H.
    The Science of Politics.

    1. Political Science--Methodology. 2.
Hypothesis. I. Woshinsky, Oliver, H. II
Title.
JA 73.065 1982   320'.01.8   82-40239
ISBN 0-8191-2652-7 (alk. paper)
ISBN 0-8191-2653-5 (pbk. alk. paper)

TABLE OF CONTENTS

INTRODUCTION

This book provides a short, simple, and systematic introduction to the use of the scientific method in the study of politics. It springs directly from several years of practical experience. For a decade we have been trying to teach students in our introductory political science courses at the University of Southern Maine how to study politics scientifically. In this attempt we have run into three problems. First, these students are, for the most part, unacquainted with the scientific method. They are often suspicious, and frequently fearful, of it. We therefore found it necessary to discover how to explain this method in an elementary, interesting and unthreatening manner.

Our second problem was the diversity of students in our courses. Most students were not political science majors. Instead, they were studying theatre or elementary education or nursing. Hence, we continually had to stress the universal relevance of a solid grounding in the scientific approach to learning. We had to show that familiarity with the scientific method was a necessary tool in modern life, not some esoteric gadget of professional political scientists.

Finally, we labored under a major constraint in teaching the scientific method. Only one-third of the course could be devoted to this material. The bulk of the course centered on the substantive findings and major approaches of modern political science. We needed a short introductory text which would cover the key elements of the scientific method without getting bogged down in arcane details. Given our broad general audience, we also hoped to find an easily-readable text which might excite the interest of, or even stimulate our students. Finding no text on the market to satisfy our needs, we found it necessary to write one ourselves.

Three basic principles underlie our work in this book. First, we believe that every college student, regardless of background or interest, can learn how to use the scientific method to study politics. Indeed, we believe it essential that they learn it. The scientific approach lies at the heart of modern civilization. No person, in our view, is truly educated without receiving a solid, systematic introduction to this way of thought. College-level students should be exposed to it early and encouraged to master it.

Second, we believe that no discipline can ever seriously be appreciated by learning only its substantive findings. We are not satisfied merely to tell students what others have discovered. We want to show them how the discoveries were made. And we want them to discover for themselves--with the same techniques used by professionals in the field. Only by using the methods of a discipline can one understand--at the deepest level--what the discipline is all about.

Third, we believe that teaching through a "hands-on" approach
is more creative and stimulating than the simple recitation of
facts and theories. When using the scientific method, students
become involved in a project of their own making. They must develop their own theory; they must discover their own data; they
must pull things together to see what it all means. Rather than
comparing the theories or citing the findings of other scholars,
they are theorizing on their own and finding on their own. True,
not all students delight in this activity. Many, however, become
wrapped up in the process of scientific investigation and discover
the joy of learning independently.

Students who complete this book will have learned how to
carry out an original social science research project from start
to finish. We begin with a general outline of what the scientific
method is. We go on to stress the importance of developing a good
theory as the basis for any valuable research. We then stress that
hypothesis-construction and hypothesis-testing lie at the core of
any science. An entire chapter is devoted to the rules for creating clear, testable hypotheses. Next, we show students how to
gather data to test their hypotheses. We present them with a few
simple but universally-used statistical devices which will help
them see what their data actually show. We suggest ways for them
to summarize their findings. Finally, we teach them how to present
their work in a formal research report which moves smoothly from
theory to hypothesis to hypothesis-testing to conclusion.

We stress two major points throughout the book. First, a good
project depends not on how much data one amasses or on how many
complex statistics one uses, but on the ideas one wishes to examine. The famous aphorism spawned by the computer specialists,
"Garbage in, garbage out," cannot be repeated too often in our
course. Only if one has a good idea from the start will one's project be of any ultimate worth.

To underline this idea, we devote an entire chapter to strategies for developing an interesting, significant theory. And
throughout the book, we return often to this key point: no matter
how conscientious your work on the other sections of the project,
without an intelligent idea underlying it to begin with, its value
is worthless. Our attitude was neatly summarized by James L. Payne,
when he expressed this hope for improved social science research:

> [The] flawed logic [of modern social science] leads
> to a system of expectations and rewards which en-
> courages highly complex measurement procedures and
> discourages simple, more manageable ones. A typical
> description of a job opening today would run like

this:

> Wanted, methodologist. Able to employ advanced techniques and sophisticated measurement designs.

Thus we appear to equate <u>complicated</u> methodology with <u>good</u> methodology. Hopefully the day will come when we see the reverse spirit displayed:

> Wanted, methodologist. Able to answer significant questions without employing advanced techniques or sophisticated measurement designs."[1]

Our primary aim in this work is not to teach "advanced techniques" or "sophisticated measurement designs" but how "to answer significant questions."

To extend this point, our book is not a compendium of statistics. We stress thinking clearly rather than memorizing formulae. With the possible exception of the advanced, graduate-school-oriented social science major, most undergraduates do not need exposure to Kendall's tau, coefficients of multiple determination, or factor analysis. We agree, however, that they do need a few simple statistical devices to help them order and evaluate their data. We present such techniques as gamma, Yule's Q, chi-square, and scattergrams; but those looking for advanced statistical methods will not find them here.

A second emphasis which colors the book is our belief in step-by-step, hands-on learning. We assume students know hardly anything at all about social science research before opening these pages. And we believe that if they learn the basics thoroughly and carefully, they will be much better suited for going on to advanced work in other courses, should they wish. The usual alternative—a hasty and superficial introduction to basic material before moving rapidly into the deep waters of advanced statistics—often leaves the student floundering and resentful, alienated from the scientific method forever.

To illustrate our approach, we spend several pages showing how to calculate the mean and the median, discussing the differences between the two, advising when to use one or the other, and providing exercises for students to practice calculating both statistics. The usual text deals with these "obvious" matters in a paragraph or two. A more serious illustration of our approach is the entire chapter we devote to the "simple" matter of just how to write a hypothesis. We develop at length eight basic rules for writing hypotheses and give students assignments requiring them to

write and recognize correctly-formed hypotheses. Learning to
write "clear, concise, and unambiguous"[2] hypotheses is not a
peripheral matter in science. It lies at the core of the scientific method. Mastering hypothesis-writing is an essential skill.
It is well worth having introductory students spend some time on
this matter. Yet no text we know of goes into the detail we devote to this issue.

     As a final example of our step-by-step, hands-on approach, we
cite one major and unique feature of the book. An entire chapter
is devoted to a lengthy illustration of how one moves from casual
observation to events in the real world of politics to the development of clear, solidly-based hypotheses ready for systematic testing. In Chapter 4, "Observation and Hypothesis-Formation: An Extended Example," we present a news story and ask students to identify hypotheses suggested by it. We then present another news
story and ask students to check on how well the original hypotheses
hold up with the additional data found in the second story. We
continue to present students with new information, so that they are
required to modify or reject some of the original hypotheses.
Finally, we ask the student to run a full-scale test of those hypotheses which are still holding up well after several observations
have been taken.

     The point of the exercise is to give the student some idea of
how researchers work--moving from slender observations to tentative
testings to the amassing of data to the final, full-blown research
project. The exercise has another aim. It gives the student some
familiarity with current political leaders and how to study them
analytically. The data presented to the student center on voting
records of 1980 U.S. Senators. The final test students are asked
to run involves evidence on all 100 Senators. By the time they
have completed the several exercises in this chapter and come to
some rather surprising conclusions, even the most recalcitrant student will find it hard to argue that scientific analysis is not
"relevant" to understanding current political trends.

     This book is aimed at the beginner--the student with little
previous exposure to the scientific method who is being introduced
to the idea that one can study politics analytically and systematically. Hence, it can be used in a variety of settings. It is
designed particularly for introductory political science courses.
But it can be useful in many undergraduate courses beyond the
first-year level. Instructors often want students to be familiar
enough with the scientific approach to carry out serious research
projects; yet they don't wish to spend half of their course teaching
students how to do these projects. And they often can't assume
that their students know what the scientific method is all about.

     Instructors in these circumstances will find our book valuable.
In concise, readable language it describes the research process

from start to finish. Middle-level undergraduate social science majors in such courses as public opinion, Congress or legislative behavior, political participation, elite analysis, policy-making, and political sociology or psychology should be able to handle the book with minimal supervision from the instructor. He could assign the book during the first week or two of the course. He might spend three or four classes reviewing its high points and then assume students will be able to use the book for guidance as they embark on their substantive research projects.

The book, in other words, would give advanced students a quick introduction to the scientific method while allowing them and the instructor to spend most of their time on the substantive matter of the course. For the small number of students in these courses who may previously have been exposed to the scientific method, the book would serve as a review of key concepts and as a reminder of how to proceed.

One final point: we have deliberately written in a clear, straightforward manner. We take our cue from "the little book" of Strunk and White, which pleads for "Clarity, clarity, clarity." "[S]ince writing is communication," they state, "clarity can only be a virtue."[3] We heartily agree. We have tried to write sentences which any college student will immediately comprehend. We have tried to spell out precisely what we mean, rather than hint or suggest or fuzz over. We believe abstruse language is never necessary--even to express complex ideas. We hope, therefore, that students will be able to read our book easily and grasp the key points without pain. Learning should be an enjoyable experience, if possible. By writing simply and clearly, we have tried to enhance whatever enjoyment students will feel as they use this book to master the scientific method.

1.   James L. Payne, Principles of Social Science Measurement (College Station, Texas: Lytton Publishing Company, 1975), p. 151.

2.   These are the requirements for good hypotheses, according to Robert A. Bernstein and James A. Dyer, An Introduction to Political Science Methods (Englewood Cliffs, N.J.: Prentice-Hall, Inc., 1979), p. 10.

3.   William Strunk, Jr., and E. B. White, The Elements of Style (New York: The Macmillan Company, 1959), p. 65.

x

CHAPTER I

THE SCIENTIFIC METHOD: WHAT IT IS AND WHAT IT ISN'T

On November 4, 1980, the American people overwhelmingly elected Ronald Reagan as their President. They did so despite the unpopularity of his party, despite his age in a country which worships youth, and despite his stands against a number of long-standing federal policies strongly favored by a majority of those same American people.

In the late 1970's the Red Brigades, a left-wing terrorist group in Italy, began going about the streets of Rome and Milan shooting prominent political and business leaders in the legs. This practice has come to be known popularly as "kneecapping."

In the early 1970's China dramatically reversed its foreign policy of virulent anti-Americanism and began making overtures of friendship to the United States. That "international imperialist gangster," Richard Nixon, quickly became "the good friend of the Chinese people."

Each of these events, at the time, shocked or surprised casual observers of the world political scene. How about you? Are you often mystified as you scan the morning paper or catch the evening news programs? Why, you may wonder, did these events take place? Can we predict whether similar events will occur again in the future? Or is politics simply a crazy business which the average person will never fully be able to comprehend?

Ultimately, what you are asking is this: can we ever understand, explain, and predict events in the real world of politics? We have written this book to give you an emphatic answer. Yes! If you master the scientific method of analysis and apply it to the study of events which interest you, you will be able to answer questions about the causes, consequences, and likely future occurrence of those events.

What exactly is "the scientific method?" To understand the concept thoroughly, you will have to read the rest of this book (and more). But we can give a brief definition at the outset. It is a method for understanding the real world--the world of facts and objects around us and inside us. It involves three steps. First, the scientist observes events in the physical world. Second, she develops theories to explain those events. And third, she tests those theories to see whether they predict other real-world events which would logically follow if the theories were valid.

Observation, theory-building, testing: these are the core

1

elements of the scientific method. And the reason for using this method? Simple. It helps us comprehend our world. We turn to the scientific method for knowledge and for explanations of how the world works. Ultimately (Jimmy the Greek take note), the scientific method can help us predict how the world is going to work.

The scientific method can be a stern taskmaster. It demands creative insight, logical reasoning, clear thinking, an ability to distinguish cause and effect, and a skill at gathering and evaluating information. Happily, it also teaches these skills. Mastery of the approach does not come automatically. It must be learned. And since it underlies the thought processes of modern humanity, it is essential that you learn what it is and how to use it.

Mastery of the scientific method will improve your ability to think. We believe that this should be a fundamental goal in any college course. It is our objective to help you to do this with this book.

A brief introduction to the scientific method
What, then, is "the scientific method?" Most of us have a hazy notion of what it entails. We have heard of it all our lives. Growing up in an advanced industrial society, we are vaguely aware that the scientific method has generated the technological progress of the last two centuries. We may even know that its principles practically define our modern mentality and set it sharply off from the mind-sets of earlier eras. Yet many citizens in developed countries have never been given an extended, hands-on introduction to the scientific method--particularly as it applies to the social sciences. We hope to do precisely that for you. We want, in the end, to make you intimately familiar with this essential tool of modern civilization.

The scientific method is a way of understanding the empirical world by developing hypotheses about that world and testing those hypotheses in a rigorous manner. But this textbook definition does not take us far. In essence, the scientific method is a process. It is a series of steps which one takes. Once all the steps have been completed, one has gained some knowledge about the physical world. To understand the scientific method, one must understand what each step entails.

The first step involves the observation of some real-world phenomenon. We notice, for instance, that liquids turn to gases when heated, that adolescent girls perform less well than boys at mathematics, or that Republicans vote to spend more money for missile systems than Democrats.

Having made some observations, we then go on to formulate a

2

theory. The theory tries to explain what we have observed. It suggests the causes of these phenomena. For example: molecules expand when heated; girls are taught to dislike mathematics; Republicans are more concerned with a Russian threat than Democrats.

From the theory we go on to develop testable hypotheses which, if the theory is correct, should be supported by the rigorous examination of additional real-world evidence. Let us carry our previous examples further. From them we might derive the following testable hypotheses: water will turn to steam when heated to 212 degrees Fahrenheit at sea-level; there will be fewer female professional mathematicians than male; and Republicans will be less likely than Democrats to support cuts in the national defense budget.*

At the core of the scientific method is the testing of hypotheses. This stage entails three major steps. First, we must operationalize the key terms of each hypothesis. That is, we must state the precise actions we will take to observe, in the real world, the phenomenon that each term in the hypothesis refers to. For example, "professional mathematician" may be defined as "anyone who is a member of the American Mathematics Association." "Republican" may be defined as "every member of the U. S. House of Representatives who is listed as a Republican in the Congressional Directory."

Once we have defined our terms operationally, we must gather the data which will allow us to test our hypotheses. If our operational definitions are clear, we will know automatically what data to gather. For instance, let us take the hypothesis that Republicans are less likely to support defense budget cuts than are Democrats. We have already defined "Republicans" as all Republican Congressmen and will define "Democrats" as all Democratic Congressmen. Let's say that we define "willingness to support defense cuts" as a Yes vote on House Resolution 9375, February 22, 1978 (the bill to cut out funds for the B-1 Bomber). Having operationally defined our key terms, we know precisely what data we need to test our hypothesis. We must simply see how each Republican and

---

*Note that these statements do not meet the rigorous criteria for phrasing hypotheses which we set forth in Chapter 3 below. We wish to avoid technical detail at this introductory stage, but for those purists among our readers, these hypotheses should be phrased in the following manner:
    -Heat of 212 degrees Fahrenheit causes water to gasify.
    -There is a positive correlation between being a male and
      likelihood of becoming a professional mathematician.
    -In the U.S., Republicanism is positively correlated with
      support for increased national defense expenditures.

each Democratic member of the U.S. House of Representatives voted on H.R. 9375 on February 22, 1978.

We now have our facts. They do not, however, speak for themselves. All we have before us at this stage is a long list of 435 names, plus a notation after each name concerning that individual's party affiliation and his or her vote on H.R. 9375. There is no easy way of telling what all this evidence means. What we must now do is to combine, manipulate, and present the data in ways that will make clear whether or not it supports the original hypothesis. For instance, we might state that 78% of Democrats, but only 22% of Republicans, supported cutting out funds for the B-1 Bomber. Or we might state that a gamma correlation of +.84 exists between being a Democrat and supporting elimination of the B-1 Bomber, thus providing strong support for our original hypothesis.* Or we might present tables, graphs, and other visual materials to summarize our evidence. Whatever we do, we must present our data in ways that clearly show whether it supports, or does not support, the hypothesis we are testing.

Having tested our hypotheses, we come to the conclusion of our investigation. We now know how well our original theory has been supported by our evidence. We must now assess our findings in detail, speculate about why the theory did or did not work, point out the relevance of the findings for other major questions in this field, and suggest fruitful avenues for future research. For instance, if we found that Republicans indeed are "tougher" on defense than Democrats, we could speculate that wars would be less likely under Republican rule; our defenses will be stronger and potential enemies will be more fearful of antagonizing us. This line of reasoning leads to an obvious new research hypothesis: wars are more likely to be started under Democratic rather than Republican Presidents.** So, ideally, our original observations lead to a supportable theory, which in turn leads to some interesting speculations, which themselves lead to an important new avenue for research.

---

* Gamma is discussed at length below in Chapter 6. At this point we need note only that gamma scores approaching +1.0 show a very strong relationship between two factors, and any gamma score over +.50 indicates a strong relationship.

** Or to put it formally, "the outbreak of wars involving the U.S. is positively correlated with Democratic control of the Presidency." See below, Chapter 3, for discussion of correct hypothesis-formation.

In short, the scientific method involves continually going from observations to theories and back to observations in a never-ending cycle. The long-term consequence is the enhancement of knowledge. As we test our theories against reality, we gain substantive information about how the world operates. To put it more simply, we _learn_.

To summarize, the scientific method involves five steps:

1. Observation of a phenomenon.
2. Formulation of a theory, based on observations.
3. Development of testable hypotheses, based on theory.
4. Testing of hypotheses:
   a. Operationalization of key terms;
   b. Gathering of data;
   c. Presentation of data.
5. Conclusion (What does it all mean?).

For long-run projects, the steps in the scientific method continue as follows:

6. Modification of original theory, or development of an entirely new theory, based on the research findings.
7. Development of new hypotheses derived from the newly elaborated theory.
8. Testing of those hypotheses.

Steps 6, 7, and 8 correspond to steps 2, 3, and 4. The round of observation, theory-construction, and hypothesis-testing continues indefinitely. Presumably, this process could only come to an end when all observable physical events have been explained --for all intents and purposes, never.

To conclude, the scientific method is not, in theory, difficult to grasp. Indeed, at its core it is simple and elegant. To apply it in practice, however, we need a much more detailed explanation. Going from casual, initial observations to a final, fully-documented research report is a complex process.

What science cannot do

Please do not take us for mad scientists. Neither are we inhuman laboratory technicians in white coats. We recognize that there are many ways of arriving at truth. The scientific method is only one way to do so--one of many. It is not always the proper method to use, even in political "science." But it is frequently an essential tool. The scientific method can tell us whether older people are more likely than younger people to vote. It can tell us what social conditions (literacy, a large middle class) are prerequisites for the development of democracy. It can tell us what the causes of war are. There are some things it can _not_ do, however. It can not tell us whether people of all ages _should_ vote, whether governments _should_ be organized as democracies, or whether nations _should_ avoid war.

To illustrate what the scientific method _can't_ do, let us suppose you are a U.S. Senator. You are trying to make up your mind about how to vote on a Congressional resolution defining life as beginning from the moment of conception. Congress considered this resolution in the spring of 1981. If such a motion were to pass, some Senators hoped, the law might effectively outlaw abortions in the United States, since the Fourteenth Amendment to the Constitution says that no "State (shall) deprive any person of life, liberty or property without due process of law."[1]

The question, of course, is: what is a person? Is it a single-celled fetus containing 48 chromosomes, or does "personhood" begin later? Does it begin when the fetus begins to sense pain—when it suffers from an abortion? That's pretty early. Perhaps a fetus becomes a person when it begins to look like a baby. That's pretty early, too. How about saying that a fetus becomes a person when it's born? That may be too late. Fetuses are capable of surviving outside the womb at 4 1/2 to 5 months. Is the fetus a person then?

Tough questions. Let's consider some related ones. How about a case in which there is serious reason for the mother not wanting to carry the fetus to term? (She's been raped, or the fetus is seriously deformed, or it will endanger her life to go on with the pregnancy.) Whose rights are more compelling: the mother's or the fetus's?

A scientist cannot answer any of these questions. Or rather, he cannot answer them in his capacity as a scientist. He can tell you, Senator, when a fetus is first capable of feeling pain, or when it is capable of surviving outside the womb, but there is no "science" that can tell you when life begins, much less whose rights—the mother's or the fetus's—ought to take precedence in abortion decisions. To answer these questions, we must turn to legal and moral reasoning, or to religious belief.

The inability of science to deal with these matters can be neatly illustrated. A scientist called to testify before a Senate subcommittee on the question of when life begins—a scientist called precisely because of his expressions of sympathy for the "pro-life" movement—became so exasperated by Senator East's unrelenting requests for a definitive statement as to when a fetus becomes a person that he finally burst out, "Senator, you're asking me to argue the unarguable."[2]

Science cannot give us spiritual or legal truths. Nor can it tell us what is just. Science can tell us only about measureable facts and the reasons for those facts. It cannot tell us about values.[3]

Beyond science, legal reasoning, moral reasoning, and religious revelation, there are other means for arriving at truth.

There is the aesthetic mode, for example. One can best comprehend the inspirational ability of political leaders such as Franklin Roosevelt, Winston Churchill, John Kennedy, Adolf Hitler, and Ronald Reagan if one listens to their speeches. One notes the words they choose, their inflection, and the resonance of their voices. One analyzes their bearing—their facial expressions and the way they hold their bodies. One evaluates the image they project to their audiences, the roles they try to carry off. One can, in short, evaluate the performances of these men in terms of the principles of good theatre.

Similarly, if one stands before David's painting of Napoleon crossing the Alps, one is struck by the sense of power, heroism and clarity of vision in the Emperor. On observing the painting, Frenchmen of the early nineteenth century felt a bursting sense of patriotism. It induced a willingness to follow Napoleon anywhere. This was no accident. Jacques Louis David was Napoleon's official court painter—in other words, his chief visual propagandist. He painted Napoleon as if the viewer were looking up at him from the level of his white charger's hoofs. This perspective compensated for Napoleon's unimposing stature. (He was a mere 5'2" tall.) It gave him larger-than-life presence. Napoleon's arm, straining and pointing his sword onward and upward over the Alps, infuses the viewer with a soaring sense of participation in a transcendent cause. The figures in the background never intrude on the centrality of Napoleon. They are painted in foggy obscurity, while Napoleon, himself, is dressed in the primary colors—red, yellow and blue. (This was another historical inaccuracy. In such a flashy uniform, he would have been an easy target for enemy marksmen.) To understand the political power of such visual propaganda, of course, one needs to understand the principles of perspective, composition, and color theory.

Such principles are understood and used by modern political propagandists who employ them in designing the imposing May Day Parades in Red Square, and even in making more prosaic choices on the color of bumper stickers to be used by candidates for the local school board. (Red signifies danger. Blue connotes coldness and conservatism. Green means calm and friendly.)[4]

In summary, there are several ways of understanding reality. The scientific method isn't much help if we're trying to understand the effectiveness of a billboard or a candidate's speech. Nor can it answer value questions. It can, however, provide us with ways of understanding and predicting observable phenomena— that is, phenomena that can be touched, tasted, smelled, heard, or seen. So the scientific method is just one of several methods for arriving at truth. But though it is not the only method, and not always the appropriate method, it is an extremely useful means for comprehending a large part of what goes on in the real world. We shall now explore each step in this process at some length.

Footnotes to Chapter I

1. U.S. Constitution, Amendment XIV, Section 1. Italics added. Note that not all Constitutional scholars would agree on the effect of such a resolution.

2. Another witness, George Ryan, M.D., President of the American College of Obstetricians and Gynecologists, stated it well when he said, "There is no question that a cell is living. But life is one thing and when it should be considered a HUMAN life is not a scientific question. It is philosophical, moral and theological." Quoted by Ann Landers (yes!) in her column of September 8, 1981.

3. Though science cannot prove values to be true or false, it can shed light on some issues involving values. When Congress decides, for example, that we should eliminate poverty in the United States (a decision on values), social scientists can evaluate policies designed to achieve that end. We can examine job training programs, income maintenance programs and welfare programs, then tell political leaders which programs achieve the main goal effectively. Science, in short, can evaluate means--but not ends.

For additional discussion of the fact-value distinction, see M. Margaret Conway and Frank B. Feigert, Political Analysis: An Introduction (Boston: Allyn and Bacon, 1976), pp. 34-38; James Q. Wilson, Thinking About Crime (New York: Basic Books, 1975), Robert A. Dahl, Modern Political Analysis (Englewood Cliffs, N.J.: Prentice-Hall, Inc., 1963 and 1976), pp. 100-107 in the 1963 edition and 12-24 and 128-39 in the 1976 edition; W.T. Jones, The Sciences and the Humanities: Conflict and Reconciliation, (Berkeley: University of California Press, 1965), pp. 175-193; and Otto A. Bird, Cultures in Conflict: An Essay in the Philosophy of the Humanities (South Bend, Ind.: University of Notre Dame Press, 1976), ch. 3 and pp. 126-7.

Those who criticize the idea of a "value-free" science argue that the scientific method rests on, and is loaded with, values. They point out that:

a. The values of an investigator influence his choice of topic;

b. The values of an investigator may influence the way he interprets his data--particularly in the "soft" social sciences;

c. Much scientific investigation takes place in societies which suppress certain avenues of investigation;

d. The method itself is imbued with certain values. These include the preference for truth over falsehood; the belief that the universe is governed by laws based on the principle of causality; the corollary belief that the universe does not operate randomly and chaotically; the preference for precision over vagueness; the belief that the more one understands about the world through generalization, the better; the belief that the proper method for validating a theory is to fail to prove it wrong, rather than to gather evidence to support it (thus building a conservative feature into theory-building aspects of science).

These points are all true. We who use the scientific method must ultimately acknowledge our irrational, "non-scientific" bases for relying on it. It answers interesting questions and appeals to our desire for order, precision, and regularity. Why do we want questions answered in an orderly, precise way? We cannot say. These are irreducible values. They are deep-seated preferences which we cannot explain, any more than Van Gogh could explain why he had to paint. However, the scientific method is no less helpful because it rests on value choices, just as Van Gogh's paintings are no less magnificent because we cannot explain why he undertook them. If the scientific method helps us to achieve our values it is useful. It may not be "objectively" true, it may not be equally valuable to all people everywhere. But it is helpful for us, here, today.

4. See Faber Birren, History of Color in Painting (New York: Reinhold Publishing Corp., 1965), pp. 139-54 (ch. 7, "The Wonders of Perception"), Birren, Light, Color and Environment (New York: Van Nostrand Reinhold Co., 1969), pp. 26-40 (ch. 4, "Psychological Reactions"); and Johannes Itten, The Art of Color (New York: Reinhold Publishing Corp., 1961).

CHAPTER II

OBSERVATION AND THEORY-BUILDING

Focusing on a problem

We have stated that we must begin any project with the observation of real-world phenomena. But first we must decide something—precisely what kind of phenomena are we going to observe? There is no easy answer to this question. Obviously the number of observable events is infinite. We notice an old man tripping on a banana peel in front of the local fire station. Shall we then take up the study of conditions under which old men are likely to trip on banana peels in front of fire stations? We see a soldier in a car failing to signal before making a left turn. Is the investigation of poor driving habits by military personnel something we should explore? Millions of potentially observable events are occurring daily. How do we narrow our focus of inquiry to one topic deserving of intensive investigation?

To begin, objective circumstances help narrow the range of topics we could focus on. Our own life situation has already, in effect, eliminated for each of us a vast range of questions capable of being explored by the scientific method. Our options for research are limited by three facts:

1. Our lack of knowledge. Many questions are ruled out because we simply don't have the expertise to explore them. The phenomenon of anti-matter is no doubt fascinating and important. Most readers of this book would, however, be unable to conduct research on that topic for one obvious reason: lack of sufficient training in advanced physics.

2. Our lack of interest. Other subjects are ruled out because we just have no personal interest in them. Many of us would be unutterably bored by such subjects as the rise of the Ming Dynasty, the quasar phenomenon, or the life cycle of the cockroach. Hence, through lack of interest we automatically rule out a huge number of subjects which are easily capable of being explored through the scientific method, but whose subject matter just doesn't do much for us.

3. Our life circumstances. The situations in which we find ourselves greatly narrow the range of phenomena we can investigate. You may, for instance, be a research chemist in a major corporation, paid to develop new perfumes or to discover new drugs to relieve the pain of arthritis. You may be a consultant for a government agency, hired to examine the efficiency of different welfare systems. Or you may be a student in a political science

course, working at a university whose library has relatively slim holdings in this field. In all these cases the objective conditions of our life radically constrict the number of phenomena which we could realistically expect to examine.

After deleting from possible consideration questions we are incapable of handling, questions which we have no interest in exploring, and questions automatically excluded by our current life circumstances, we are left with a relatively small number of topics for investigation. But "relatively small" is a deceptive term. Even with their focus of interest narrowed, the research chemist, the government consultant, and the political science student have anywhere from a dozen to a hundred projects they could actually undertake. How does one narrow the choice of topics down from this number to one?

Although the question remains difficult, we can suggest a few strategies which may prove helpful.

1. The topic must be interesting to you personally. Let's say that you have narrowed your possible research subjects down to 1) the determinants of voting behavior in rural America and 2) the relation between organized crime and political corruption in major American cities. If you have lived all your life in Plains, Georgia, the first topic might be one you can really sink your teeth into. The second might seem quite distasteful to you. By all means, choose topic number one. Or if you are a New Yorker through and through, the first topic might bore you to tears, while the second might appear fascinating. Don't hesitate to choose topic number two. In other words, pick a subject you care about, one that means something to you. Good research was never done by a bored investigator.

2. Don't pick a subject for which no data exist. Or to put this in a milder form, don't pick a subject for which data exist but are difficult or impossible to obtain.

The point seems obvious, yet students frequently fall into this trap. Let's say you wish to test the hypothesis that paranoid Presidents are more likely to start wars than non-paranoid Presidents. On the surface, this looks like a good subject. It interests you personally (thereby meeting criterion one) and seems like an important question (thereby meeting criterion three --see below). Nevertheless, the project must be discarded. You will simply not be able to test this hypothesis. Why? For one clear reason--no data now exist on the extent of paranoia among American Presidents. The subject has hardly been studied. Those psychological analyses of American Presidents that do exist have produced no consensus among the community of Presidential scholars about the degree (if any) of paranoia in our past leaders. We

12

cannot label past Presidents "paranoid" or "non-paranoid." We cannot rank them on a scale from 1 (non-paranoid) to 10 (very paranoid). We simply have nothing to say about Presidents on this (admittedly important) question. The data we want do not exist. Therefore, we cannot test this hypothesis.

The average student is likely to be affected by a milder version of this problem. Let's say you have developed the hypothesis that "aggressive" Congressmen are more likely to be reelected to the House than "passive" ones. As one measure of aggressiveness you decide to gather data on the use Congressmen make of the Congressional recording studios. These studios help Congressmen make video and radio tapes which can be used for publicity purposes back in their district. The service is cheap. It represents one of many perquisites Congressmen have at their disposal for bolstering their image among constituents and incidentally helping their reelection chances. Aggressive Congressmen, you reason, would be more likely to use this device than passive ones.

So far, you are on excellent ground. The topic seems to meet all possible criteria. It represents an interesting and important question. As a campus politician, you yourself are personally intrigued by it, since you have your own plans to run for Congress some day. And finally, you know that the data exist. You read an article about this point. It stated that the amount of money each Congressman spends on the House recording studios can be discovered in a publication entitled Quarterly Report of the Clerk of the U.S. House of Representatives.

There's just one little hitch. You are attending a small Methodist college in northwestern Iowa and your library barely has funds to subscribe to Time Magazine. It has never purchased such esoteric material as the above-mentioned House document. In short, the data are still unobtainable, as far as you are concerned.

The point of all this is simple. It is crucial at the outset of any project to make certain that the data you need to explore your topic, to test your hypothesis, are easily available to you. Ideally, the material should exist in your local college library. Occasionally, your professor can lend you material. And sometimes you can get data through your own efforts--travel to a nearby library, writing away for material, conducting your own poll, etc. But make sure early that the data you want do exist and can be obtained well before the due date for any assignment.

One way to check on the availability of evidence is to talk with your instructor about possible projects. Her job is to steer you away from those which cannot be done. Another way to see if the information you need exists is to drop in to the library and browse through major data collections. In Chapter 5 we discuss basic data sources held by most libraries. Spend some time becoming familiar with these sources. A knowledge of these key collections will provide you with many ideas for research projects, as well as assure you about the availability of the necessary data. We cannot overstress the need for this preliminary investigation. You cannot undertake a project for which no data exist. And you cannot know whether the data exist until you have actually come across them yourself. This preliminary stage of investigation is crucial for the success of the entire project.

3. Choose a topic that is interesting to a broad audience. This point differs substantially from our earlier point that the topic must interest you personally. Now we are saying that it must also seem important to others. You may, for reasons of your own, be terribly excited about the relationship between sexual attractiveness and belly-button lint. Most professors would, nevertheless, give you little encouragement to conduct research on this subject. They would probably tell you that the hypothesis lacked any "theoretically interesting ramifications." We are going to take some time to explain precisely what they mean by this phrase, since "choosing an interesting question" is the most important step in any research project. The point may seem obvious, but in practice the vast majority of poor student papers (and failed professional research) falters on this key issue.

An interesting question, to begin, is one that leads beyond the basic facts under investigation. Let's say you actually discover that men who are attractive to women have a greater amount of normal belly-button lint than men unattractive to women. So what? Does this help us understand anything else about society? About sex drives? About patterns of interaction between the sexes? Precisely what difference does it make now that we have uncovered this information? What we are suggesting by these questions is this: the topic of the research is trivial and, even though data can be gathered and a hypothesis tested on the subject, no serious thinker cares about what the findings might be or believes that they would add one iota of useful information to our sum of knowledge about human behavior.

Although this example may seem ridiculous, students (and professors) are continually coming up with trivial, noninteresting hypotheses, which they then set about testing. An unfortunate effort goes something like this:

"I was told to develop a hypothesis from my observations. In my dorm I have noticed that English majors are always working away in the library, but Theater majors are constantly over at Joe's Bar getting drunk. From this observation I derive the following hypothesis:

14

Theater majors drink more beer than English majors."

One is left with the feeling that this is not quite what research should be about. Yet it is hard to explain precisely why. Let us look at a more extended example to suggest what is wrong with the hypotheses on belly-button lint and beer-drinking.

Let's say that you live in a small town which contains six important families: the Smiths, the Whartons, the Zissises, the Chandlers, the Anthonys and the Carters. Over the years you have casually observed that members of the Smith, Wharton, and Zissis families seem to take radical political positions on most issues, while members of the Chandler, Anthony and Carter families generally take conservative positions. Let's say you conduct extensive interviews with all living members of these families, examine all available evidence on past political participation by other members of these families for the past five decades, and, sure enough, come up with this finding: people in East Succotash named Smith, Wharton, and Zissis are likely to be radical in their political behavior; people named Chandler, Anthony, and Carter are likely to be conservative. When you publish these results, what general reaction do you expect to occur?

We can speculate that it would be underwhelming, to say the least. Most people would have no interest in your results. The research provokes more questions (and yawns) than it answers. Most people would have not the slightest interest in your results. For those who bothered to pay any attention at all, the most likely response would be, "So what?" And some might even be angered at the waste of money exemplified by this "typical" scientific project. One more example of cash being spent to discover the obvious or the unimportant, they would say. Senator Proxmire might even be called upon to hand your study the "Golden Fleece of the Month" award--for the most ridiculous waste of taxpayers' money during the past 30 days.

What do these reactions imply? They suggest that your findings are simply not very interesting. They are such low-level generalizations, so unrelated to any of the broader questions that intrigue thinkers, scholars, and political participants, and so unlikely to lead to any significant additional discoveries in this field that they leave us cold. So, we might say, out of the four billion members of the human species, we now know something about the political behavior of six nonpowerful families in one unimportant, small, rural town. Why is this worth knowing? What benefits have we gained from our study? How has our knowledge of human social and political behavior been enhanced?

It would appear, at first sight, that no positive answer can be given to these questions. Our findings appear to have no

15

broad significance. They lead nowhere. They are, in short, uninteresting. Can there be any justification for having conducted
such a study? There can, but only if one important condition is
fulfilled. The findings must be placed in some kind of theoretical context. That is, we must have some general idea as to why
the findings occurred, or else postulate that some other phenomenon can be explained as a result of these findings. In short,
we want to know the reasons why our observed phenomenon took place
and we want to know what additional effects this phenomenon itself
brings about. Only by examining cause and effect relationships
do we give significance to any bare set of facts.

This point cannot be exaggerated. No single finding is important in and of itself. Even the statement, "Ronald Reagan has
just been shot by a lone gunman," would be meaningless to a visi-
tor from Mars or to a Rip Van Winkle just awakening from a 50-year
sleep. This fact is meaningful only because all of us instantly
have a context within which to place it. We have some ideas as to
why he was shot (powerful people are often the target of disgrun-
tled social marginals), and we have some idea of the likely consequences of his being shot (disruption of government policy-making,
national outrage, public displays of support and sympathy, etc.).
In other words, a fact is important only to the extent that some
theory tells us why it is important—what factors caused it to
come about or what effects it is likely to have on other events
in the real world.

Developing a theory

A theory is an attempt to explain facts. Let's return to the
example of voting in East Succotash. By itself the finding is
either forgettable or confusing. "Why do people vote in the manner you have observed?" You might answer, "I dunno. They just do.
That's enough, isn't it?" This response negates the utility of
your study. It evades an explanation for your findings. Without
a theory to put them in perspective they are eminently forgettable.
No wonder your parents ask themselves why they are spending all
their hard-earned money on your education!

O.K., you say to yourself, I know I've got to have a theory.
So you postulate some explanation out of the blue. Perhaps, you
say, the Chandlers, the Anthonys, and the Carters vote conserva-
tively because they differ in ethnic origins from the Smiths, the
Whartons, and the Zissises. But this response doesn't take us far.
It appears that all the families have identical ethnic origins, except perhaps the Zissises. You are grasping at straws. If you
are to make anything of these findings, you need a more solid theoretical base than you have yet provided.

Suppose that we have done more than simply observe the voting

16

behavior of these six particular families. We have, in addition, noticed an intriguing pattern of behavior in this town. Schools there require children to be seated alphabetically. Children whose names begin with A, B, and C sit near the front of the room, and children whose names begin with W, X, Y, and Z sit at the rear. We observe also that children are allowed outside for recess in alphabetical groups--beginning with the A's and ending with the Z's. They further go to lunch in the same order: A's first, Z's last. Indeed, for all occasions--presenting awards, passing out tickets for school events, participating in trips to museums, concerts, and so forth--the same order is rigidly followed.

Under these conditions how might the Z's begin to think and behave? First, of course, they might develop resentment about their situation. Why are they always last in line for the goodies? Life is unfair! The teachers are unfair! The school system is unfair! The government that allows this is unfair!

Second, since they are always sitting at the back of the room, they would have more opportunities to misbehave and to express their resentment. It is physically easier for students at the rear to pass notes, converse, throw spitballs, and cheat on tests than it is for students at the front. And what would the teachers think about these recalcitrant Whartons and Smiths? Why, naturally they are unmanageable and ineducable! For the students perceiving these negative expectations, each occasion on which they are called upon to answer a question becomes an unpleasant experience, during which they either confirm their teacher's expectations or surprise him--if their answer is correct--by an exception to their "normal" behavior.

Since the teachers provide no real support for the academic achievements of students at the end of the alphabet, these students will in fact begin to perform poorly. So we have the classic vicious circle. An expectation on the part of the teacher that certain students are incorrigible and ineducable leads to incorrigible behavior and poor academic performance by these students, which in turn confirms the teacher's expectations.

Over the years these students will gravitate toward the lower part of their class. Their grades will be too low for many of them to enter college. Their employment prospects will be dimmer than those of the lucky A, B, and C students, who graduate from college and go on to high-paying and interesting jobs.

What we have produced, then, is an underclass of people who are condemned to poor jobs; who are resentful because everyone else has always had first crack at life's rewards; and who have become alienated from the social and political system which has always treated them poorly. How would we expect them to vote?

For candidates representing "the establishment" or for those who give voice to their alienation (i.e., radicals)? The answer is clear.

Furthermore, we suspect that what we have learned has some important implications. We might conclude that societies run on a strictly alphabetical basis are more unstable than others: they create a permanent group of alienated, disaffected citizens who are susceptible to radical appeals to overthrow the system. We might also conclude that any purposefully-created social inequality creates the potential for political unrest. Any alienated group, after all, is likely to feel angry at its status and may wish to express its anger at the society which created its alienation in the first place.

We have gone, then, from a seemingly insignificant—and exceedingly dull-finding to one of the most important questions in the realm of politics: what are the causes of political instability?

Now our original hypothesis—that Zississes, Whartons, and Smiths are more radical than Anthonys, Chandlers, and Carters—assumes some significance. We know the causes for the phenomenon that we have observed, and we have an idea of how important our findings are. In short, we have put the hypothesis in a theoretical context. We have, as you are aware, picked a farfetched example, but we did so purposely to illustrate our point. Any fact can become significant if placed in context by a well-reasoned theory.

We hasten to add that merely placing a finding within a theoretical context does not automatically make it interesting and significant. Suppose, for example, we were to hypothesize that Republicans eat slightly more meat per week than do Democrats. We could probably construct a theoretical context for this notion. (Republicans have slightly higher incomes than Democrats and can therefore afford more expensive food.) And we might test the hypothesis and find that—yes—Republicans consume an average of 3.89 pounds of meat per week compared to 3.82 for Democrats. But is such a finding important? Is it worth your time doing research on? Can't you find something better for a term paper?

In choosing a topic for research, then, you must not only focus on one with theoretical implications. You must choose one with "important" or "significant" implications. Researchers call this the exploration of an "interesting question." Unfortunately, there are no easy guidelines for determining what research is "worth doing" and what isn't. Your ability to choose an interesting question is at least partly a function of your own imagination and interpretive skills. (No one thought the question of why

18

apples fall out of trees was important until Newton thought about it and developed an answer that stood at the heart of scientific knowledge for the next three centuries.)

There is no textbook answer to help you choose a topic. Nevertheless, the following suggestions may be useful as you search for questions worth pursuing.

1. Your hypothesis should have broad ramifications. That is, it should have importance beyond itself. Finding that "Republicans eat a little more meat than do Democrats" is just an isolated fact. Does it help explain anything about politics anywhere? We suspect it does not. On the other hand, the finding that "alphabetical discrimination causes alienation" has importance for school administrators, for school boards, for parents, for economists, and perhaps for state legislators.

2. A hypothesis is probably interesting if it passes a rough rule of thumb that we call "the-average-man-in-the-street reaction." Imagine how your family would react if you went home and gave them a 30-second sketch of your research project. You might tell them: "Today I discovered that poor people tend to own few yachts;" or "My research shows that Social Welfare majors living at home and coming from small families buy 2.57392 more ounces of toothpaste each year than Criminal Justice majors living on campus and coming from large families;" or "People who are in good health are more likely to vote than people in hospitals." Their reaction would probably vary from "Huh???" to "So what?" to "You mean that's the sort of nonsense you're learning in school? What's education coming to these days?"

On the other hand, suppose you tell them: "Today I learned through my research that there is a direct relationship between a person's likelihood of committing violent crimes and his belief that he will be punished for those crimes. The more certain people are that they will be punished, the less likely they are to commit crimes. If criminals are swiftly caught and swiftly punished, crime will diminish. This means that the way to reduce crime is not by trying to abolish poverty or by trying to rehabilitate criminals, but by increasing the number of police on the street, speeding up court procedures, and making jail sentences mandatory for certain crimes."

In this case, the average, reasonably intelligent, non-student will probably find your research interesting, even stimulating. The "Ho hum" or "So what?" reactions are now much less likely.

Note that the above "findings" are purely hypothetical. The "facts" are hotly disputed by researchers in this field. Nevertheless, the hypothesis is clearly interesting and important. It

19

does have broad implications. The average person can understand why it is worth pursuing. Hence, the hypothesis is a strong candidate for classification as "an interesting question." It appears important enough to justify an in-depth research project.

3. Almost by definition, a hypothesis is interesting and worth pursuing if it is one that scholars in the field think, talk and write about a lot. In this regard the student, as a beginner, must make a blind leap of faith. Suppose you are taking a course in political science. You should assume, at this stage in your studies, that political scientists are studying interesting topics. If many of them have conducted research on a given subject, then it probably is, in fact, a significant area for research. (If you later go on to more advanced work in political science, you may reach a point at which you can disagree with other scholars about what is interesting; or you may be able, on your own, to discover questions that are interesting; but at this stage the best thing is to accept established wisdom in the discipline.)

It is usually quite acceptable, then, to conduct research on any topic you read about in any of your social science courses. (The exception to this rule is obvious: if your instructor or your textbook author mentions a topic only to suggest its worthlessness, better forget it.) You may even engage in a "replication" of past studies. That is, you may pursue the same topic and use the same methods (even the same poll questions) as other social scientists. If you choose to do a replication, however, you must: a) give credit to the person whose work you are trying to duplicate; and b) apply his methods to new data which you yourself have gathered.

A corollary of this third point is that readings in your courses can suggest research topics. A basic text in any field summarizes or alludes to dozens of studies conducted by other scholars. Any one of these studies could form the basis for your own research project. Careful review of course readings, then, could help you discover a good topic. Following up footnote or bibliographic references can also lead to project ideas. Or you may simply head to the library and explore, among the vast array of studies already done by others, for a topic which strikes you as especially fascinating.

Recapitulation

Let's summarize. There are four steps involved in formulating a problem.

1. You must find a problem that is interesting and important. It should have broad ramifications and should pass the "man in

the street" test.

2. You must show that you are aware of the findings of others who have written about this problem. You should tell what questions remain unanswered by previous research.

3. You must develop a theory explaining why you think your hypothesis will be supported by actual evidence. Remember, you are trying to go beyond merely establishing that a relationship exists between two phenomena (seating order in school and later voting behavior, for example). You are also trying to explain why the relationship exists.

4. You must state your hypothesis or hypotheses. The proper way to express hypotheses will be discussed in the next chapter. For now, let's just say that a hypothesis is a statement expressing the relationship between two phenomena--education and political participation, for example, or age and beauty. Hypothetical statements could be phrased as follows:

> Higher education causes above-average levels of
> political participation.
>
> or
>
> Age is negatively correlated with beauty.

Focusing on a problem and developing a theory: an example

Let's see how, in practice, a student might go about developing some interesting hypotheses. She might begin her paper in the following manner.

[Step 1: finding an important problem.]
Politics, when you come to think of it, is not that lucrative. True, Congressmen earn more than $65,000 a year. But these people are highly educated and skilled at presenting themselves to large groups. They could earn much more as insurance salesmen or lawyers than they do in politics. In addition, the typical politician puts in long hours during the day, then attends lots of meetings at night. He has virtually no free time. Compared to other jobs a Congressman could have, that of politician seems characterized by long hours and relatively low pay.

Why, then, do people run for public office? I believe that a variety of personal needs lead people into professional activities of all sorts. Some of these needs are so pronounced for some individuals that they can be satisfied only in the

field of politics--a field that most people with
their capabilities avoid because the demands are
high, the financial rewards insubstantial, and the
future uncertain.

I further suspect that there are several types
of personalities who participate in politics. Each
of these types is characterized by the possession
of a particularly strong incentive, or drive, that
compels him or her to run for public office. It is
significant that differing drives exist. This fact
helps explain why politicians behave differently
from each other in similar circumstances.

If we can understand the connections between a
politician's emotional incentives and his actions,
we can make predictions about how he will behave when
he is in office. This psychological information
could serve as a better guide to a politician's
behavior than the promises he makes in an election
campaign. After all, President Johnson promised
that he wouldn't send Americans to fight in
Vietnam, President Nixon promised to restore
integrity to government, and President Reagan
promised a balanced federal budget.

These paragraphs illustrate Step 1. That is, they focus on
an interesting problem with broad ramifications. What is it that
compels people to engage in political activity? The student
argues for some deep-seated emotional cause, since politics is
demanding and doesn't provide the objective rewards most people
look for in their jobs. The possible ramifications of this
approach are broad. The student suggests that there are
different kinds of politician, based on differing psychological
needs. Knowing what need a politician has, therefore, might help
predict how he will behave. And knowing his motivation could also
help us control that behavior.

Yes, the research proposal has significant implications. It
also passes the "man-in-the-street" test. In the first sentence
the student challenges commonly-held opinions and then goes on to
raise some interesting questions about the psychological
underpinnings of political behavior.

Let us follow the student on to step 2:

[Step 2: summarizing the literature.]
Several studies of incentives have been conducted
over the past few years.[1] They have discovered a
limited number of motivational types. Particularly

significant are the status type and the program type.
Both are common to most political settings, yet differ
dramatically in motive and behavior.

The status type is preoccupied with social standing,
prestige and fame. He is in politics to be somebody, to
make a name for himself, or even to go down in history.
Status participants are concerned with their "image",
with making a good impression. They pay careful attention to the tactics of personal advancement, to publicity
techniques, to the development of public speaking skills.

The program type is a horse of a different color. He
actually enjoys working on specific policy problems.
While the status type will say little about specific policies, rarely going beyond popular cliches, the program
type plunges into detailed (and often boring) analyses
of specific problems. The program participant is relatively uninterested in the mechanics of getting elected
and is not a particularly astute manipulator of other
individuals--or of large groups, such as voters.

So far, incentive analysis has focused on attempts
to explain why people engage in political activity.
There has been relatively little effort made to see
whether these incentives can predict the behavior of
officials once they have been elected.

---

1. The major studies of incentives include: James L.
Payne, Patterns of Conflict in Colombia (New Haven: Yale
University Press, 1968); Payne, Incentive Theory and Pol-
itical Process: Motivation and Leadership in the Domini-
can Republic; (Lexington, Mass.: D.C. Heath and Company,
Lexington Books, 1972); Oliver H. Woshinsky, The French
Deputy: Incentives and Behavior in the National Assembly
(Lexington, Mass.: D.C. Heath and Company, Lexington
Books, 1973); Payne and Woshinsky, "Incentives for Political Participation," World Politics 24 (July, 1972):
518-46; Payne, "Show Horses and Work Horses in the U.S.
House of Representatives," Polity 12 (Spring, 1980):
428-56; and Payne, "The Personal Electoral Advantage
of House Incumbents, 1936-1976," American Politics Quarterly 8 (October, 1980): 465-82. For other works which
suggest the importance of studying leaders' emotional
needs, see Harold Lasswell, Psychopathology and Politics
(Chicago: University of Chicago Press, 1930); James
D. Barber, The Lawmakers: Recruitment and Adaptation
to Legislative Life (New Haven: Yale University Press,

1965); Barber, <u>The Presidential Character: Predicting Performance in the White House</u> (Englewood Cliffs, N.J.: Prentice-Hall, Inc., 1972); and Michael Maccoby, <u>The Gamesman: The New Corporate Leaders</u> (New York: Simon and Schuster, 1976).

The preceding paragraphs follow Step 2. They briefly summarize the findings of scholars who have worked on this topic. In addition, they describe the research question (the reasons for participating in politics) and tell what issues have been raised by past studies (for example, can incentives predict post-electoral behavior?).

The paper goes on:

[Step 3: building a theory.]
The characteristics of these two types lead me to assume that their political behavior will differ dramatically. The status type will surely spend more of his time making public speeches (to become better known), while the program type will spend his time reading, studying, speaking with experts, and working out solutions to policy problems with like-minded specialists in quiet committee rooms. As a result of these different routines, the status type is likely to get more publicity than the program type and will indeed become better known.

Here is Step 3: the building of a theory. The student gives her <u>reasons</u> for believing that the status type will behave one way, while the program type will behave in another. We cannot overstress the importance of this stage in the research paper. <u>You must state, clearly and logically, the reasons why you believe your hypotheses will be supported by your data</u>. This is the point at which you are setting forth the theory that either makes your work interesting and convincing, or fails to do so. The most important thing you can do, at this early stage in your paper, is to explain the factors which justify, in your opinion, the hypotheses which you are about to test.

Finally, to conclude the introductory section from this student's paper:

[Step 4: stating the hypotheses.]
These speculations lead to the following hypotheses, which I plan to test in this paper:
]. The status incentive causes publicity-seeking behavior.
2. The program incentive causes problem-solving behavior.
3. The status incentive is correlated with the

achievement of broad name-recognition.
4. The program incentive is negatively correlated
   with the achievement of broad name-recognition.

Here the student completes Step 4: the formal statement of a
series of hypotheses that emerge from her theory. Now she will go
on to test these hypotheses in the remaining sections of the paper.

Conceptualization, as this first section of a research paper
may be labeled, is the most difficult step in the use of the scientific method. The world "out there" is dizzyingly complex. It is
difficult to narrow your thinking down to one small aspect of it
and formalize the questions you want to ask. This process re-
quires clear-headed rationality. Skill in using it can only be developed through practice.

How do you go about developing this skill? The best way is
to look carefully at some event--the most recent Congressional
elections, for example, the development of a new, peaceful relationship between historic enemies Egypt and Israel during the late
]970's, or the attempt on President Reagan's life in April,]981--
and ask yourself two questions. First, what did I learn from this
event? And second, what is the explanation for what I have observed?

Let's think a bit about the assassination attempt. Why did
John Hinckley, Jr., fire the shots? Was he trying to stop President Reagan from cutting back on programs aiding the poor, perhaps,
or protesting the Administration's policy in El Salvador? No. He
pulled the trigger in order to get a famous actress to notice him
and to fall in love with him, for God's sake! There was apparently no political motivation at all. That's striking. That's
one important thing I learned from the event.

Now, let's move on to the second question--what is the explanation for what I observed? How could anyone imagine that shooting a President would accomplish the goals that Hinckley set? (By
the way, he was not completely unsuccessful. Jody Foster now
knows his name.) What personality configurations allowed him to
pull the trigger? John Hinckley was apparently a very lonely man
who was socially so inept that he sabotaged his own attempts to
form human contacts. He dropped out of school, started to wander
around the country, stopped bathing and shaving regularly, shaped
his expression into a permanent scowl, began wearing "odd" cloth-
ing, and took up the habit of muttering angrily to himself. Perhaps he thought that his obvious "differentness" would make people
interested in meeting him. Naturally, it had the opposite effect.
So, at the same time that he was becoming increasingly lonely, he
was becoming increasingly repulsive to potential acquaintances.

25

He began to do bizarre things to gain attention. At first he simply slipped notes under Jody Foster's door. As he became increasingly isolated from society, however, he began to consider actions that would gain him attention because they were outrageous. He began to buy guns. Taking his small arsenal to Washington on the evening of March 29, 1981, he rented a hotel room, went out for dinner at McDonald's, came back and slept, arose the next day, wrote Jody Foster a final love letter, then went to the Washington Hilton and shot the President, his Press Secretary and a Washington police officer.

Let's review. First, what did we learn from this event? The attempted killing of the country's premier politician was done by a man apparently without any political motivation. Second, what is the explanation? The shooting was done by a lonely man who wanted to be noticed. Is that odd? Thankfully, it is. Those of us who are depressed about being lonely can usually come up with better ways of attracting attention. There aren't many of us whose deranged reasoning and moral deficiencies allow us to kill someone. But there are some. How about the other assassins in American political history? John Kennedy's killer seemed to fit the Hinckley "type." So did Robert Kennedy's. So, for that matter, did those who attempted to kill George Wallace and Gerald Ford.

It looks as if we're really on to something here. We are developing a theory that may explain why some people try to assassinate political leaders in America. (We may even be on to some research leads which would allow us to predict whether individuals with certain personality traits are likely to become assassins; but that's way down the road.) The hypothesis that we'd try to test would read, "Assassinations are correlated with feelings of desperate loneliness on the part of the assassin." Or perhaps: "the likelihood of committing a political assassination is positively correlated with the degree of one's personal isolation from society."

What we've done is to focus on an interesting problem (the causes of attempts on a President's life), state a hypothesis, and offer our reasons for believing that it is true.

Let's try it again. Isn't it peculiar that Israel's Prime Minister Begin and Egypt's late President Sadat—both regarded in their early careers as hard-nosed and implacable enemies—made such strides towards reconciliation between their two countries? And how was it possible that men who built up a reputation for being foreign policy "hawks" somehow wound up as peacemakers? Does that happen often? Well, President Nixon, who for 20 years was regarded among the chilliest of cold war warriors, ended the War in Vietnam, initiated the process of détente with the Soviet

Union (in cooperation with that other hard-liner, Leonid Brezhnev), and visited China (ruled, then, by the rabidly anti-imperialist Mao Zedong). Odd. . . .

O. K. What the peace treaty between Israel and Egypt has done is to trigger some ruminations on peace-making in general. It leads me to the _observation_ that foreign policy conservatives are better able to _make peace_. It's a tentative observation, of course, and it may not be supported by data I collect when I go out to test it; but it's what I've learned so far from thinking about the peace negotiations.

Now, _why_ would it be the case that hard liners are peace-makers? Perhaps they have freer hands at those moments in history when the outstanding issues between nations diminish to the point where peace becomes possible. After all, their reputations for dealing firmly with the enemy are unassailable within their own countries. Since they've always "talked tough," they're judged unlikely to sell their country down the river in any negotiations. Doves, on the other hand, often have their hands tied, because the domestic opposition is suspicious of their capacity to stand up to the enemy. In order to avoid any appearance of weakness, they must be wary of making concessions. Consequently, they are less likely to reach any agreements.

What we have, now, is an observation (hard liners are more likely to be peacemakers) and an explanation as to why it is true (their hands are freer). The observation is interesting (because it challenges common assumptions about who is likely to make peace) and has broad ramifications (for explaining and predicting the success or failure of negotiations).

We could go through the same procedures for the Congressional elections held in the most recent non-Presidential year. Turnout was very low. (That is my observation.) Why was it low? Perhaps people don't think that the Congress is as important as the Pre-sidency. If that's the case, the marginal voters—those who aren't terribly interested in politics in the first place—are more like-ly to vote in Presidential elections, but to stay home in the off years. (That's my theory.) And it's interesting because it means that the views of those who are less interested in politics—those who are poor or have little education—are underrepresented in off-year Congressional election campaigns. (Here we have it again, in very abbreviated form—an observation, an explanation and an assessment of ramifications.)

Now let's see you do it.

Assignment #1: Focusing on a problem and developing a theory.
Take one event. Those mentioned above suggest the possibili-

ties. Or consider these: the election of France's first Socialist President, the rise and fall of the Solidarity Movement in Poland, the Soviet invasion of Afghanistan, terrorist activities in Latin America, the relations between South Africa and her neighbors, or the failure of John Anderson to promote a serious third party movement in 1980. Or open your newspaper and pick some other event.

Ask yourself _what_ you learned from one of these events, _why_ the phenomenon took place, and whether your line of thought _is interesting_.

Now go through steps 1-4.

Step 1: Describe an observation and show why it is interesting and important. Would an inquiry into this problem have broad ramifications? Would it pass the "man-in-the-street" test? Do scholars write about it? Does it interest you?

Step 2: Summarize the findings of others and discuss the questions left open by their research.

Step 3: Provide a theory that explains your observation. Remember, a theory is nothing more than your resons for believing that the observation is true. _Be thorough!_ Don't leave gaps in your reasoning. And _be creative!_ Remember, the great advances of the past have been made by people like Galileo, Newton and Einstein. Imagination is the key ingredient in scientific investigation.

Step 4: State your hypothesis. The proper form for a hypothesis is discussed in the next chapter. Let's say, for now, that a hypothesis is one sentence describing a relationship between two things—motivation and action, age and beauty, height and weight.

CHAPTER III

FORMULATING HYPOTHESES

Was Step 4 in the previous chapter difficult? Did you come up with something like this?

> The fringes of society tend to produce Democrats, unless people come from broken homes, in which case they are likely to end up as non-voters, although in the South they often become members of the Ku Klux Klan, when if they vote it is for Democratic candidates, but not at the federal level, if they vote at all.

Sorry about that!

Maybe it was unfair to ask you to write a hypothesis before going through an explanation of how it is done. But the scientific method includes a number of steps, each of which must be mastered before going on to the next. To master a step, you must practice until you are comfortable with it. If you feel good now about your ability to conceptualize, let's move on to the next step--formation of hypotheses.

A hypothesis is a statement containing the smallest bit of information that can be tested. Each book you will read in political science contains hundreds of hypotheses--some tested, some not. Some are not even stated as hypotheses. They should be, however, since a real science of politics, or a science of anything, consists of a body of propositions that have been formally tested and shown to be supported.

You must learn to recognize hypotheses, even when they appear in disguised form (as they often do). And you must learn to formulate them yourself. That is, you must learn how to devise testable statements about the world in which you live. Writing hypotheses will become easy for you, but it will take practice before you get the hang of it.

Formulating a hypothesis is an exercise that seems simple at first glance--and eventually will be. It's awfully easy though to fall into the fuzzies at this stage; and if you do, it will sabotage your efforts to come up with an interesting finding that your audience will accept.

Let's consider just what a hypothesis is.

To begin, since a hypothesis is a statement containing the

29

smallest bit of information that can be tested, it should contain two, and only two, variables. A variable is any object or observable phenomenon that can have two or more values. (That is, its value can "vary.") Income, for example, is a variable. A person can be as rich as a Rockefeller or as poor as a student. The variable, "income," then, has several million possible values.

Party identification is another variable. An Austrian voter can identify with the Socialist Party, the People's Party, the Freedom Party, the Communist Party, or with no party at all. Party identification for an Austrian has five possible values.

In opposition to variables are "constants." Pi equals 3.1416 (rounded) always and forever. It never changes. Likewise, the distance from Fargo to Cheyenne is a constant: 909 miles. But the actual concept of "distance" is a variable. Its value can change dramatically, depending on the particular distance we are referring to.

A special type of variable is the one with only two values. The variable, war--as in the hypothesis, "Anti-foreign propaganda is positively correlated with war "--has two values: war and non-war. To test this hypothesis, we would measure the amount of anti-foreign propaganda produced in a sample of nations, then see whether those nations producing the largest amount of this material were in a state of war or non-war (colloquially known as "peace;" sorry, scientific jargon is not always terribly elegant!).

A hypothesis can be precisely defined as follows: it is a statement describing the relationship between two variables. One of these is the "independent" variable; the other is the "dependent" variable. The independent variable is presumed to influence the dependent variable. In essence, a hypothesis asserts that when something happens, something else is changed by it. Or to put it another way, when the independent variable changes, so does the dependent variable. If a nation produces a mountain of anti-foreign propaganda, then it will soon be at war. Or if I pass my next geology quiz, then my mood will improve.

In these hypotheses the second variable (war, mood) is the dependent variable. Its value (war/non-war, happy/sad) depends on the other variable (high amount of propaganda/low amount of propaganda, pass my quiz/fail my quiz). I am asserting that if I look at cases in which there is very little anti-foreign propaganda produced, I expect to find nations at peace. On the other hand, if I change the value of the independent variable to "high amount of anti-foreign propaganda," I expect the value of the dependent variable to change along with it (to war). I am hypothesizing that the existence of war or peace depends upon the amount of anti-foreign propaganda produced.

Similarly, if I want to test my second hypothesis, I would prepare for some of my quizzes and not for others. I would then record changes in my post-quiz mood to see whether it was dependent on the results of the quiz. (Go ahead, try it! Your geology instructor will understand that it's just an experiment you're conducting for a political science course.)

Rules for hypothesis-formation

We have developed some simple rules to guide you in writing hypotheses. Each rule is designed to avert typical problems students encounter in trying to form hypotheses.

One problem that crops up occasionally in political research is illustrated by the following hypothesis: "Minor party candidacy is correlated with loss of a presidential election." This looks like a testable proposition. It is clearly stating a relationship between two terms. It is saying, in essence, that minor-party candidacies (the independent variable) produce losses in presidential elections (the dependent variable).

To test this hypothesis, we might go back through American presidential elections defining a minor party as one whose candidate received less than 10% of the electoral vote. Then we would see whether any of these candidates ever won an election. We would find the following data:

Table III-1
THE RELATIONSHIP BETWEEN MINORITY PARTY STATUS
AND VICTORY IN AMERICAN PRESIDENTIAL ELECTIONS

	Won a Presidential Election	Lost a Presidential Election
Major Party Candidate	48	65
Minor Party Candidate	0	161

Voila! We have a finding. Our hypothesis is borne out by the data! In each Presidential election, there have been two, and sometimes three, major nominees for President. One of these has always won; the other one (or two) have lost. But minor party candidates lose every time! We conclude that a candidate cannot win unless he is nominated by a major party. The dependent variable (victory/defeat) clearly depends squarely on the independent variable (nomination by major/minor party). The hypothesis is strongly supported. We are ready to rush into print with our findings.

Or are we? Isn't there something fishy about this hypothesis? How have we defined a minor party? As one whose candidate receives less than 10% of the electoral vote. But no candidate can become President without winning a majority of the electoral vote.[1] A

minority party candidate is therefore, <u>by definition</u>, a loser.
The hypothesis means nothing more than "losers are losers." You
can see this clearly when we take the original hypothesis and fill
in our definitions for the terms:

Minor party candidacy   correlates with   loss of election.
Winning under 10%
   of electoral vote   correlates with   loss of election.
Losing the election   correlates with   loss of election.

   To summarize, this hypothesis has only one variable. A hypothesis with this characteristic is called a <u>tautology</u>. When
constructing hypotheses, be alert for this pitfall. Make sure
that you have two variables and that the two do not share the same
definition.

   Tautologies are sometimes easy to recognize, as in these
statements:

   Inflation is positively correlated with rising prices.
   Poverty is positively correlated with lack of money.
   Liberalism is negatively correlated with support for
      President Reagan's economic policies.

On the other hand, it is easier than you might think to construct
a tautological hypothesis. Some famous post-World War II research
on fascism and personality found a remarkable correlation between
an individual's paranoia and his belief that various ethnic groups
were plotting his economic ruin.[2] And public opinion researchers
found during the 1950's that people who were poorly adjusted to
the world were politically conservative.[3]

   In the first case, the research was faulty because paranoia
was defined as the belief that people were plotting behind one's
back. The belief that this plotting was done by Jews or Blacks,
or by Wall Street millionaires, was no more than expression of this
paranoia. We can see the problem when the argument is outlined:

Paranoia   correlates with   hatred for Jews, Blacks,
                                              and other ethnic groups
                                              who are plotting my ruin.

The belief that peo-   correlates with   hatred for Jews, Blacks,
   ple are secretly   and other ethnic groups
   plotting against me   who are plotting my ruin.

   In the case of the finding that conservatives were poorly adjusted, poor adjustment was defined as the sense that the individual was losing control over his life because changes were happening too quickly. Political conservatism was then defined as

hostility to change. Observe:

| Poor adjustment to the world | correlates with | political conservatism. |
| The belief that I am losing control of things because of rapid social changes | correlates with | dislike of rapid social changes. |

It's hardly surprising that these two variables were highly correlated with one another!

The point that we want to make is this: the independent variable and the dependent variable should not share the same definition. To put it another way, a hypothesis in the form, "A causes B," or "A is correlated with B," is acceptable. A hypothesis that really means, "A causes (or is correlated with) A," is not. This leads to our first rule for hypothesis construction.

Rule #1: The hypothesis must not be a tautology.

A second characteristic of the correctly-written hypothesis is that it focuses on two, and only two, variables. Take the sentence, "Senators are people who work longer hours than the average office worker, though most people don't believe it."[4] How would we test this hypothesis? First, we'd want to learn whether it is true that Senators work longer hours than the rest of us. To do that, we might follow a sample of Senators around for a week, then figure out the average number of hours that a Senator works. Then we'd compare this information with the U.S. Census Reports on the average work week for white collar workers.[5]

Next, we'd want to know whether people actually believed Senators were hard-working. For this information we would turn to public opinion polls.[6]

Suppose we found that the average Senator worked 48.1 hours per week, that the average office worker put in 39.2 hours weekly, and that 56.5% of the people believed that Senators were hard-working. Is the hypothesis supported? No, because the second clause ("most people don't believe it") isn't borne out by the data. Should the hypothesis be rejected? Not entirely, because Senators are indeed hard-working. The problem is that we have a compound hypothesis--two hypotheses in one. We must break it into its component parts and test them separately. Broken down, the two hypotheses read this way:

Hypothesis 1: Senators work longer hours than the average office worker.

Hypothesis 2: Most people don't believe that Senators work
long hours.

Hypothesis 1 would be tested in the manner described above.
So would hypothesis 2. But note that its verification has nothing
to do with whether Senators really do work long hours or not. Hypothesis 2 tests for the factual existence of a belief, not the
belief itself. People have believed many things that are not true
(the world is flat, Hitler is peace-loving, Mars is peopled by
little green men). In 1970 most Americans believed that the Vice-
President of the U.S. would not dream of taking a bribe, even
though at the time Spiro Agnew was accepting long brown envelopes
stuffed with dollar bills in the basement of the White House. So
be sure to keep separate in your mind belief statements and factual statements, We can test for the sociological characteristics
of those who believe that all welfare recipients are cheats. We
can also test to see whether welfare recipients in fact do cheat.
The two issues—a belief that they cheat, and whether they actually
cheat—are entirely separate.

Not all compound hypotheses involve facts and beliefs mixed
together in an impermissible way. They may involve two factual
statements or two belief statements. The assertion, "American
Governors have usually been powerful and popular," is a compound
factual proposition. To test it, we must break it down into two
statements:

Hypothesis 1: American Governors have usually been powerful.
Hypothesis 2: American Governors have usually been popular.

A compound belief statement must also be broken into two belief
propositions. We cannot test the hypothesis, "Most people believe
politicians are outgoing and corrupt," since it is really two
hypotheses:

Hypothesis 1: Most people believe politicians are outgoing.
Hypothesis 2: Most people believe politicians are corrupt.

The important point here is simple. Hypotheses contain the
smallest bit of information that can be tested. It is impossible
to test compound hypotheses, hypotheses containing three or more
variables. Always break your hypothesis down into its simplest
possible form: two variables and the asserted relationship between
them. If you would like to test relationships between three or
more variables, split your assertions into separate hypotheses.
This point leads to our next rule.

Rule #2: A hypothesis must contain two,
and only two, variables.

Now, another question arises. What purpose does it serve to phrase an assertion in the form of a hypothesis? What are we aiming at here? What kinds of relationships are we trying to describe? Well, in order to be useful, a hypothesis must predict or explain phenomena we can observe repeatedly. In the first instance, it can help us to predict whether, given a certain set of circumstances, a particular event will follow. In the second instance, it can move beyond mere prediction and help us understand why an event occurs. Take the example of a child playing with crayons. Suppose he decides to see what the wall of his room would look like with purple stripes on it. His father comes in, discovers the crime and gives him a spanking. "Aha!" says the child to himself. "Today Daddy gave me a spanking after I drew purple lines on the wall. I guess I shouldn't draw purple lines there." The next day the child tries green circles--to the same response from his mother. "Today," says the child, "Mommy spanked me after she saw green circles on the wall. No more green circles for me."

Learning in unconnected bits and pieces is characteristic of a child's process of comprehension. As the child matures, though, he begins to learn to experiment with putting things together. "Last month," he says, "I got spanked after Daddy and Mommy saw my purple lines and green circles. I wonder what'll happen if I draw some red squiggles on Granny's wall when we go over for dinner." The next day the child learns that red squiggles produce a similar effect at Granny's.

"What's going on here?" he says to himself. "I know that Daddy likes purple, because that's the color of the yarn he crochets with. And Mommy likes green, since that's the color of her sports car. And Granny's motor cycle is red. Hm... Maybe I'd better play it safe. It seems that if I draw on walls then I'll get a spanking, even if the grownups like the colors... Yes, that's it! I've got it! I can feel myself hypothesizing! Mommy! Daddy! Listen to this--my first generalization. 'Drawing on walls is correlated with spankings.'"

What our young scientist has done is to move onto a new plane with his thinking. Instead of merely collecting scraps of information, he's integrating them. He realizes that if he takes a certain type of action, he will produce a particular sort of reaction. Not only does he know now that purple walls bring a certain response from Daddy, that green ones produce the same from Mommy and that red ones draw it from Granny; he knows that if he draws on any walls with any color, he'll have a sore fanny. Learning to generalize--to predict that certain things will occur, given similar sets of circumstances--is an important step for us. It allows us to move through the world efficiently and effectively. We know that the sun will rise tomorrow morning. We know, if we turn the ignition key, that not only the car we're used to driving, but all cars will start. We know that if we throw a ball--even one we've never seen before--into the air, it will come down again. Or we know that in the aftermath of an assassination attempt, reporters and doctors will minimize the danger of a wound to a political leader.

Generalization, then, is an important tool. In many ways, one has to generalize in order to get along in the world. But, we should be clear on what generalization does not mean. Sometimes you'll hear professors cautioning you to avoid generalizations. What they're saying, of course, is that you should avoid making statements whose meaning is so general that it is not clear or specific. "President Reagan is a jerk," or, "My philosophy is, 'power to the people,'" are assertions that are unclear. Is President Reagan a jerk because he eats jellybeans or smears his hair with Brylcream--that is, is he jerk because of his personal characteristics? Or is he a jerk because of his policies? And what is a "jerk," anyway? Similarly, does "power to the people" mean a social, economic and political system in which all the goods of society are distributed equally? Does it mean power to a particular group of people? If so, who are the "people?" Do they include doctors, lawyers and bankers; or by "people" do we mean only poor, Black sharecroppers from Walthall County, Mississippi?

A real generalization--in a scientific sense--is a very precise statement. "Being a Catholic is correlated with being a Democrat," "education is correlated with income," and "height is correlated with weight" are statements in which each term--"Catholic," "Democrat," "education," "income," "height" and "weight"--can be defined very specifically. These sentences are also generalizations. They mean that, while one can always find exceptions (Catholic Republicans, Ph.D.'s on welfare or short sumo wrestlers), most Catholics will be Democrats, a person who's gone through more years of schooling will earn more money than one who hasn't, and taller people are usually heavier than shorter people. Each of these hypotheses may be rephrased in the form, "If the circumstances are characterized by X, then one will generally find Y."

Hypotheses, then, can offer a prediction. They can answer the "whether" question. But they can also answer the "why" question. We can assert not only that if we find X, we will find Y; but also that the presence of X causes Y to happen.

Let's go back to our budding 3 year old scientist. He has just made a discovery--that all lines, circles and squiggles that he draws on walls produce a sore bottom. Unsettled by this curious finding (After all, Granny insisted on the red motorcycle in the showroom.), he ponders. "What's going on with these grownups? I used all their favorite colors, and they still got mad... I know... It's because they hate me." Testing this hypothesis by putting on his cutest expression and standing in front of each

36

grownup in turn, he finds that that particular theory doesn't hold
water. This time he gets hugs. "What is it then?" he asks.
Tossing the problem around in his mind for a few weeks, he begins
to notice that Mommy, Daddy and Granny all enjoy showing their
houses to friends, that they seem to sit down and glance around
their living rooms from time to time with satisfied smiles on their
faces. "They must really enjoy things the way they are--the way
they planned them," he thinks. "Oh well, as I've heard my uncle,
the Latin teacher, say, 'De gustibus non est disputandum!' Now I
see that it makes them feel bad when I do something to change what
they've arranged. And when they feel like this, they want to make
me feel bad, too; so they spank me. Yes, that's it! Mommy, Daddy,
I'm hypothesizing again! Listen: 'Frustration causes aggression.'"

   A good hypothesis in its proper theoretical setting should
provide the same sort of helpful guidance for us. It should explain what has been observed, and it should predict that under the
same conditions the phenomenon should recur. To illustrate, we
ask you which of the following is the better hypothesis:

   Hypothesis 1:   Severe ideological disagreement between the
                   North and the South caused the U.S. Civil War.
   Hypothesis 2:   Severe ideological disagreement between sec-
                   tions of a nation causes civil war.

   The first hypothesis purports to explain one event. The second hypothesis also explains that event, but goes further. It predicts that in similar circumstances in other times and places, we
can expect to find civil wars. In addition, the latter hypothesis
can be tested. (We would take a variety of nations, examine newspaper reports, diaries, political speeches, etc., to ascertain the
degree of ideological cleavage, and then determine whether civil
war has broken out in those nations with the most severe ideological splits.) The first hypothesis is not testable. (Historians
are still arguing--more than]00 years after the event--about
whether the American Civil War was caused by disagreement over
slavery, or by Northern industrial expansion.[7])

   Hypotheses which focus on specific events are less interesting than those which generalize to broad patterns; but beyond that,
they are not even testable, as are the general-statement hypotheses. The sentence, "John voted Democratic because he is a worker," can never be supported to anyone's satisfaction. Someone will
argue that John's beloved mother was a lifelong Democrat, hence
John's devotion to the party. Someone else will remind you that
John always detested his Republican father; his Democratic leanings
follow from his Oedipal rebelliousness. Others will point out that
John lives in a Democratic neighborhood, or that he was raised in
the Democratic South, or that he's always been a strong admirer of
John F. Kennedy, or whatever. The argument about why John voted

Democratic can never be resolved.

But if we notice that John is a worker and also that he votes Democratic, then we can test a broader and much more interesting hypothesis: <u>people like John</u> vote Democratic because they are workers (or workers vote Democratic). This statement <u>can</u> be tested. One way to do it would be to find two different groups of people who are alike in every way except one: some are workers, others are not. We would then see whether the working-class group had greater sympathy for the Democratic Party than the other group did.

So hypotheses focus on general patterns, events which can be viewed repeatedly, not individual cases. We wish to generalize about "civil war," not just about the U.S. Civil War. We are interested in the voting habits of workers, not just those of John. Our desire to generalize leads us to this rule:

> Rule #3: Both terms in a hypothesis must be general;
> that is, they must describe recurring phenomena.

There are two qualifications to Rule 3. For one thing, terms in the hypothesis must not be so general as to be impossibly vague. We deal with this problem in the next section. Here we take up another qualification: it may in some cases be necessary to <u>state limits</u> to the general applicability of the hypothesis. This need arises when you suspect that your hypothesis does not work at all times in all places. You may wish to qualify the hypothesis by stating the circumstances in which you expect it to be supported.

For instance, after reviewing the evidence, you conclude that "IQ is positively correlated with life span in modern nations." The qualifying words "in modern nations" are added for various reasons. Perhaps you could simply find no evidence about the relationship between IQ and life span in developing countries. Or perhaps the evidence about that relationship was unclear. Or perhaps you are not a specialist on developing countries and did not even bother to investigate existing data in those places. For whatever reason, the words "in modern nations" show that you are not yet ready to say that IQ is correlated with life span everywhere at all times.

A more extended example may make our point clearer. Let's say that you conducted a study of all members of the Ways and Means Committee of the U.S. House of Representatives in the 1890 to 1900 period. Among your principal discoveries in this finding: congressmen with more seniority on the committee were more likely than those with less seniority to get committee acceptance of their bills and amendments. You conclude that the findings support this hypothesis: "seniority on the job is positively correlated with job effectiveness."

On the surface your conclusion is perfectly justified. As you think about it, however, you begin to wonder. Haven't you extrapolated to an awfully broad universe (all workers in the entire world throughout all of history) from a rather small sample (a few dozen American congressmen in one 10-year period of history)? Placing some limits on the applicability of the hypothesis would appear to make sense. The hypothesis could, in fact, be re-phrased in dozens of ways. Following are some examples, ranging from narrow to general:

> In committees of the U.S. House of Representatives in the late 19th century, seniority in committee is correlated with effectiveness in committee.

> In 19th-century American politics, seniority in legislative committees is correlated with effectiveness in committee.

> In American politics, seniority in a political position is correlated with effectiveness in that position.

> Among male legislators* in democratic systems, seniority in committees is correlated with effectiveness in committees.

> Among legislators everywhere, seniority in committee is correlated with effectiveness in committee.

> Among political leaders, seniority is correlated with job effectiveness.

> Among workers, seniority is correlated with job effectiveness.

These re-statements of the hypothesis do not exhaust the possibilities. (Quick! Think of three additional ways, congruent with the original findings, to phrase the hypothesis.) How does one decide what limits, if any, to place on the applicability of a hypothesis?

---

* Remember that the original study focused only on males. It dealt with 19th-century legislators in the U.S., among whom no women can be found.

There is no simple answer to this question. Researchers usually rely on a combination of intuition and general knowledge of the subject matter. We suggest these guidelines: your hypothesis should apply to 1) as broad a set of phenomena as possible, given 2) your interests and 3) your knowledge of findings from related studies. For instance, faced with the study of U.S. members of the Ways and Means Committee, the authors of this book would opt for the following hypothesis:

> Among political leaders, seniority in a political institution is positively correlated with effectiveness in that institution.

In choosing this formulation, our reasoning goes something like this:

1. We wish to make as broad a generalization as possible. (Remember, the narrower the hypothesis, the less interesting it is.) So we don't want to limit the hypothesis merely to Americans, males, or 19th-century politicians.

2. Furthermore, we are familiar with other political studies which suggest that seniority in politics increases job effectiveness.[8] Politics is a complicated business. It takes time to master the unwritten norms, the "rules of the game," which exist in any political institution. It makes sense (and other research confirms) that politicians who have been part of a political body for a long time understand their colleagues better than newcomers and are hence better able to gain peer acceptance for their own political goals. So our general knowledge of politics makes us willing to take the leap from one small unit of politicians to all politicians in general.

3. On the other hand, we are not familiar enough with findings from outside political science (nor, perhaps, are we bold enough) to extend our generalization. We are not ready to say it applies to all workers everywhere. Besides, we have long-standing personal interests in the characteristics of political leaders. We are content to apply our hypothesis to that group alone. (Note that this limitation does not make the hypothesis an "uninteresting" one. A generalization which applies to all political leaders everywhere surely meets the significance test.)*

Other researchers with different interests from ours might have come up with a different set of limits to the hypothesis derived from the Ways and Means Committee study. Someone concerned with sex roles, for example, might have derived this generaliza-

---

* For a hypothesis which probably fails the significance test, see the first hypothesis on page 39, above.

tion:

> Among males, job seniority is positively correlated
> with job effectiveness.

An historian might have chosen this statement:

> In 19th-century industrial societies, job seniority
> was correlated with job effectiveness.

In all these cases the basic hypothesis remains the same. What
changes are the conditions under which one expects the hypothesis
to apply. If no conditions are set forth, it shows that one
assumes the hypothesis to apply in all circumstances.

Our examination in this section has led to our fourth rule:

> Rule #4: Always specify the conditions (if any) which
>   limit applicability of the hypothesis.

We have said (Rule #3) that both terms in a hypothesis must
be general, but noted a qualification to this statement in Rule
#4. We must now qualify Rule #3 in a second way. Yes, the terms
in a hypothesis must be general, but they must not be so broad as
to be meaningless or fuzzy. A good deal of the writing (and thinking) about politics that one encounters in daily life is pretty
sloppy. What might a fragment of a conversation between two
students (maybe two professors) sound like?

> Bill . . . . "President Reagan is really a turkey."
>
> Gene . . . . "I agree with you. But you can't say
>   that just about him. Politicians are
>   all alike."
>
> Bill . . . . "Uh, huh . . . I wish--just once--that
>   we'd get a President who would do some-
>   thing about all the problems we have."
>
> Gene . . . . "Yeah . . . me, too . . . these guys are
>   nothing but a bunch of rejects. I agree
>   with you 100%."

What is Gene agreeing to? Bill said, "President Reagan is
a turkey." Does he mean that the President has gone through a
physical metamorphosis and is now walking around, bedecked with
feathers, saying "gobble, gobble" and introducing anti-Thanksgiv-
ing legislation in Congress. What is a "turkey?" Well, it's
clearly something negative. Does it mean that President Reagan
is stupid? That he is wrongheaded about an issue? That he is

41

mean-spirited about something? We don't know. The term is too
vague.

Bill wants a President who will "do something" about our problems, but what does he mean? Should the President ask Congress
to provide more generous assistance to people on welfare, or
should he ask Congress to pass legislation punishing all those
welfare cheats?

And just what is Gene saying when he declares that "politicians are all alike?" Are they crooked? Cowardly? Unimaginative?
Self-interested?

This conversation is nothing but political elevator music
that reassures us about our social surroundings while it tells us
nothing. While they seem to be forthright and aggressive, these
statements are in fact so tentative that they reveal nothing of
the substance of Bill's or Gene's thoughts. Much of what passes
for political wisdom is stated in such terms. You should avoid
making statements such as, "Minority groups are satisfied with
symbolic political gains," or "The 1976 presidential election
represented a victory of the New Politics," without specifying
exactly what you mean by "symbolic political gains" or "the New
Politics." Better, avoid such terms altogether. They are loaded
with so much emotional baggage that the reader's prejudices keep
him from understanding, even if you try to offer a clear concetu-
al definition. Use terms whose meaning is clear _and_ generally
understood.

Rule #5: Each term in a hypothesis must have a clear,
               generally understood meaning.

There are two exceptions to this rule. First, when you are
dealing with a concept that you yourself have discovered, you may
have to invent a term to describe it.

Let's say you have observed, for example, that in the latter
half of the 20th century most voters have lost their religious
convictions. Religious fervor, however--you go on to say--is a
basic human need. Some voters, you argue, have replaced their
attachment to a religion with their attachment to the state. For
them, politics is a stage upon which the forces of good and evil
contend. Certain politicians are the functional equivalent of
angels, others of devils. They achieve psychological salvation by
engaging in politics on the side of goodness and truth.

You might develop a series of hypotheses that spring from
this line of thought. One of them might read: "Religio-political
fervor is correlated with a drop in church attendance." "Religio-
political fervor" is an invented term--one that is not heard in

everyday conversation. You made the term up. It describes well, you believe, the concept you had in mind after observing the real-world pattern of detachment from religion and attachment to politics. No other term will do, for you are breaking new ground. Either no one else has observed the pattern you discovered, or else no one has yet thought of a satisfactory term to describe it.

Since you invented the concept, it will be new to all readers. Most will find it nonsense until you clarify its meaning. Inventing terms is a risky business. Creativity--venturing outside the tried and true paths--always carries risks. Before inventing a term, you had better be certain that it stands for a real phenomenon which you have observed, which you can describe for others, and which has not already been given a descriptive name by someone else. And be sure to define your term clearly immediately following your first usage of it.

There is a second exception to the rule that terms in a hypothesis must be clear and generally understood. Some terms commonly used in political discussions can have several meanings. "Alienation" is one. It can refer to: 1) people's feelings that political leaders don't care about them personally; 2) a sense that the political system in which they live is incapable of dealing with the major issues of the day; 3) a judgment that they are being repressed by the political system; 4) a revulsion against the political style of the national leadership; 5) non-voting.

In a developed scientific discipline relatively vague terms such as "alienation" would be out of place. But political science is not yet as "hard" a science as, say, biology. Central ideas in political science discourse are expressed by words like "alienation," "instability," "legitimacy," and "political efficacy." One cannot always avoid using these terms. But be cautious when doing so. When working with "alienation" and similar concepts, be sure to specify <u>exactly</u> the meaning you want to assign to the word in your theory and in your hypothesis.

> Rule #6: When a term which may not have a clear, generally understood meaning cannot be avoided, be sure to clarify its meaning just before or just after your statement of the hypothesis.

Another rule in hypothesis-construction follows from a point made in Chapter 1: science cannot prove or disprove individual values. Therefore, terms in a hypothesis should not be value-laden. For instance, the assertion, "Democrats are scoundrels," cannot be subjected to a scientific test. The word "scoundrel" is a perjorative term expressing an individual value preference: against Democrats (and presumably for Republicans). It has no place in scientific analysis. A Democrat could just as easily argue that "Republicans are scoundrels." Neither person could convince the other of the correctness of his hypothesis, no matter how much "evidence" was gathered, because they would be in fundamental disagreement on the meaning of the word "scoundrel." For each, "scoundrel" means "someone who disagrees with my basic values." But there is no way of proving or disproving that someone who disagrees with your basic values is a scoundrel. This is simply a term you find emotionally satisfactory to make a negative value judgment about another person.

We can, of course, test factually-based statements about Democrats and Republicans. All of the following propositions are capable of being supported or invalidated:

> Democrats are more likely than Republicans to support higher minimum wages.
> Democrats are more likely than Republicans to support federal aid to minority groups.
> Republicans are more likely than Democrats to support less government control over the economy.
> Republicans are more likely than Democrats to support a "hard-line" anti-Soviet foreign policy.

If evidence did in fact support these propositions (which it does), then we could use that information to make our individual value judgments about the two parties. We might, for instance, just happen to *like* higher minimum wages or aid to minority groups. These preferences follow from our own values which, remember, cannot be proved correct or incorrect. Once we have identified our own values, the scientifically-supported statements about where the two parties stand on matters relating to those values are useful to us. Since Democrats support things we like, we will make a value judgment that Democrats are "the good guys" and Republicans the "scoundrels."

Of course, if you happen to like a free-market system and a tough defense posture, then, for you, Republicans would wear the white hats, Democrats would be "the bad guys." The point is: be sure to distinguish between empirical propositions—on which factual evidence can be brought to bear—and value statements, which simply reflect your own personal inclinations.

The "scoundrel" example we have been using is an obvious case of imposing value judgments into scientific discourse. Even at higher levels of political sophistication, however, this error is often made. Most of us have heard the statement, "Democracy provides a better way of life than dictatorship." This too is a pure value assertion. It is a "better way of life" only if your core values include respect for the individual, belief in freedom of speech, preference for liberty over state control, and so forth. If you prefer (as many do) order, hierarchy, state power, submission of the individual to community values, and so forth, you might well come down on the side of dictatorship. We cannot prove one or the other is better. We can only point out the human behavior patterns usually found in one and the other system and leave it to each observer to decide which system best promotes her own values.

> Rule #7: Neither term in the hypothesis should be
> value-laden, nor should the hypothesis as
> a whole state a value judgment.

As you must have observed from the previous discussion, writing hypotheses has to be done pretty precisely. So far, we have discussed the manner in which to choose variables and describe them. Now you must specify exactly what the relationship between your two variables is. You have two alternatives. Either you are saying that variable A causes variable B, or that variable A is correlated with variable B. If you can establish the former type of relationship, you will have explained the relationship between two phenomena. One brings the other about.

If you cannot establish that one variable causes the other but is simply correlated, or found with it, you are showing merely that when your independent variable undergoes a change, your dependent variable does too. This does not always mean that the independent variable is causing the change in the dependent variable. In fact, a third variable may be the cause of change in both your independent and dependent variables.

The alternatives can be seen in the following diagrams, where the arrows represent causality.

Alternative 1: Variable A causes Variable B.

$$A \longrightarrow B$$

Alternative 2: Simultaneous changes in variables
A & B are caused by variable C.

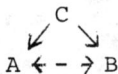

$$C$$
$$\swarrow \quad \searrow$$
$$A \leftarrow - \rightarrow B$$

Alternative 1 describes a pretty straightforward relationship. In the real world, you might encounter statements such as, "A high level of political interest causes greater voter turnout," or, "Governmental repression causes revolutions."

The second type of relationship is a bit more complicated.
In Chapter 2 we discussed a theory concerning the relationship
between the emotional incentive for political involvement (the
status drive versus the program drive) and various forms of behavior. The theory predicts that the status type will spend most of
his time seeking publicity, while the program type devotes his
efforts to the problem-solving work that goes on in legislative
committees. The status type has neither the time nor the interest to devote himself to committee work. The program type would-
n't take the time or have the inclination to generate publicity
for himself.

It's difficult to learn the incentives of U.S. Congressmen.
You can't simply write letters asking them to tell whether they
are more interested in accumulating status for themselves or in
solving problems.

Actually, in order to establish these incentives, you would
have to go to Washington and take several months to interview
members of Congress--spending perhaps an hour or two with each
one, then coding their discussions according to a list of characteristics found in the conversations of the two different types.
While it may be interesting for you to do so, practical barriers
are pretty obvious.

For the purposes of a research paper, you would have to find
a roundabout way of establishing congressmen's incentives. It
turns out that the program incentive causes low levels of publicity-seeking and high levels of committee activity, while the
status incentive causes high levels of publicity-seeking and low
levels of committee activity. Where one finds congressmen with
high levels of publicity, therefore, one would also expect to
find low levels of committee work. The high level of publicity
did not cause the low level of committee work. Rather, both
patterns were caused by the third variable: the status incentive.

Similarly, where one finds a low level of publicity, one
would expect to find high levels of committee work. You are not,
obviously, claiming that active committee work causes less publicity, that not doing committee work causes one to become known.
If that were the case, a congressman could get a lot of press
coverage even if he didn't get out of bed in the morning. No, you
are saying merely that the two variables are correlated with each
other and that their correlation is the product of a third variable which you cannot measure directly--the emotional incentive.
The relationship is represented by the following diagram:

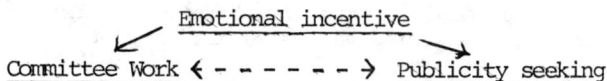

Emotional incentive

Committee Work ← - - - - - - → Publicity seeking

The actual hypothesis which follows from our discussion would go something like this: "For U.S. Congressmen, the amount of committee work done is negatively correlated with the level of national publicity achieved." Or, by employing our third variable, we could say: "The status incentive causes high levels of publicity," and, "The status incentive causes low levels of committee work."

So we have two types of relationship which can be tested in a research paper: a causal relationship or a correlational one. And this point leads to Rule #8:

> Rule #8: The relationship between two variables must be expressed either by the verb, "to cause," or by the phrase, "is correlated with."

It is important to restrict yourself to one of these two connectors. Others may be misleading. Let's look at the problems that can arise when different connectors are used.

1) "Doctors are Republicans."
2) "Education leads to a trust in government."
3) "If a community has a high level of poverty, then it will have a high level of crime."

Does the first statement say that a person's occupation causes her to associate with the Republican Party? Probably. But it could also be the case that the amount of wealth in a person's family makes it possible for her to afford medical school costs and also makes it likely that she will be a Republican. In that case the relationship between occupation and party identification is a correlational rather than a causal one. It would diagram this way:

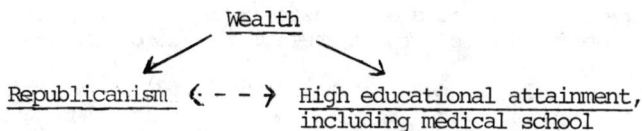

```
                     Wealth
              ↙               ↘
Republicanism  ⟨ - - ⟩  High educational attainment,
                        including medical school
```

Statement 1, all things considered, is an evasion. Its author is failing to tell us whether he believes there is a causal or a correlational relationship between his two variables. As a result we cannot really test the hypothesis, and it ends up being useless.

How about the second statement? Education may "lead to" a trust in government in the sense that it causes it. On the other hand, education may lead first to the accumulation of wealth. This wealth may in turn bolster the individual's faith in the political system under which he was able to achieve success and security. So the relationship is not one of direct cause and effect. It is indirect or "developmental." Diagrammed, it takes this form:

A   causes →   B   causes →   C

Education   causes →   Wealth   causes →   Trust in government

What we now have in effect is a compound hypothesis, and that's something to be avoided (see Rule 2).

And the third hypothesis? Does being poor <u>cause</u> one to be a criminal? Maybe. But it may be that the restricted intellectual environment in poor areas causes both crime (through the failure of families and schools to deliver appropriate moral standards to children) and poverty (by preparing children poorly for school, thereby making their academic and economic success unlikely). Again, it's unclear whether a causal or a correlational relationship is being described. The statement as phrased could be diagrammed in either of two ways:

1. Poverty ————————→ crime

2.   Third variable
     (e.g., restricted intellectual environment)
      ↙   ↘
   poverty ← – – – – – – – → crime

The "if . . . then" form represented by statement 3 should be avoided. Mathematical hypotheses are commonly phrased in this way. That's all right, because in mathematics one is seeking to establish only a statistical association—disregarding causality entirely. But in political science, we want to be able to distinguish between correlations and causes. The "if . . . then" format obscures the difference between these two relationships.

Statements 1, 2, and 3 above are not useful as written. They need to be re-phrased in line with the eight rules enunciated in this chapter. Correctly expressed, they look like this:

1) "Being a doctor is correlated with Republican Party membership."
2) "Education causes trust in government."
3) "In any community, the level of poverty is positively correlated with the level of crime."

"Being a doctor is correlated with Republican Party membership" sounds more awkward than "Doctors are Republicans." But the former statement is more specific than the latter, and in a genuine science of politics we must sometimes sacrifice elegance

48

and the economy of language for clarity. Look at it this way.
"y = mx + b" is not an especially lovely way to describe the slope
of a line. Nor is "$e = mc^2$" a poetic evocation of the relationship between mass and energy. But these statements are accurate
and useful. We want to make the same kind of statement in political science and therefore beg the same tolerance enjoyed by
mathematicians and physicists.

One final note about the interpretation of hypotheses written
in the fashion we have suggested is in order. If we go on to test
our "being a doctor is correlated with Republican party membership" hypothesis and unearth the following data, is our hypothesis
proven?

Table III-2
THE RELATIONSHIP BETWEEN OCCUPATION AND PARTY
IDENTIFICATION

Occupation	Party Identification		
	Republican	Democratic	Independent
Doctors	50	25	25

Maybe. But suppose someone wished to compare our findings
with a survey she completed among a random sample of people who
were not physicians, and she gathered the following data:

Table III-3
PARTY IDENTIFICATION AMONG A RANDOM SAMPLE OF NON-
PHYSICIANS

Occupation	Party Identification		
	Republican	Democratic	Independent
Non-physicians	60	20	20

Looking at the two tables together, one can see that, indeed,
doctors are more likely to be Republican than they are to be anything else, but that our original hypothesis is a misleading half-
truth, because the non-physicians are even more likely to be
Republicans.

The moral: Be careful. When you say that Variable A is
correlated with Variable B, it is understood that you are also
saying that Variable A is more strongly correlated with Variable B
than is Variable non-A. The data cited in Tables III-2 and III-3
would actually disprove the hypothesis.

If all this sounds a bit complicated, let's cite a few examples of hypotheses and their interpretations.

Hypothesis	Interpretation
1. Being a doctor is correlated with being a Republican.	1. Being a doctor makes you especially likely to be a Republican.
2. Being male is correlated with a high level of political participation.	2. Men are more likely to participate in politics than are women.
3. High income is correlated with political conservatism.	3. Wealthy people are politically more conservative than poor people.

Phrasing our observations about the world in terms of hypotheses is difficult at first. Once you get the hang of it, though, it becomes easy. And it's worth developing this ability, because it enhances our powers of induction and sensitizes us to the need to support our statements with data from the real world.

Assignment #2: Formulating Hypotheses
The ability to form hypothese comes only through practice. Your second assignment is to construct five hypotheses, making sure that in each case you follow the rules for hypothesis formation. We'll repeat them here:

Rule #1: The hypothesis must not be a tautology.
Rule #2: A hypothesis must contain two, and only two, variables.
Rule #3: Both terms in a hypothesis must be general; that is, they must describe recurring phenomena.
Rule #4: Always specify the conditions (if any) which limit applicability of the hypothesis.
Rule #5: Each term in a hypothesis must have a clear, generally understood meaning.
Rule #6: When a term which may not have a clear, generally understood meaning cannot be avoided, be sure to clarify its meaning just before or just after your statement of the hypothesis.
Rule #7: Neither term in the hypothesis should be value-laden, nor should the hypothesis as a whole state a value judgment.
Rule #8: The relationship between two variables must be expressed either by the verb, "to cause," or by the phrase, "is correlated with."

Your instructor will give you detailed information about what material to consult in making up your hypotheses. You could turn to current events again, as you did for the exercise in Chapter 2. We prefer an alternative. Turn to the substantive material you have read in other texts for this course and make up hypotheses based on evidence presented in those works. For example, if you have learned that wealthier countries are more likely to be democratic than poorer ones, you might state:

> Among nations, there is a positive correlation between wealth and democracy.

Or if you have learned that incumbent congressmen are more likely to win elections than their challengers, you might conclude:

> In democratic elections, being an incumbent is positively correlated with likelihood of electoral victory.

The number of conceivable hypotheses you could derive is large, even if you are a newcomer to the study of politics. Finding five should be easy. Review the eight rules, review the texts you have read, and go to it.

Assignment #3
Learning to recognize correctly-written hypotheses is as important as learning how to write them. This assignment tests your ability to tell whether a hypothesis is set down in the correct form and, if it isn't, to say why not.

A. Which of the following are _correctly-written, testable hypotheses?_ Circle the number of all sentences which meet the formal criteria for correct hypotheses. Whether the hypotheses would or would not, in your estimation, be supported by actual evidence is immaterial. The statement, "Indian rain dances cause rain," may be a _testable_ hypothsis, although it will very likely turn out to be an _unsupported_ one. We want to see here whether you can recognize _testable_ hypotheses, not whether you have the substantive knowledge to tell which hypotheses have empirical support behind them. So, circle the testable hypotheses.

1. The legitimacy and stability of any regime is correlated with the industriousness and common sense of its people.

2. Political leaders are ambitious.

3. The shooting of an Austrian prince caused World War I.

4. Working-class status is positively correlated with left-wing voting.

5. War causes economic destruction.

6. Holding political power is correlated with having male chauvinist pig tendencies.

7. President Reagan is correlated with being a conservative.

8. In electoral campaigns, participation rates are correlated with media campaign coverage.

9. Historically, the decline of social trust has led to the downfall of great civilizations.

10. Vast disparities between rich and poor are correlated with revolutionary upheavals.

11. The lack of money is correlated with poverty.

12. Powerlessness among freshman legislators causes rebellion against the legislative leadership.

13. The revolt against authority has taken a curious turn in this century.

14. Education causes tolerant attitudes toward racial minorities.

15. Between any two nations, the likelihood of war is negatively correlated with the amount of trade between those nations.

16. Ronald Reagan will cause a decline in our living standards.

17. Having a professional status in society is correlated with having conservative political attitudes.

18. Living in rural areas causes political apathy.

19. Being a female is correlated with the taking of anti-war political positions.

20. Poverty is negatively correlated with participation in politics.

21. Being an only child is correlated with rapid upward mobility.

B. Each of the following statements violates _one_ of six rules enunciated in this chapter for correct hypothesis-formation. Write, before each statement, the number of the rule which is *being violated. (The rules are set forth on page 50.) Note that Rules 4 and 6 are irrelevant to this exercise, so you can ignore them as you work on this part of the assignment.*

1. *Conservative attitudes are correlated with evil political leaders.*

2. *Quasi-political economics is correlated with nationalistic recidivism.*

3. *Happiness is correlated with a state of inner joy.*

4. *Revolutions have a tendency to bring about dictatorships.*

5. *The Russian invasion of Afghanistan caused increased international tensions.*

6. *Racist attitudes are positively correlated with voting for deplorable political candidates.*

7. *Social status is connected in an important way with the construction of our self-image.*

8. *War and famine are caused by intolerant attitudes.*

9. *Antidisestablished demagogic autarky causes disruption of rigidified mobility.*

10. *Level of education is positively correlated with number of years of schooling.*

11. *High levels of wealth are correlated with conservatism and personal ambition.*

12. *War is caused by violent confrontations between nations.*

13. *Solid, time tested institutions that people believe in are a bulwark of political stability.*[9]

FOOTNOTES TO CHAPTER 3

1. Actually, there is one exception to this statement. If no Presidential candidate receives a majority in the electoral college, the President is then chosen by members of the U.S. House of Representatives. This situation has occurred twice in the 48 American Presidential elections--in 1800 and in 1824. But the development of the modern two-party system has rendered its chances of happening unlikely. Indeed, no election has gone to the House--that is to say, no candidate has failed to get a majority of the electoral votes--for over 150 years.

2. Theodore W. Adorno, Else Frenkel-Brunswick, Daniel J. Levinson, and R. Nevitt Sanford, The Authoritarian Personality (New York: Harper & Row, 1950).

3. Herbert McClosky, "Conservatism and Personality," American Political Science Review 58 (1958), pp. 27-45.

4. This example is suggested by a reading of James L. Payne's treatment of the same topic; see his Foundations of Empirical Political Analysis (Chicago: Markham Publishing Company, 1973), p. 6.

5. See U. S. Department of Labor, Employment and Earnings: States and Areas, 1938-78 (Washington, D.C.: Government Printing Office, 1979).

6. See, for example, the vast amount of material in the following: George H. Gallup, The Gallup Poll: Public Opinion, 1935-1971, 3 vols. (New York: Random House, 1972); Gallup, The Gallup Poll: Public Opinion, 1972-1977, 2 vols. (Wilmington, Del.: Scholarly Press, Inc., 1978); and Elizabeth Hann Hastings and Philip K. Hastings, eds., Index to International Public Opinion, 1978-1979 (Westport, Conn.: Greenwood Press, 1980).

7. One historian has collected 92 different perspectives on the causes of the American Civil War. See Kenneth M. Stampp, ed., The Causes of the Civil War (Englewood Cliffs, N.J.: Prentice-Hall, Inc., 1965). Stampp concludes that "...after a century the debate [over the causes of the war] is still inconclusive...." (Stampp, p. 4.) See also Thomas J. Pressley, Americans Interpret Their Civil War (Princeton, N.J.: Princeton University Press, 1954) and Edwin C. Rozwenc, ed., The Causes of the American Civil War (Boston: D. C. Heath & Co., 1961).

8. See, for example, Donald R. Matthews, U. S. Senators and Their World (New York: Vintage Books, 1960), p. 175.

9. We're cheating, There are two violations here. See whether you can spot both errors, The hypothesis is taken from Michael G. Roskin, Countries and Concepts: An Introduction to Comparative Politics (Englewood Cliffs, N.J.: Prentice-Hall, Inc., 1982), p. 378.

CHAPTER IV

OBSERVATION AND HYPOTHESIS-FORMATION:
AN EXTENDED EXAMPLE

Let us now illustrate--through a concrete, detailed example--
how one develops hypotheses. As we have said, the trick is to go
from real-world observations to theoretical generalizations. One
type of observation in political science is simply to watch a
politician and see what he does. You go to a city council meeting
and see that the Mayor is brusque and arrogant with the council-
lors. You attend a session of the state legislature and notice
that members from rural districts vote for dairy subsidies, members from urban districts vote against.

For most of us, unfortunately, it is impossible to observe
politics in this first-hand way most of the time. We must rely on
others to observe for us. We can then use their observations for
our own purposes. A number of people in modern societies are paid
for the precise purpose of observing politics close up and inform-
ing the rest of us about it. Reporters are the most well-known
of these individuals. They are trained to be accurate observers,
and their profession postulates objective reporting of day-to-day
events as its highest ideal. We can, for the most part, assume
that the stories of experienced reporters in reputable news
sources are reasonably accurate observations about what goes on
in the world of politics.

This assumption allows us to draw on a much broader set of
observations than we ourselves could ever make. It allows us to
use the observations found in news stories as the basis for hypotheses of our own about the political world. Let us illustrate
how this can be done. Imagine that the time is January, 1981, and
that you have come across the following story on page 1 of the
New York Times:

> Rating members of Congress has become an important
> activity for American interest groups. These groups
> have settled on a sure-fire way to see whether Congress-
> men support their goals. They check on voting records
> in Congress and give each legislator a score ranging
> from 0 to 100. The scores reflect each Congressman's
> roll-call voting behavior on issues of central concern
> to the interest group. The higher the score, the more
> frequently the Congressman voted to support goals fa-
> vored by the group.

Two prominent interest groups have recently released their ratings for the year 1980. One, the Americans for Democratic Action, is perhaps the group with the longest record of rating political leaders. Founded in 1947 by such charter members of the liberal establishment as Hubert Humphrey and Eleanor Roosevelt, it has come, almost by itself, to define what liberalism stands for at any given moment. Few would dispute the conclusion that a rating of 70 or better from the ADA automatically denotes someone as a genuine American liberal. No one doubts that a person consistently rated under 30 by the ADA must be seen as a dyed-in-the-wool conservative.

A second prominent organization which rates congressmen is the AFL-CIO (American Federation of Labor-Congress of Industrial Organizations). Its ratings represent the interests of organized labor. A "high" score on the AFL-CIO rating scale suggests someone who is friendly to labor and the positions taken by labor leaders. A "low" score identifies someone opposed to organized labor's aims.

For any rating system people with scores in the middle range can be considered as "moderates" with respect to that particular set of issues.

Some interesting results appear as one browses through the 1980 ratings. For instance, among Senators 78-year-old Democrat John Stennis of Mississippi, Chairman of the Armed Services Committee, received an ADA score of 17 and a rating of 38 from the AFL-CIO. On the other hand, the 39-year-old Democrat Paul Tsongas, who holds no chairmanship, received ADA and AFL-CIO ratings of, respectively, 89 and 84.

The article continues on page 39, but you pause a minute, before turning the pages, to ponder what you have read. Let's say that you know next to nothing about American politics. (This assumption may even be correct.) Still, if the data you have found here are representative of all Senators, you can draw a number of tentative conclusions from the reporter's observations. One obvious point emerges from the article. Senator Tsongas is much younger (39) than Senator Stennis (78); he is also much more liberal (89 to 17) by ADA ratings. Thus, our first conclusion would be that younger Senators are more liberal than older Senators.

We now want to state this conclusion as a hypothesis. Remember that a hypothesis is a statement about the relationship between two variables which follows the eight rules enunciated in Chapter 3. The following statement should serve us adequately:

H-1: Among political leaders, age is negatively correlated with liberalism.

Let us examine this sentence carefully to see how it conforms to all the rules of hypothesis-formation.

1. Rule 1 says the statement must not be a tautology. It seems clear, on the surface, that age does not mean the same thing as liberalism, so we do not have a tautology on our hands. (We must be on the lookout for a tautology again, however, when we start talking about testing our hypothesis and defining its terms operationally. If "liberal" is defined as "anyone under 30," then we have indeed constructed a tautology.)

2. Rule 2 says that the statement must be about two, and only two, variables. We meet this requirement. Our statement centers on two variables only--age and liberalism.

3. Rule 3 calls for general terms. Age and liberalism are surely general terms. (The following statement illustrates non-general terms: "Senator Tsongas is correlated with having an ADA rating of 89.")

4. Rule 4 specifies that we should state any conditions which limit applicability of the hypothesis. In this case we have decided to limit our generalizations to "political leaders." The reasoning for this decision can be found on pp. 40-41 above. Several other limiting conditions, or none at all, might have been chosen by other researchers with different interests or dispositions from ours.

5. Rule 5 says that each term in a hypothesis must have a clear, generally understood meaning. We seem to meet this condition. Age (how old you are) and liberalism (support for government programs to promote egalitarianism) have reasonably clear meanings to informed American citizens.

6. Rule 6 applies only when one or both terms in a hypothesis have no clearly understood meaning. Since both terms are clear, in this case, rule 6 does not apply.

7. Rule 7 states that the two variables must be connected by either a causal or a correlational statement. We say the terms are "negatively correlated," thus meeting the requirements of this rule.

8. Rule 8 holds that value judgments must not be expressed in a hypothesis. Our hypothesis projects no value position. We aren't saying that age should be correlated with liberalism. We aren't saying that age is good or bad, that liberalism is glorious or abominable. We are simply making an objective statement. When you find old politicians, they will probably also be conservative ones.

After some effort, we have now come up with one hypothesis stated in a clear, correct manner. The attentive reader will have noticed that a number of additional hypotheses can be gleaned from the first five paragraphs of our hypothetical news story. Before you read further, try this little exercise.

Assignment #4
Go back and re-read the news story on pages 57 and 58. Then write down at least three other hypotheses which would clearly follow from information presented in the article. Do this now. Don't look ahead, or the exercise will lose all its value to you. And make sure that your hypotheses conform to our eight basic rules.

Writing hypotheses: the first formulation

Did you have any trouble coming up with three hypotheses? You shouldn't have, but we admit that hypothesis-construction takes practice. In fact, 14 additional hypotheses can be constructed from this single article—even before we turn to page 39 for the rest of it!

How is this possible? Well, let us stop a minute and examine the article in detail. Note the different pieces of information we are given about each Senator. We learn about his age, his party, the state he represents, whether he holds a chairmanship or not, his ADA rating for 1980, and his AFL-CIO rating for 1980. To show clearly just what information we have gleaned from the story, let us present it in tabular form:

Table IV-1. SELECTED DATA ON U.S. SENATORS, 1980

Senator	State	Party	Age, 1 Jan 1980	ADA rating, 1980	AFL-CIO rating, 1980	Committee Chairman?
Stennis	Miss.	Dem.	78	17	38	Yes
Tsongas	Mass.	Dem.	39	89	84	No

We have, all told, six different pieces of information about each Senator. Each of these information "bits" represents one

variable. So we have six variables, each of which can be correlated with all of the other variables. It is possible, therefore, to construct a total of 15 hypotheses--all from the information contained in three sentences of one newspaper story! (Once
you catch on to it, you will see that we are surrounded by enough
casual information to construct an infinite number of hypotheses.
You will also be struck by how easy they are to make up.)

All 15 hypotheses are set forth on the next page.

A few comments on the wording of these hypotheses are in
order:

1. Notice that we do **not** say, "Age is correlated with being a committee chairman," but rather "with the holding of top
power positions." This decision follows from our often-stated
aim--to make interesting hypotheses. "Being a committee chairman" is a specific, low-level, and not very exciting phenomenon.
It implies sitting at the head of a room shuffling papers during
endless hours of boring meetings (ho-hum). It might be important,
however, if it had broader ramifications than those conjured up by
this image. In fact, it is well known that having a committee
chairmanship in the U.S. Congress means having political power.
And "having political power" is an important and interesting
phenomenon. So the significant fact about Senator Stennis is not
his particular title, but the reality underlying it. Senator
Stennis is powerful. Thus, when we make up hypotheses relating
to his holding of a chairmanship, we phrase them in such a way as
to reflect the real meaning of a chairmanship--namely, that it
confers political power.

2. By the same reasoning we do not say, "Age is correlated
with an AFL-CIO rating of 70 or better." This statement again
avoids the real meaning of the rating, which is, simply, a measure
of a congressman's support for organized labor. We are not concerned with particular numbers, but with the general concept,
"degree of support for labor."

3. The reader should now understand why we do not say,
"Age is correlated with representation of the state of Mississippi." (Stop a minute. Can you say in your own words what is
wrong with that way of phrasing the hypothesis?) What is important is not one, specific state, but some borader, general phenomenon which that state might represent. What broader phenomenon
does Mississippi suggest? Anyone remotely familiar with American
politics knows the answer. Mississippi is part of the country's
most distinctive region. It represents the poorest region, the
least industrialized region, the region with the most distinctive
culture, the only part of the country to lose a war and be occu-
pied by "foreign" troops--in short, it represents the American
South. Regional differences have always played a major role in

61

SELECTED HYPOTHESES DERIVED FROM
A NEWS STORY ON U.S. SENATORS

H-1: Among political leaders, age is negatively correlated with liberalism.

H-2: Among political leaders, age is negatively correlated with support for labor.

H-3: Among political leaders, age is positively correlated with the holding of top power positions.

H-4: Among political leaders in the U.S., age is positively correlated with representation of a Southern district.

H-5: Among political leaders in the U.S., there is no correlation between age and party.

H-6: Among political leaders in the U.S., there is no correlation between party and regional representation.

H-7: Among political leaders in the U.S., there is no correlation between party and liberalism.

H-8: Among political leaders in the U.S., there is no correlation between party and support for labor.

H-9: Among political leaders in the U.S., there is no correlation between party and the holding of top power positions.

H-10: Among political leaders in the U.S., liberalism is negatively correlated with representation of a Southern district.

H-11: Among political leaders in the U.S., support for labor is negatively correlated with representation of a Southern district.

H-12: Among political leaders in the U.S., representation of a Southern district is positively correlated with the holding of top power positions.

H-13: Among political leaders, liberalism is positively correlated with support for labor.

H-14: Among political leaders, liberalism is negatively correlated with the holding of top power positions.

H-15: Among political leaders, support for labor is negatively correlated with the holding of top power positions.

American politics. The most significant of these regional differences has been that between the South (traditionally defined as those states which formed the Confederacy during the Civil War) and the rest of the country. One major difference between Senator Stennis and Senator Tsongas, then, is that Stennis is a "Southerner" and Tsongas is a "non-Southerner."

4. Note that some hypotheses postulate "positive" correlations between variables and others suggest "negative" correlations. A positive correlation means that the two variables move upward or downward together. The more you have of one, the more you get of the other. Likewise, when one diminishes in value, so does the other. A negative correlation means an _inverse_ relationship exists between the variables. As one increases in value, the other diminishes. Or as one gets smaller, the other gets bigger. For instance, H-2 ("Age is negatively correlated with support for labor") means that as a leader gets older, he is _less_ likely to support labor. Conversely, the "less old" (younger) he is, the _more_ he is likely to support labor.

Sometimes we omit the modifier, "positive," to describe a correlation. For example, we might say, "Level of education is correlated with participation in politics." In this case it is simply understood that the two variables are _positively_ correlated. The hypothesis means that the more education you have, the more likely you are to participate in politics. All hypotheses are assumed to state positive correlations, unless "negative" or "no" correlation is specifically mentioned.

5. Be aware that "no correlation" between variables is a distinct possibility. When X and Y are "not correlated with each other," it means that a change in one has no impact at all on the other. Take the relationship between annual yearly rainfall in Thailand and the likelihood of political revolution in Bolivia. We assume that no correlation exists between these two variables. That is, no matter whether it rains a lot or not at all in Thailand, Bolivia's chances of having a revolution are affected in no way whatsoever. "No correlation" means the two variables increase and decrease in ways completely independent of each other. In our hypothesis H-7 we postulate no correlation between party and liberalism because, from the preliminary evidence, whether you are high or low on the liberalism scale seems to have no bearing on your party affiliation. Tsongas, the liberal, and Stennis, the conservative, are both Democrats.

6. Notice that we have placed two different limits on the applicability of these hypotheses. In some cases we generalize to all "political leaders." In others we generalize only to "political leaders in the U.S." Why the dichotomy?

63

To begin, we want to generalize to all political leaders, if possible. (The more general the hypothesis, the greater its significance, remember?) But some of our data derive from circumstances very specific to the United States. For instance, parties vary dramatically from country to country. Each party belongs to a specific culture and historical era. We hesitate to generalize about parties beyond our borders without having a good deal more evidence than we find in this single news story.

In the same way, the American South is a special region, shaped by unique historical, social and political circumstances. It hardly seems likely that the southern parts of most other countries would also happen to be the most conservative parts of those countries. So we would not want to conclude that "leaders from the south everywhere are more conservative than leaders from the north."

When hypotheses included concepts specific to American circumstances, then, we applied them only to "political leaders in the U.S." But most of our concepts had broader applicability. "Degree of support for labor" is a phenomenon to be reckoned with in every country, as is "age of leaders," "degree of liberalism," and "the holding of top power positions." When hypotheses dealt only with these concepts, we felt they could be applied to political leaders everywhere.

It is not impossible to make broad hypotheses out of information concerning American political parties or the American South. One would like first, however, to have some knowledge about political trends in other countries. Our own background allows us to make hypotheses such as the following:

> Among political leaders, coming from a left-of-center
> party is correlated with support for labor.*

---

* This hypothesis might strike some political scientists as tautological. "Support for labor" is seen by many as automatically denoting a left-of-center position. This does not have to be the case, however. Juan Peron and other rightist dictators have at times taken positions ostensibly in favor of the labor interests in their country. And such great leftists as Lenin, Stalin and Brezhnev often repressed labor union leaders to the detriment of labor interests in the U.S.S.R. and elsewhere. "Support for labor" and "leftism" do not necessarily go together. But to avoid a tautology, one must take care in defining the two terms. If "support for labor" is defined as "support for better working conditions, better wages, and improved benefits for workers," while "leftism" is defined as "support for political movements which seek to use state power to redistribute social values (power, status, education, money, skills) in a more egalitarian manner," then the two variables are not identical and hence do not form a tautology.

Among political leaders, representing a rural district
is correlated with conservative position-taking.

These hypotheses are broad and significant. It even turns out
that there is a good deal of evidence to support them. They could
not, however, have been derived solely from information presented
in the newspaper article. They depend on (a) some additional
knowledge about American society (e.g., Democrats are more often to
the left than to the right of center, Mississippi is a rural state)
and on (b) knowledge of trends in other countries (e.g., the left
in most places is associated with support for labor, rural areas
are usually more conservative than industrialized areas).

In making up hypotheses H-1 through H-15, we acted as if we
were students without a great deal of additional information about
American politics beyond that presented in the newspaper article to
show what you, yourself, could do, faced with those data. The more
sophisticated hypotheses presented above show what you may be able
to achieve with a little practice as you continue your study of
politics.

7. As we mentioned earlier, scientific language is not
always elegant. At its best, it is clear and explicit, but it
takes getting used to. We suspect you will not instantly grasp the
meaning of some of our 15 hypotheses. But getting used to the
correct phrasing of hypotheses is important. We urge you to go
back, re-read all of these hypotheses, and make sure you understand exactly what they mean. Make sure, also, that you understand
why each hypothesis follows from the data presented in Table I.

Assignment #5
*Here is a simple exercise you should find useful. Write out
"in English translation" exactly what each hypothesis means. That
is, state the hypothesis in your own words. Central to the scientific method is the ability a) to state hypotheses in correct language, and b) to understand what hypotheses mean when they are
stated in correct language by others. Only when you can switch
back and forth with ease will you have mastered this major step in
the scientific method.*

*To guide you in this task, we have "translated" the hypotheses
ourselves. That is, we have stated them another way in non-scientific language. Check to see how your paraphrasing corresponds
with ours. (Of course, there are many ways to do this, so you
aren't necessarily "wrong" if you don't duplicate our statements
exactly.) Before going any further, make sure you understand why
each hypothesis on page 62 has the meaning we give it below.*

65

THE 15 HYPOTHESES "TRANSLATED"

H-1: Older politicians are more likely to be conservative than younger ones.

H-2: Older politicians are less likely to support labor than younger ones.

H-3: Older politicians are more likely to have powerful political jobs than younger ones.

H-4: Politicians from the American South are generally older than their Northern counterparts.

H-5: No one age group is clearly over-represented in the leadership element of American political parties.

H-6: No one region is clearly over-represented in the leadership element of American political parties.

H-7: Within the same political party American national leaders can be either liberal or conservative.

H-8: Within the same political party American national leaders can be either labor supporters or non-supporters.

H-9: Among American politicians, your political party does not necessarily determine whether you obtain a powerful political job.

H-10: American politicians from the South are less likely to be liberal than non-Southern American politicians.

H-11: American politicians from the South are less likely to be supporters of labor than non-Southern American politicians.

H-12: American politicians from the South are more likely to have powerful political jobs than non-Southern American politicians.

H-13: Liberal politicians are more likely to be supporters of labor than conservative ones.

H-14: Politicians who hold powerful political jobs are less likely to be liberal than non-powerful politicians.

H-15: Politicians who hold powerful political jobs are less likely to be supporters of labor than non-powerful politicians.

Writing hypotheses: the second formulation

Let us return to our 15 hypotheses. On viewing this imposing array of conclusions, the reader may wonder how a small set of facts about two individuals can generate this number of assertions. Two points may assuage the reader's concern. First, we remind her that hypotheses are precisely what the word implies: provisional conjectures, working suppositions, conditional guesses. They are not "iron-clad laws" or "solid research findings." Hypotheses remain conjectural until tested by means of elaborate, full-scale studies. So even though we have stated a number of hypotheses, even though they are stated in a rigorous, analytical format, we still have no evidence whatsoever that any of these hypotheses will be supported in practice.

Our second point is that these particular hypotheses must be seen as very tentative generalizations. They are first approximations, gropings in the dark, early attempts to make sense of some real-world observations. We clearly need more data before we can feel any confidence in these hypotheses.

This point suggests what our next step must be. Our news story example illustrates how easy it is to generate hypotheses. Making them up is simple. Testing them, however, is another matter. One can spend days, weeks, years, testing any given hypothesis. And you obviously don't want to spend all that time and energy testing hypotheses which you could see from the beginning were fanciful or erroneous. Sensible researchers, then, test only those hypotheses solidly backed by preliminary evidence, only those which they are fairly confident will work in practice.

What does "solid preliminary evidence" look like? There are two answers to this question. First, the student can never go wrong adopting as a working hypothesis the research findings turned up in other studies. Thus, one is on solid ground in choosing hypotheses such as the following:

1. Among nations, there is a positive correlation between literacy rates and the existence of democratic institutions.[1]

2. There is a positive correlation between socio-economic status and degree of trust in government.[2]

3. There is a negative correlation between degree of authoritarianism and level of education.[3]

Since a number of studies have found support for these hypotheses, they are eminently worth examining again with new data and under different circumstances. But a student would be mistaken in trying to test these hypotheses:

4. There is a negative correlation between likelihood of participating in politics and level of education.

5. There is a positive correlation between being left-handed and likelihood of voting for left-of-center political parties.

In the case of number 4, we have a solid mass of evidence which shows precisely the opposite of the hypothesis as stated.[4] There is absolutely no "solid preliminary evidence" to suggest it is worth while to test the hypothesis. Number 5 is a frivolous hypothesis. Since no evidence has ever turned up to suggest a correlation between left-handedness and left voting, it would simply be a waste of time conducting serious research on the subject.

There is a second way of deciding whether preliminary evidence warrants further testing of a hypothesis. This method is used when the subject is new or for other reasons has not been thoroughly studied. Reliance on the findings of others then becomes impossible. Or circumstances may prevent the examination of other studies--for example, a student may be given only a short time to write an original research paper. In these cases one relies on one's own resources to weed out the unlikely hypotheses. One does this by conducting a series of impressionistic tests of the original hypotheses. Those which continue to be supported after several stages of the testing process are presumed worthy of formal, systematic testing.

Let's say that you draw this conclusion after conversations with three Republican dorm mates:

Being a Republican is correlated with being a liberal. Then it turns out that the next ten Republicans you meet all call for an end to the food stamp program, a dramatic increase in defense spending, and a return to the old family values. You obviously would have to develop serious doubts about the utility of the original hypothesis. On the other hand, if you conclude after one semester in college that

being a professor is correlated with holding left-of-center opinions,

and six of the next seven courses you take are from radical or socialist instructors, you may feel that your hypothesis has some basis in reality.

The point is simple. Never remain satisfied with an early, rapidly-formed conclusion. Always look for ways to gather additional evidence, ways to check on the usefulness of your tentative

generalizations. And conduct a series of additional simple tests
so as to weed out those hypotheses which are clearly unworthy of
your precious time. In the following pages we will show you how
this can be done, by making use once again of the news story with
which we began this section.

Let us return to our original 15 hypotheses. We have said
that those were tentative hypotheses, developed on the basis of
very little solid evidence. Let us gather some more evidence to
see how well those hypotheses stand up. We shall do this casually,
at first, since we don't want to waste a lot of research time on
frivolous endeavors.

The first thing we could do is to finish reading the rest of
the Times news story. Although most of this article focuses on
interest group power and fails to present us with relevant information, we do come across some interesting data in one paragraph.

> The Democratic Party remains sharply divided between its
> liberal and conservative wings. Typical of the former is
> Washington's Senator Warren Magnuson. The 75-year-old Mag-
> nuson, Chairman of the powerful Appropriations Committee,
> scored 72 on the ADA rating system and a solid 89 with the
> AFL-CIO. On the other hand, Louisiana's J. Bennett Johnston,
> Jr., rated scores of 33 from the ADA and 41 from the AFL-CIO.
> Johnston, young for the Senate (48), has not yet obtained any
> powerful position in that seniority-oriented body.

Several new pieces of information appear in this paragraph. We
can use them to check on our original hypotheses. The first step
is once again to systematize our data:

SELECTED DATA ON U.S. SENATORS, 1980

Senator	State	Party	Age, 1 Jan. 1980	ADA rating, 1980	AFL-CIO rating, 1980	Committee Chairman?
Stennis	Miss.	Dem.	78	17	38	Yes
Tsongas	Mass.	Dem.	39	89	84	No
Magnuson	Wash.	Dem.	75	72	89	Yes
Johnston	Louis.	Dem.	48	33	41	No

We now proceed to check each hypothesis against the totality
of the data given above—to see whether our first impressions are
confirmed or undermined. Notice, in passing, how helpful it is
to put our information into systematic form. The table above shows
us instantly just what we know about each Senator. Our knowledge
is well organized and easy to work with. This clear format sums

up the basic data presented in six rambling paragraphs. The student who gets in the habit of organizing what he knows will find his studies (and his life) a lot easier to deal with.

We now turn to each of the 15 hypotheses. Let us walk through an examination of three of them with you, by which time you should be able to check on the others by yourself. Hypothesis H-1 states that age is negatively correlated with liberalism. That is to say, the older Senators should be conservatives, the younger ones liberal. Is this the case? Senator Stennis is "old" (78) and also "conservative" (ADA rating of 17). Senator Tsongas is "young" (39) and "liberal" (ADA rating of 89). But when we turn to the next two men, we find our hypothesis turned upside down. Senator Magnuson is "old" (75) and "liberal" (ADA rating of 72), while Senator Johnston is relatively young (48) and relatively conservative (ADA rating of 33).

We can look at it another way. Of the two older Senators, one is conservative (50%), while one of the two younger Senators (50%) is also conservative. Our hypothesis so far looks weak. There is one other way to check on its validity. We could take the two older and the two younger Senators and find their average ADA scores. It turns out that Stennis and Magnuson average 44½ on the ADA ratings, while Tsongas and Johnston average 61. The difference is not overwhelming. Both numbers are in or close to the 40-60 range often used to characterize "moderates" in American politics. Still, a not insignificant spread does exist and in the predicted direction.

How do we sum up our re-evaluation of Hypothesis H-1? We are surely less comfortable with it than we were before, yet we are not quite ready to throw it out altogether. We might phrase our conclusions in this way:

Re-interpretation of original hypothesis after first examination of new evidence

H-1: The new data throw some doubt on the original hypothesis and make us less confident of it.

Having stumbled once, let us try again. How well do we fare on Hypothesis H-2? This one states that older Senators will be less likely to support labor than younger Senators. Again, let us look at our two older Senators, Stennis and Magnuson. The former does not rate very high in labor's eyes (AFL-CIO rating of 38); the latter is beloved by labor (AFL-CIO rating of 89). The pattern is almost identical for the two younger Senators. Johnston is luke-warm for labor (AFL-CIO rating of 41), while Tsongas is red-hot (AFL-CIO rating of 85). Once again, 50% of the older Senators are pro-labor, as are 50% of the younger Senators.

When we use average rating scores by age, we find again no
difference between young and old. The two older Senators average
63½ in their scores for labor, compared to 62½ for the younger
Senators. The older men are just slightly more pro-labor than the
younger ones, whereas they should be a lot less pro-labor if the
hypothesis is to be supported. The evidence is in and clearly
leads away from the orignal hypothesis. We conclude:

Re-interpretation of original hypothesis
after first examination of new evidence

H-10: The new data strongly support the original
hypothesis and strengthen our confidence in it.

Assignment #6

*Are you starting to understand how to make simple tests of hy-
potheses? Good. In that case why not try to do a few on your own?
Here's a simple exercise. Take the 12 other hypotheses listed on
page 68. Using the data on page 78, check to see how well each of
these hypotheses is now supported. For each hypothesis state
briefly your conclusion (as we did for H-1, H-2, and H-10). You
will find this a useful exercise. When you have finished, you can
check your conclusions against ours (see next page).*

Writing hypotheses: the third formulation

We now have a better feel for the value of each of our original hypotheses. Some are standing up, others look doubtful. But
we are still basing our judgments on a small amount of evidence.
Let us persevere. The day after you read the original story in
the Times, let us say that you come across an article in U.S. News
and World Report on the growing conservative nature of the Republican Party. One paragraph leaps out at you:

> The growing conservative mood among Republicans cuts
> across all age levels and sections of the country. Out
> West in Arizona, Senator Barry Goldwater, 71 years old, racks
> up an ADA rating of 0 and gets a score of 18 from the AFL-CIO.
> On the other side of the country, Senator Gordon Humphrey of
> New Hampshire (only 39) is rated a mere 6 by both ADA and AFL-
> CIO. Finally, smack in the middle of the country is Kansas
> Senator Robert Dole. The 56-year-old Midwesterner scores 22
> on the ADA rating system and 28 on the AFl-CIO's.

You are delighted at the quantity of new information which
has just been made available to you. Breaking your date for the
evening, you dig up those original 15 hypotheses and start fever-
ishly to work re-testing them. As usual, you first put your data
into an organized format: (see p. 73)

Re-interpretation of original hypotheses
after first examination of new evidence

H-1:   The new data throw some doubt on the original hypothesis and make us less confident of it.

H-2:   The new data fail to support the original hypothesis and make us much less confident of it.

H-3:   The new data strongly support the original hypothesis and strengthen our confidence in it.

H-4:   The new data fail to support the original hypothesis and make us much less confident of it.

H-5:   The new data strongly support the original hypothesis and strengthen our confidence in it.

H-6:   The new data strongly support the original hypothesis and strengthen our confidence in it.

H-7:   The new data strongly support the original hypothesis and strengthen our confidence in it.

H-8:   The new data strongly support the original hypothesis and strengthen our confidence in it.

H-9:   The new data strongly support the original hypothesis and strengthen our confidence in it.

H-10: The new data strongly support the original hypothesis and strengthen our confidence in it.

H-11: The new data strongly support the original hypothesis and strengthen our confidence in it.

H-12: The new data fail to support the original hypothesis and make us much less confident of it.

H-13: The new data strongly support the original hypothesis and strengthen our confidence in it.

H-14: The new data throw some doubt on the original hypothesis and make us less confident of it.

H-15: The new data fail to support the original hypothesis and make us much less confident of it.

SELECTED DATA ON U.S. SENATORS, 1980

Senator	State	Party	Age, 1 Jan 1980	ADA rating, 1980	AFL-CIO rating, 1980	Committee Chairman?
Stennis	Miss.	Dem.	78	17	38	Yes
Tsongas	Mass.	Dem.	39	89	84	No
Magnuson	Wash.	Dem.	75	72	89	Yes
Johnston	Louis.	Dem.	48	33	41	No
Goldwater	Ariz.	Rep.	71	0	18	No
Humphrey	N.H.	Rep.	39	6	6	No
Dole	Kansas	Rep.	56	22	28	No

Before, proceeding, we must note that one piece of information presented in the table above was not given in the U.S. News and World Report article. We had to infer, from our own store of political knowledge, that Goldwater, Humphrey, and Dole were not Committee Chairmen in the U.S. Senate of 1980. In the U.S. Congress the minority party never gets a committee chairmanship. (Majority parties or majority coalitions in nearly every country allocate all chairmanships to their own members.) Since Republicans were in the minority in the 1980 U.S. Senate, there was no possibility that one of these three Republicans could hold a chairmanship.

We can now re-examine our 15 hypotheses a second time. Let us pick up H-1 again. Remember that we have already lost some confidence in this hypothesis. This second re-evaluation shows it to be a real loser. This is the hypothesis that says younger politicians will be liberals, older ones conservatives. Before we do any statistical juggling, we already have a sinking feeling that this cannot be correct just by a casual inspection of the data on our three new Senators. These men fall into three distinct age groups. Goldwater is relatively old (71), Dole is middle-aged (56), and Humphrey relatively young (39). Yet each man is a solid conservative. The ADA rates the three 0, 22, and 6, respectively. So we see at a glance that age makes no difference at all in your level of conservatism. Whether you are 39, 56, or 71, you can still be extremely conservative.

Let us move on to sift the evidence more systematically. As we did before, let us divide the Senators into old and young and see which group (if any) is more liberal. Magnuson, Stennis, and Goldwater can all easily be considered "old" (all over 70). Tsongas, Johnston, and Humphrey (all under 50) would appear to be "young." Of course, everything is relative. To a college student Johnston (48) might seem decrepit. But he was, in 1980, among the youngest third of U.S. Senators. The average age of American Sen-

73

ators has hovered around 55 for decades. For a U.S. Senator, then, Johnston is definitely "young."

But how do we classify the 56-year-old Senator Dole? Is he "old" or "young?" This question raises an inevitable corollary: Why do we have to classify people into one of two categories at all? Although answers to this question can become extremely complex, almost metaphysical, let us deal with it here on the simplest possible level. Briefly, categorization is essential to the scientific method and, indeed, to human thought processes. We are always categorizing people and things all the time and could not continue to live without doing so. Survival depends on knowing who is a "friend" and who is an "enemy," on recognizing what substances are "edible foods" and which are "poisons," on knowing who is your "boss" and who is your "subordinate." We are constantly dividing people we know into categories such as "intelligent" or "stupid," "aggressive" or "passive," "friendly" or "hostile." What's more, we act on the basis of our categories, because we find them useful. The tendency to label and type people, things, and events would appear to be a deeply ingrained and necessary human trait, not some private mania of the odd-ball scientist.

What the scientist does is to elevate the human tendency—the human need—to categorize to a more systematic, a more analytical, plane. Simply stated, science itself—that is to say, the testing of hypotheses—could not exist without categories. We divide blood cells into red and white, tumors into benign and malignant, soils into acidic and alkaline. And then we check to see whether these differentiated species behave differently in similar situations, react differently to similar stimuli. And when we see that they do behave differently, we have learned something important—for example, that maple trees produce a sweetish syrup when tapped, but elm trees do not.

So far, we have spoken of categorization in its simplest form, the dichotomy. Things are either black or white, hot or cold, big or small. Dichotomies are useful intellectual devices. (Imagine how hard your life would become if you could never divide parts of the world into either one thing or the other.) Still, we all recognize that the world is often more complex than the dichotomy would have it. We often need more than two categories. In Canada there are three national political parties. According to one famous study, there are four different kinds of Presidents.[5] Another study found that marriages fall into one of nine different patterns.[6] And a well-known psychologist has discerned twenty-six different human personality types.[7] So our need to categorize does not necessarily mean a need to dichotomize.

We do not, in short, have to divide all U.S. Senators into the categories of "young" and "old." We could divide them into

"young", "middle-aged," and "old." Or we could divide them into
"young,""young middle-aged," "middle-aged," "old middle-aged," and
"old." Or into these categories: "30-39," "40-49," "50-59,"
"60-69," and "70 and over." Or into any other set we might find
useful. And for some statistical purposes, as we shall see, we
could simply classify each one according to his actual age and end
up with a very large number of categories. (For Senators, the
number of categories would be around 40, since the age of most
Senators is between 35 and 75. But if one were categorizing people according to income, the number of categories would be enormous
—since income presumably ranges from zero to several billion.)

Categories, then, are essential for any kind of thinking and
especially for scientific research. But despite the variety of
categorizing schemes, most people find that typologies presenting a
small number of cases are the most useful. The human mind can carry only so much baggage. If I tell you that there are 87 different kinds of politicians, you would never be able to remember them
all. They would end up a confused jumble in your head, and the
categories would be quite useless to you. If I tell you that
there are three kinds of politicians--the aggressive-ambitious-
driven type, the quietly-efficient-bureaucratic type, and the con-
genial-backslapping-good-old-boy type--you can remember the terms,
you can apply them to real-world politicians you encounter, and
you may actually find them helpful in distinguishing among different kinds of political leaders.

The world is inordinately complex, and the human mind constantly seeks ways to simplify it in order to make sense of it.
Categorizing schemes which involve large numbers of categories
usually complicate rather than simplify reality. As a general
rule, typologies--to be useful--should limit the number of categories to single numbers; and the most famous typologies usually
divide people or events into a mere two to five categories.

The dichotomy, then, is a perfectly legitimate and widely-
used intellectual device. It is also the simplest. The beginner
can understand and work with it easily. So let us not shy away
from the dichotomy. Later we shall develop more complex categories, but the dichotomy is a good jumping-off point for the student just getting seriously into scientific research.

Having developed the rationale for our endeavor, let us return
to our attempt at classifying Senator Dole as either "young" or
"old." What we would really like here is some kind of general
rule for classifying all Senators as either "young" or "old." Indeed, we would like a general rule for classifying as "higher" or
"lower" on a given variable all cases we might be studying involving numbers (income levels, density of stars, rainfall averages).
Luckily, there is one simple general rule--one we are all familiar

with—to aid us in making classifications. It involves using the "average." We can say that all those cases <u>at or above</u> the "average" will be put into one category. Those <u>below</u> the "average" go into another.

As usual, nothing is as simple as we would like. We have placed quotation marks around the word "average" because—are you ready for this one?—there are two kinds of average! Each one can give a different result and is used for different purposes. Let us examine both kinds of "average."

You are surely familiar with the most common way of calculating an average. You take all the numbers in a group, add them up, and divide by the total number of cases. The result of this calculation is an average called the <u>mean</u>.

Let's say you are an ardent baseball fan. You wish to check on the average hitting abilities of the players on your favorite team, the Peoria Purple Sox. As part of your examination you decide to calculate the mean number of home runs hit by the nine starting players (including the designated hitter). First, you set down your data, as follows:

Home run hitting,
Peoria Purple Sox, 1982

Player	Number of home runs
Tackhammer	12
Finkelstein	11
Brzycahtzsz	10
Trillantino	10
Jones	9
Krautmeister	8
Lemachin	7
Watchnikoff	7
Arbuthnot	7

Then, you add up all the home runs hit by these nine players and get the figure 81. You divide 81 by the total number of players (9) and end up with 9. This number is the mean number of home runs for the nine starting hitters on this baseball team. One way to summarize what you have found is to say: "The players in the starting line-up of the Peoria Purple Sox hit, on the average, nine home runs each year." Or: "The average Peoria Purple Soxer hits nine home runs a year."

Notice how <u>useful</u> the mean is for descriptive purposes. If someone asks, "How does the Peoria team do in the home run department?" and you answer, "The mean player hits nine four-baggers a

year," you have conveyed helpful information. The listener con-
jures up an image of a number of players hitting around nine home
runs a year. In fact, this image will be accurate. All of the
players hit within three home runs of this figure. One simple
number sums up a good deal of information.

There are times, however, when the mean distorts our data and
conveys a positively misleading impression. Take the case of the
Peoria team's arch-rivals, the Chattanooga Butterflies. Here are
the home run statistics for the Butterflies' starting line-up:

Home run hitting,
Chattanooga Butterflies, 1982

Player	Number of home runs
Bletchnikovsky	58
White	5
Heath	5
Pierce	5
Smith	4
Snow	3
Roy	1
Foss	0
Black	0

It turns out that this team has precisely the same mean number
of home runs as the Purple Sox! So why are we dissatisfied at the
conclusion that "Chattanooga and Peoria players both hit an average
of nine home runs a year?" We have the distinct impression that
the number 9 does not do a good job of describing home run hitting
by any player among the Butterflies. Eight of these players don't
even come close to hitting nine home runs a year, and one hits over
six times as many a year. So we have an image in our head of a
number of players around the nine mark, and that is totally erroneous. Surely we can find a better way to summarize the home run
hitting abilities of the Chattanoogans.

There is a better way. It is a second way of calculating
averages called the median. We turn to this method when one or a
few numbers pull the majority out of line to create the kind of
distortion we have just witnessed. The median is defined simply
as the middle number in a consecutive series. That is, when numbers are arranged from highest to lowest, the median is the number
exactly in the middle. Exactly half the numbers in a series are
above it, exactly half are below.

In the case of these two baseball teams the middle number
(the median) will be easy to identify, for we have already listed
the players in order of their home-run-hitting abilities. For

Peoria the middle number is 9. There are four numbers above 9
(12, 11, 10, and 10) and four below (8, 7, 7, and 7). We conclude
that Jones, with his nine home runs, represents the median hitting
ability of the team. We also see that when there is a reasonably
even dispersal of numbers, the mean and the median are very similar (identical, in this case).

Before reading further, try to identify for yourself the
median number of home runs for the Chattanooga Butterflies. You
should have chosen the number 4. If you did not, re-read the previous two paragraphs to make sure you understand how a median is
arrived at.

We now have another way to describe the average home-run
talents of the Butterflies. The median Chattanooga player hits 4
home runs a year. Note how much more useful the median is than the
mean in this case. Eight of the nine players hit four or close to
four home runs a year. This number gives a more correct image of
the team than the mean of 9 does. We now see the Butterflies as a
bunch of losers, rather than as a group of moderate abilities.
True, one player is not well described by our new average number,
but--what the heck!--you can't have everything. We might conclude,
"Except for the incredible Bletchnikovsky, the median Butterflies'
player hits a mere four home runs a year."

Two cases arise when finding the median becomes slightly more
complicated than just "finding the middle number." One case involves an even set of numbers. To illustrate, let's look at that
great baseball team, the 1949 Boston Red Sox. (This team had
everything going for it and should have won the pennant, but
managed to blow it at the last minute--thereby inaugurating the
"September collapse" with which all Boston fans are familiar.)
Since "designated hitters" did not exist in 1949, only eight players can be defined as regular starting batters that year. They
performed as follows:

Home run hitting,
Boston Red Sox, 1949

Player	Number of home runs
Williams	43
Stephens	39
Doerr	18
Zarilla	9
DiMaggio	8
Tebbetts	5
Pesky	2
Goodman	0

What is the median home run output for this group? It can't

be the middle figure, since there is no middle figure. There never will be a middle figure when we have an even group of numbers. Instead, we have two middle figures. Here, 9 and 8 are the two middle figures. (There are three numbers above 9: 18, 39, and 43. There are three numbers below 8: 5, 2 and 0.) The way to calculate the median in this case is to take the average of the two middle numbers. The result is 8 1/2. We would say that the median number of home runs for starting hitters on the 1949 Boston Red Sox team is 8.5. Incidentally, what is the mean number of home runs for this team? Which number do you prefer for describing the team's home run performance? Why?

A second complication can arise with the median. There may be ties. What if Prof. Goodfellow gives two quizzes in his seminar on sub-atomic particles, with the following results?

Prof. Goodfellow's Quiz #1		Prof. Goodfellow's Quiz #2	
Student	Grade	Student	Grade
John	92	John	87
Mary	84	Mary	86
Brenda	79	Brenda	83
Wilhemina	79	Wilhemina	79
Chip	79	Chip	79
Engelbert	73	Engelbert	78
Bathsheba	57	Bathsheba	45

In both cases there is no one middle number, but two or three. But 79 is clearly the number we would call the median in both these cases. It is not so clear in the next case:

Prof. Goodfellow's Quiz #3	
Student	Grade
John	96
Mary	91
Brenda	85
Wilhelmina	79
Chip	79
Engelbert	74
Bathsheba	(dropped course)

Bathsheba having dropped out, we are left with six students--an even number. Ordinarily, the median in this case would be the average of the two middle numbers. But we actually have three middle numbers, because of the tie between Wilhemina and Chip. Here the median is calculated by averaging all three of the middle numbers, or: 85 + 79 + 79 divided by 3. The median for this quiz turns out to be 81.

In the final analysis, when do we use the mean and when do we use the median for describing an average? Normally, the mean is preferable. It is easier to calculate, and it has a number of useful mathematical properties not possessed by the median. In addition, if the numbers are at all large (20 or more), it takes time to calculate the median because of the need to place all the numbers in arithmetical sequence. For numbers of 100 or more, putting them all in order becomes an enormous chore. Furthermore, if you are working with a fairly large set of numbers, the distorting effect on the mean of extreme cases will usually be negligible. For example, if three students in a class of four score 70 each on a quiz and the fourth student scores 100, the perfect student pulls the class mean up to 77½. But if we have thirty students in the class, all of whom score 70, one additional student with a perfect score pulls this group's mean up to a mere 71 (a perfectly acceptable description of the group's performance).

In another case, however, even one extreme value can distort the average for a large group of people. Say you had 99 factory workers making $10,000 a year each. Add the factory owner, who makes $1,010,000 a year. The mean yearly income for this set of 100 people turns out to be $20,000! The median income for this group is, of course, $10,000. Which figure better describes the group? Our conclusion is: be cautious. Normally, use the mean for obtaining average, but if this figure will produce strong distortions of the data, discard it for the median.

If you have a good memory, you will recall why we have spent the last few pages discussing averages. We are trying to classify seven U.S. Senators as either "young" of "old." Those at or above the average would be called "old": those below the average would be called "young." So it became necessary to find the average. We can now return to the table of page 73 and look hastily at the ages of the seven Senators. The ages appear to be scattered between 39 and 78, with no particular extreme to distort the picture. We can feel safe in opting for the mean as our average. It turns out to be 58. (Means are a breeze to calculate in this day of the $10 pocket calculator.) At last we can classify our recalcitrant Senator Dole! We can place this 56-year-older in the "young" category.

What if Senator Dole had been 58, identical to the average? A simple rule can handle this fairly common occurrence. When defining "old" and "young", you need merely state that ages at or above the average will be considered "old;" those below the average will be considered "young". Using a clear definition of this sort, you will always know how to classify each case in any group of data you are working with.

We can finally proceed with the next phase of our test. You

may (or may not) remember that we are working on Hypothesis H-1, which states that the older you are, the more conservative you will be. We can now check on the ADA scores of our four young and three old Senators.

Young Senators	ADA scores	Old Senators	ADA scores
Tsongas	89	Stennis	17
Johnston	33	Magnuson	72
Humphrey	6	Goldwater	0
AVERAGE (mean)	37.5	AVERAGE (mean)	29.7
AVERAGE (median)	27.5	AVERAGE (median)	17

The difference between old and young Senators is now even less than it was before, and the average for both groups rests in the moderately conservative range.* Still, younger Senators remain, on the whole, slightly more liberal than older ones. We note, however, that only 25% of the younger Senators are liberal, compared to 33% of the older ones. The case is perhaps not yet closed, but we are hardly very confident of our hypothesis. We draw this conclusion:

Re-interpretation of original hypothesis
after second examination of new evidence

H-1: The new data fail to support the hypothesis, and our lack of confidence in its value has been reinforced.

How does our second hypothesis fare? H-2 says older Senators will be less supportive of labor than younger ones. Our first re-examination showed no support for this hypothesis. This second effort should make us ready to throw the hypothesis into the wastebasket. The table below tells the story. We see instantly that

Young Senators	AFL-CIO Scores	Old Senators	AFL-CIO Scores
Tsongas	84	Stennis	38
Johnston	41	Magnuson	89
Humphrey	6	Goldwater	18
Dole	28		
AVERAGE (mean)	39.8	AVERAGE (mean)	48.3
AVERAGE (median)	34.5	AVERAGE (median)	38

* Note that we have provided information on both types of average: the mean and the median. Normally, you will choose to work with one or the other. However, when you have small numbers and it is easy to calculate both of them, you will find it useful to do so. If the mean is far out of line from the median, you would then

young Senators are somewhat _less_ likely than older Senators to support labor, whereas the hypothesis states they should be more likely to do so. The average AFL-CIO ratings (both mean and median) are somewhat higher for old Senators than for young Senators. What's more, 33% of the older Senators can be called strong labor backers; only 25% of young Senators rate that description. Our conclusion:

Re-interpretation of original hypothesis
after second examination of new evidence

H-2: The new data again fail to support the original hypothesis and make us feel increasingly confident that it has no merit.

We turn now to the third hypothesis we have been examining: H-10. This one says that Southern politicians are less likely to be liberal than non-Southerners. The hypothesis worked well during our first re-examination. A glance at the new data, however, makes us uneasy. None of the three Senators added to the data set (Goldwater, Humphrey, Dole) are from the traditional South, yet all are strongly conservative. Still, let us examine the data systematically before giving up on the hypothesis. As usual, we construct a simple table to see what we have:

Southern Senators	ADA Scores	Non-Southern Senators	ADA Scores
Stennis	17	Tsongas	89
Johnston	33	Magnuson	72
		Goldwater	0
		Humphrey	6
		Dole	22
AVERAGE (mean)	25	AVERAGE (mean)	37.8
AVERAGE (median)	25	AVERAGE (median)	22

Clearly, the data are not overwhelmingly strong in favor of the hypothesis. Yet, we are hardly ready to discard it. Although the median ADA scores are about even, the non-Southern Senators still have a clear lead on the mean ADA ratings. Further, notice that _all_ Southern Senators (100%) are conservative, while only 60% of non-Southern Senators are. A case can still be made that Southerners are more conservative than others. But our concern that the case for this hypothesis is weakening must be expressed in our conclusion:

---

want to examine the data-set carefully to see which (if either) of your two averages best sums up the information.

Re-interpretation of original hypothesis
after second examination of new evidence

H-10: The new data weaken the hypothesis and undermine our confidence in it, although we are
not yet ready to reject it.

Assignment #7
*It is again time to send the ball into your court. Go through
the remaining twelve hypotheses with the data on page 73. See how
well the new data support each hypothesis. Then write out your
twelve conclusions. When you have completed the exercise, check
the next page to see whether your analysis agrees with ours.*

Having spent this much time on these 15 hypotheses, you should,
if you are a true scientist, feel a growing interest in their outcomes. What is the real story? Are conservatives really no older
than liberals? Are Southerners likely to be Democrats rather than
Republicans? Is power all in the hands of the elderly? Curiosity
and an eagerness to answer questions lie at the heart of all good
research. Let's say curiosity gets the better of you and you head
to the library for more information. Delving into publications
such as The Congressional Quarterly Almanac,[8] the Almanac of American Politics[9] and Congressional Directory,[10] you dig up information on four more Senators whose names pop out as you flip through
the pages--Ribicoff, Long, Leahy, and Percy. You add this information to your other material and come up with the following data-
sheet:

SELECTED DATA ON U.S. SENATORS, 1980

Senator	State	Party	Age, 1 Jan. 1980	ADA rating, 1980	AFL-CIO rating, 1980	Committee Chairman?
Stennis	Miss.	Dem.	78	17	38	Yes
Tsongas	Mass.	Dem.	39	89	84	No
Magnuson	Wash.	Dem.	75	72	89	Yes
Johnston	La.	Dem.	48	33	41	No
Goldwater	Ariz.	Rep.	71	0	18	No
Humphrey	N. H.	Rep.	39	6	6	No
Dole	Kans.	Rep.	56	22	28	No
Ribicoff	Conn.	Dem.	70	56	77	Yes
Leahy	Vt.	Dem.	40	83	83	No
Long	La.	Dem.	61	28	50	Yes
Percy	Ill.	Rep.	60	39	41	No

Now that you are becoming an old hand at examining evidence,
we should be able to fly through this third re-examination of the

Re-interpretation of original hypotheses
after second examination of new evidence

H-1: The new data fail to support the hypothesis, and our lack of confidence in its value has been reinforced.

H-2: The new data again fail to support the original hypothesis and make us feel increasingly confident that it has no merit.

H-3: The new data again support the original hypothesis and make us feel quite confident that it is a useful one.

H-4: The new data offer slight support for the original hypothesis; we are not yet ready to reject it.

H-5: The new data very strongly support the original hypothesis and make us feel quite confident that it is a useful one.

H-6: The new data definitely undermine the hypothesis and weaken our confidence in it.

H-7: The new data definitely undermine the hypothesis and weaken our confidence in it.

H-8: The new data definitely undermine the hypothesis and weaken our confidence in it.

H-9: The new data definitely undermine the hypothesis and weaken our confidence in it.

H-10: The new data weaken the hypothesis and undermine our confidence in it, although we are not yet ready to reject it.

H-11: The new data weaken the hypothesis and undermine our confidence in it, although we are not yet ready to reject it.

H-12: The new data marginally reinforce the hypothesis but do not leave us very confident in it.

H-13: The new data strongly support the hypothesis and make us feel quite confident that it is a useful one.

H-14: The new data throw increasing doubt on the original hypothesis and further weaken our confidence in it.

H-15: The new data throw increasing doubt on the original hypothesis and further weaken our confidence in it.

hypotheses. First, we trot out H-1 which links age to conservatism. Before we can analyze the data, we must remember that the new pieces of information will produce different averages for each of the variables. That is, what is "old," what is "liberal," and so forth, will now have a different numerical definition. The last time we examined H-1 (with information on seven Senators), the mean age for the group was 58. The new data hardly change this mean at all. The mean age for all eleven Senators becomes 57.9. This lack of change is merely a coincidence, however. It turns out, for instance, that the addition of the four new Senators changes the mean AFL-CIO score from 43.4 to 50.5. Remember, whenever you add new data to existing data, be sure to re-calculate group averages.

Young Senators	ADA Scores	Old Senators	ADA Scores
Tsongas	89	Stennis	17
Johnston	33	Magnuson	72
Humphrey	6	Goldwater	0
Dole	22	Ribicoff	56
Leahy	83	Long	28
		Percy	39
AVERAGE (mean)	46.6	AVERAGE (mean)	35.3
AVERAGE (median)	33	AVERAGE (median)	33.5

In our final pre-test analysis of data on this hypothesis we come away relatively unimpressed by it, though not ready to reject it out of hand. The table above shows a slight tendency for older Senators to be more conservative than younger ones. The mean ADA rating for older Senators is 35.3; that for younger Senators is 46.6—a clear, if not overwhelming difference. One-third (33.3%) of the older Senators (Magnuson and Ribicoff, of the six) are liberals. Two-fifths (40%) of the younger Senators (Tsongas and Leahy, of the five) are liberals. Again, we see a difference in the expected direction, but hardly a dramatic one. We note finally that median ADA scores for the two groups are just about identical (old: 33.5; young: 33). We conclude that there may be a slight tendency for younger political leaders to be more liberal than older ones, but nothing more. Stated formally:

Re-interpretation of original hypothesis after third examination of new evidence

H-1: The new data lend slight support to the hypothesis; we are not yet ready to reject it, but have no great confidence in it either.

We turn now to Hypothesis H-2. This assertion, that age is negatively correlated with support for labor, has not held up well

with the addition of new data. This latest set of evidence leads
to rejection of the hypothesis altogether. As you can readily see,
almost no difference exists between AFL-CIO scores of young and old
Senators, but what difference does exist leans in the "wrong" direction. Older Senators are slightly _more_ pro-labor than younger
ones.

Young Senators	AFL-CIO Scores	Old Senators	AFL-CIO Scores
Tsongas	84	Stennis	38
Johnston	41	Magnuson	89
Humphrey	6	Goldwater	18
Dole	28	Ribicoff	77
Leahy	83	Long	50
		Percy	41
AVERAGE (mean)	48.4	AVERAGE (mean)	52.2
AVERAGE (median)	41	AVERAGE (median)	45.5

We have re-checked H-2 three different times. Each time the
new data fail to support the original proposition. We are not only
ready to reject H-2, but are indeed becoming confident of a new
hypothesis relating age to labor support--namely, no correlation
exists between the two variables. We draw our conclusions in this
manner:

Re-interpretation of original hypothesis
after third examination of new evidence

H-2: The new data lead us tentatively to reject
the hypothesis and to assert this new one:

H-2': Among political leaders, no correlation
exists between age and support for labor.

This last set of data raises a delicate point. When does a
"difference" really make a difference? This seemingly nonsensical
question lies at the heart of a major problem in research--how to
interpret one's findings. We see in the previous table, for instance, a difference of 3.8% between mean AFL-CIO scores for young
and old Senators. Is this difference "important?" Would a 7.8%
difference be important? A 17.8% difference? What guidelines,
finally, do we have to see what we have discovered?

In a later chapter we will take up some statistical devices
which will help answer these questions. But even after using the
most sophisticated statistics, once we have the results we must
fall back on our own individual interpretations to say what the
data mean. Although many extensive studies have been carried out,
scientists are still arguing the question of whether cigarettes

kill you or not. Interpretation is everything. Looking at the
same evidence, one person will "see" an important correlation,
another person will not. We must often rely on our common sense,
but one person's common sense is not the same as another's.

With these discouraging words as preface, let us return to
our immediate case to see what we can make of it. We shall use
what "common sense" we can muster. A 3.8% difference must be considered in terms of the total potential difference between young
and old Senators. There could have been a difference of 100% between the mean scores of these two groups. (One group could have
averaged 0%, the other group 100%.) On a continuum of 100, 3.8
doesn't seem like much. Even an 8% or 9% difference seems less
than striking.

On the other hand, a 20% difference feels like a fairly big
gap between two scores. We can't prove that 20% is an important
difference. That's just the way it feels to us, after having
played around with statistics in this way for a number of years.
We believe many other researchers would agree with us, although
surely some would not. As an argument for our rough "20% rule,"
we show below how its use can delineate six easily-recognized
types in American politics:

USING THE 20% RULE TO DEFINE THE POLITICAL
POSITIONS OF AMERICAN POLITICIANS

ADA rating	Ideological positions
Around 0%	Strong Conservative
Around 20%	Conservative
Around 40%	Moderate, Leaning Conservative
Around 60%	Moderate, Leaning Liberal
Around 80%	Liberal
Around 100%	Strong Liberal

Few observers would disagree with our characterization of
Senators at these particular points on the ADA scale. This suggests (though it can't prove) that 20% is a reasonably good
dividing-point. The closer a difference gets to 20%, the more
likely it is to reveal an important gap between two groups.
Scores under 10% show next-to-no difference between two groups.
Scores in the 10%-20% range present ambiguous evidence, which
you will unfortunately have to interpret on a case-by-case or
seat-of-the-pants basis.

Don't go away thinking that a difference of 3.8 never means
anything. Everything is relative, as we have suggested before.
3.8 on a scale of 100 doesn't look like much. But on a scale of
5 it would look enormous. Suppose you learned that poor women in

your state had an average of 5.2 children in their lifetime, compared to 1.4 children per rich women? Does that seem like a major
difference? Absolutely! And you feel it's important because you
know that the number of children women produce rarely gets much
above 10, and more often than not in our times stays under 5. So
a 3.8 difference in the number of children found in one set of
mothers compared to another hits us in the face.

On the other hand, a difference of 20, which may seem important in comparing two Senators' ADA ratings, would seem insignificant in comparing two Americans' yearly income. If Bill Suttle-
meyer earns $15,170 a year and Wallace Wainwright earns $15,190,
we would see no real difference between the two--nor would they.
In comparing income levels, only $500 differences would seem worth
bothering about. And in comparing distances between the earth and
various stars, a difference might not seem important until it
reached 10 light-years or more.

We reiterate that there are no hard-and-fast rules for interpreting data or statistics. All we can say at this point is the
following: look closely at your data and ask yourself, "What kind
of difference between these groups would really seem important,
given the possible range of values I am working with?" Then go
ahead and make a judgment. Just be ready to back it up if someone
(like your professor) disagrees with your "judgment call."

We promise no additional digressions before concluding our
tests of the original hypotheses. The third hypothesis we have
been looking at is H-10, the proposition that liberals are unlikely to come from the American South. At the last test this hypothesis was barely holding up. The new infusion of evidence, however,
re-invigorates our faith in this assertion. The difference between

Southern Senators		ADA Scores	Non-Southern Senators		ADA Scores
Stennis		17	Tsongas		89
Johnston		33	Magnuson		72
Long		28	Goldwater		0
			Humphrey		6
			Dole		22
			Ribicoff		56
			Leahy		83
			Percy		39
AVERAGE	(mean)	26	AVERAGE	(mean)	45.9
AVERAGE	(median)	28	AVERAGE	(median)	47.5

the average liberalism ratings of the two groups is now just about
at the 20% mark. Further, none of the Southerners are liberal,
while 50% of the non-Southerners are. So after several casual

analyses, all tending in the direction of support for our hypothesis, we are now ready to conclude that it is worth conducting a full-scale test on this particular proposition. We put it this way:

Re-interpretation of original hypothesis
after third examination of new evidence

H-10: The new data strongly support the hypothesis
and make us confident that a major test of
this proposition would not produce evidence
to refute it.*

Assignment #8
It's your turn again. Analyze the remaining 12 hypotheses in light of the evidence on page 83. What conclusions do you draw? Be sure to undertake this exercise before looking at our re-interpretations!

Re-interpretation of original hypotheses
after third examination of new evidence

H-1: The new data lend slight support to the hypothesis; we are
not yet ready to reject it, but have no great confidence
in it either.

H-2: The new data lead us tentatively to reject the hypothesis
and to assert this new one:
H-2': Among political leaders, no correlation exists
between age and support for labor.

H-3: The new data overwhelmingly support the hypothesis; a major
test is warranted, and we are confident that it would produce evidence to support the hypothesis.

H-4: The new data lend slight support to the hypothesis; we are
not yet ready to reject it, but have no great confidence in
it either.

H-5: The new data strongly support the hypothesis; a major test
is warranted, and we are confident that it would produce
evidence to support the hypothesis.

---

*   We could also have phrased it this way: ". . . a major test
of this proposition would produce evidence to support it." For a
discussion of how to phrase conclusions after scientific testing,
see pp. 187-90 below.

H-6: The new data lead us tentatively to reject the hypothesis and to assert this new one:
  H-6': Among political leaders in the U.S., a correlation exists between representing a Southern district and being affiliated with the Democratic Party.

H-7: The new data lead us tentatively to reject the hypothesis and to assert this new one:
  H-7': Among political leaders in the U.S., a correlation exists between being liberal and being a Democrat.

H-8: The new data lead us tentatively to reject the hypothesis and to assert this new one:
  H-8': Among political leaders in the U.S., support for labor is correlated with being affiliated with the Democratic Party.

H-9: The new data lead us tentatively to reject the hypothesis and to assert this new one:
  H-9': Among political leaders in the U.S., membership in the Democratic Party is correlated with holding top power positions.

H-10: The new data strongly support the hypothesis and make us confident that a major test of this proposition would not produce evidence to refute it.

H-11: The new data lend some support to the hypothesis; we are moderately confident that a full-scale test would not produce evidence leading to rejection of the hypothesis.

H-12: The new data strongly support the hypothesis; a major test is warranted, and we are confident that it would produce evidence to support the hypothesis.

H-13: The new data overshelmingly support the hypothesis; a major test is warranted, and we are confident that it would produce evidence to support the hypothesis.

H-14: The new data tentatively lead us to reject the hypothesis; indeed, there appears to be some slight support for the opposite of the original hypothesis, namely:
  H-14': Among political leaders, liberalism is positively correlated with the holding of top power positions.

H-15: The new data tentatively lead us to reject the hypothesis; indeed, there appears to be strong support for the opposite of the original hypothesis, namely:
  H-15': Among political leaders, support for labor is positively correlated with the holding of top power positions.

Summing up

It is time to review what we have done and see where to go
from here. An important step in the scientific process might be
labeled as "fiddling around." You make casual observations of
some phenomena that interest you, you conduct preliminary, low-
level tests, you build up tentative impressions about the variables
which might be influencing the outcomes you are observing; you
poke, you prod, you guess, you follow your nose. In this process
you play the role of tourist in a new land, a laid-back amateur.
At some point (and no one can define precisely when that point is
reached) you become familiar enough with the problem, the evidence,
and the methods to shuck your role of tourist and amateur. You
now become the seasoned traveller, the hard-boiled professional.
In short, you have learned enough to know what questions should be
followed up in earnest, and which show no promise. It is time to
get serious.

We have reached that stage. After several attempts to relate
new evidence to the original fifteen hypotheses, we find that some
of these hypotheses have held up well and others look weak. Indeed, some of the original hypotheses have had to be revised for
one simple reason: much of the later evidence failed to support or
even ran counter to the hypotheses as first stated. Having matched new pieces of information to the fifteen initial hypotheses, we
now find ourselves left with varying degrees of confidence in those
hypotheses (or, in some cases, their revised versions).

In any scientific endeavor it makes sense to concentrate limited resources (time, money, etc.) on the most promising avenues
for research. Those hypotheses showing the strongest initial support in preliminary investigations would logically be those to
which we would first commit the resources of a full-scale test.
When a number of leads appear equally promising, we would want
first to choose the more "interesting" hypotheses. (Remember the
discussion in Chapter 2.) In fact, our personal preference is to
choose an interesting hypothesis which has obtained only moderate
preliminary confirmation over a more prosaic hypothesis which has
obtained strong support in early investigations.

Given these two criteria of "preliminary confirmation" and
"interestingness," we would personally undertake full-scale
testing of these fifteen hypotheses in the following order:

GROUP I, KEY HYPOTHESES TO TEST:	H-10:	Being Southern correlates with being conservative.
	H-12:	Being Southern correlates with power-holding.
	H-6:	Being Southern correlates with being Democratic.

GROUP II,	H-14:	Liberalism correlates with power-holding.
INTERESTING	H- 7:	Liberalism correlates with being Democratic.
HYPOTHESES,	H- 9:	Being Democratic correlates with power-
SHOULD BE		holding.
TESTED IF AT	H- 8:	Being Democratic correlates with support
ALL POSSIBLE:		for labor.
	H-15:	Support for labor correlates with power-
		holding.

GROUP III,		
MODERATELY		
SUPPORTED OR		
MODERATELY	H-13:	Liberalism correlates with support for
INTERESTING		labor.
HYPOTHESES;	H-11:	Support for labor correlates with being
TEST IF TIME		non-Southern.
ALLOWS:		

GROUP IV, LESS	H- 3:	Age correlates with power-holding.
INTERESTING	H- 5:	Age does not correlate with party.
HYPOTHESES;	H- 2:	Age does not correlate with support for
HARDLY WORTH		labor.
TESTING:		

GROUP V:		
POORLY	H- 1:	Age negatively correlates with liberalism.
SUPPORTED,	H- 4:	Age correlates with being Southern.
UNINTERESTING		
HYPOTHESES;		
FORGET THEM:		

Not all scholars would choose our precise ordering, but we suspect that most would not be far out of line from the listing above. How did we arrive at these judgments? Let us review the groupings:

1. The first set contains hypotheses which have been strongly supported during preliminary investigation and which involve important political concepts. If one region of a country is different from the others and is more powerful, a number of important political implications follow. And these three hypotheses (if supported) do lead to this conclusion: the American South is more conservative, more supportive of the Democratic Party, and more powerful than the rest of the U.S. These are, as veteran observers of American politics know, three of the most central facts about our system; as such, they deserve extended analytical treatment well before most other propositions about the American scene.

2. The second group contains hypotheses not quite as strongly supported as the first group, but nearly as interesting. They center on the quintessential political question--who holds power?

The answer they suggest is that liberals, supporters of labor, and (in the U.S.) Democrats are most likely to hold power. Since political outcomes and national policies would differ drastically if the opposite were true (if conservatives, labor opponents, and Republicans held power), the testing of these hypotheses would appear to be an important task.*

3. The third group contains an interesting hypothesis (that labor supporters are non-Southern) which is only partially supported by preliminary evidence; and a less interesting hypothesis overwhelmingly supported by casual early tests (that liberals are pro-labor). One therefore feels less urgency about testing either of these hypotheses than one did for those in the first two groupings. Neophytes to political science may disagree with our placing of the liberals-are-pro-labor hypothesis in this category. We argue simply that a liberal-labor alliance is such a natural element in the political scene of most democratic countries that it hardly seems like the most pressing of topics for further research.

Indeed, in the U.S. liberalism and pro-laborism seem, on the surface, almost equivalencies. Some might argue that the statement borders on the tautological. (But see our discussion on page 64, footnote.) We hasten to point out that the evidence presented in this chapter allows us to avoid a tautology when we assert that "liberalism is correlated with support for labor." Liberalism is defined as "scoring high on the ADA rating system." "Support for labor" means "scoring high on the AFL-CIO rating system." Only if those two measures were constructed in essentially the same way would we be faced with a tautology. And for the most part the measures are independent of each other.

The ADA used the way Senators voted on 18 bills, and the AFL-CIO used 19 bills, in constructing their 1980 ratings. Three of these votes were identical; the others were on unrelated issues.[11] There is, admittedly, some overlap. But over 80% of the data used to construct one index is unrelated to the other index. Liberals are not, by definition at least, labor supporters. And the slight overlap in definition of the two terms may explain partially, but by no means entirely, the strength of the correlation between them. Even if we had omitted these three votes from the rating, liberalism and pro-laborism would show a strong correlation with each other. (Doubters are invited to challenge this assertion—which

---

* The difference between American politics in 1980 and 1981 illustrates the importance of this question: who holds power? Between those two years a major power shift occurred. Power, which had indeed been in the hands of liberals, labor supporters, and Democrats, shifted to conservatives, labor opponents, and Republicans, as a consequence of the 1980 election. The result has been a drastic change in the kind of national policies Americans are receiving from their new political leaders.

we admit we have not tested--by going back to the original data source [see footnote 11] and re-calculating ratings after omitting the three votes common to both rating systems.)

4. The last five hypotheses all have one variable in common-- age. In our judgment, this is not a particularly interesting variable. Whether one is old or young seems much less important in politics than whether one is liberal or conservative, pro-labor or not, pacifistic or aggressive. And few studies have ever shown that age correlates with any other important variable. Indeed, our own preliminary investigations here suggest that age does not correlate with such key concepts as party affiliation or support for labor. In short, the age question is probably the least salient of all those taken up in this chapter. Hence, variables relating to age are least worthy of being tested in full-scale research analysis.

You might wish to dispute our assessment of this variable when it comes to H-3 (older politicians are more powerful than younger ones). But if you think about it a minute, even this hypothesis is not terribly exciting. It simply says that one of the top rewards from political activity goes to those who are older. In what human organization (outside of sports and perhaps show business) is this not true? In almost all human endeavors those who have seniority, experience and time to acquire skills and knowledge are more highly rewarded than those lacking these traits. In businesses, in the university, in churches--everywhere older people have more power, more money and more recognition than do younger people. In our judgment the finding that such a common human pattern holds also in politics is not the most "interesting" finding we could concern ourselves with.

5. The only difference between the two hypotheses relating to age in Group 5 and the three relating to age in Group 4 is this: the Group 4 hypotheses at least have a good deal of support behind them in our initial examinations. Those in Group 5 are barely supported at all. Hence, they fall into the unhappy category of hypotheses which aren't particularly interesting to begin with and which aren't supported by much empirical evidence either.

A newcomer to the study of politics may disagree with our assessment of age as a variable of minor importance. It flies in the face of some popular stereotypes. After all, most people think of young politicians as flaming liberals and olders ones as crusty conservatives. Yet in the real world older people can be ardent liberals or radicals. Mao Zedong was in his 70's when he inaugurated the Chinese Cultural Revolution; John Brown was nearing 60 when he led the raid on Harper's Ferry. And young people are not immune to the appeals of conservatism. Think of David Stockman, who at 34 became the principal implementer of President Reagan's anti-liberal economic policies. Or note that seven of the eight under-30 members of the U.S. House of Representatives in 1981 were strong conservatives.[12]

Your instructor may discuss in class the reasons why age is not necessarily correlated with one's political beliefs. Since the issue lies in the realm of substantive matters, it goes beyond the scope of this book, but we can provide a brief rationale for the absence of the expected pattern. The growing-conservatism-with-age theory is right in one sense: one changes one's ideas less as one grows older. One's basic values and philosophy of life are heavily influenced by experiences while young. Some (Freudians) argue that the period from three to five, or even earlier, is crucial; others talk of the importance of the early adult years (18-25). But all seem agreed on one fact: after 25 or 30 one's basic outlook on the world changes little.

What counts, then, is what you have learned before, say, 30. If you grew up in a liberal household, went to a liberal college, and socialized continuously with groups of liberals in your 20's, then you are going to be a liberal for life. On the other hand, if all your early experiences lay in the conservative camp, you will remain a conservative for the rest of your days. And remember Lenin, who became a Communist before he was 20 and stayed one until he died. The reason we have old liberals, middle-aged radicals, and young conservatives, then, is because people cling to the ideas they develop early in life and don't change much as they get older.[13]

We will admit that destroying popularly-held misconceptions can be useful. For this reason some readers might give the group of hypotheses dealing with age higher priority than we assign it. Our judgment here derives from our experience as scholars. Many studies show age to be a less significant variable than the others we have been examining. We downgraded it accordingly.

But don't take our word for it. Please check up on us. That's what the scientific method is good at: settling arguments about factual matters. Take any of these age-related hypotheses and test them. Use either the data we provide in Appendix 1 or any other data you want to dig up. Good luck! And please let us know what you discover.

The next step in our study of political leaders is simple. We test those hypotheses which, according to our trial-run analyses, now merit testing. In the "real world" you would head to the library, comb through a variety of reference sources, and dig up the necessary information on all U.S. Senators to test one or more of these hypotheses. We will shortly give you some exercises along those lines. At this point, however, we provide the information for you. We ourselves have gone to the library and accumulated all the information needed to test each hypothesis. This evidence is presented in Appendix 1. The rest is up to you. (Please note the following points concerning the data on U.S. Senators. Senator Byrd of Virginia is an Independent. Simply leave him out of all tests involving the party variable. In addition to committee Chairs, party leaders are also powerful. We have indicated the four most powerful party leaders; they should be included with committee chairmen when you are testing for power-holding. Finally, we have done some calculations to save you time in this first major exercise. We have calculated means and totals for you. Naturally, in your own research you will have to undertake this task for yourself.)

Assignment #9
    Take one (or more, depending on instructor's wishes) of the most "serious" hypotheses (preferably in Groups 1 or 2) and test it, using _all_ the available data in Appendix 1 relevant to that hypothesis. These tests should be conducted exactly as we have done throughout this chapter, using means and percentages. Once you have completed the test, present all your evidence and state, preferably in one clear sentence, your conclusion regarding the hypothesis in question. To give you an example of what your results should look like, we present a sample exercise sheet below, testing what appeared to be the least interesting hypothesis, H-4.

THE RELATIONSHIP BETWEEN AGE AND REGION OF ORIGIN AMONG AMERICAN POLITICAL LEADERS

TEST OF HYPOTHESIS H-4: Among political leaders in the U.S., age is positively correlated with representation of a Southern district.

Mean age of all U.S. Senators, 1 January 1980: 53.8
Senators 54 and over will be defined as "old."
Senators 53 and under will be defined as "young."

"Southern" = a Senator representing one of these twelve states:
    Texas, Louisiana, Arkansas, Mississippi, Alabama, Georgia, Florida, South Carolina, North Carolina, Virginia, Tennessee, Kentucky
"non-Southern" = a Senator representing one of the other 38 states.

Mean age of Southerners =   54.9
Mean age of non-Southerners =   53.5

24% of all Senators are Southern
29.5% of old Senators are Southern
18.4% of young Senators are Southern

76% of all Senators are non-Southern
70.6% of old Senators are non-Southern

81.6% of young Senators are non-Southern

51% of all Senators are old
62.5% of Southern Senators are old
47.4% of Northern Senators are old

49% of all Senators are young
37.5% of Southern Senators are young
52.6% of Northern Senators are young

NOTE: 5 Southern Senators (20.8% of all Southerners) were exactly
        54 years old, or just slightly above the mean, leading them
        to be classified as "old." If even two or three of these
        had been a few months younger, the percentage differences
        between Northerners and Southerners would have been virtu-
        ally wiped out. Only one Northerner (1.3% of all Northern-
        ers) was age 54. In short, a minor change in definition
        could have the effect of wiping out the already small dif-
        ferences in age between Northerners and Southerners.

WE CONCLUDE: Extensive testing has produced little evidence to
support H-4. There may be a slight tendency for Southerners to be
a little older than Northerners, but this tendency is so slight
that we are forced to the following conclusion:

> H-4':   Among political leaders in the U.S., there is no cor-
>   relation between age and region of political origin.

   Once you have completed an exercise such as this one, you
should feel a certain sense of accomplishment and of curiosity
satisfied. You will have conducted a major test of an important
idea. As a result you will know something which you didn't know
before. And that, after all, is the whole purpose behind scientific research: learning.

   For instance, in the example just presented (H-4), we learned
that Southern Senators are scarcely any older than Northern Senators. Even this prosaic finding is mildly interesting, since
there is a mythology among observers of the American political
scene that Southern congressmen are doddering old mossbacks compared to energetic young Northerners. Whatever truth there may
have been to that image in the past, we can now state emphatically
that it does not describe differences among U.S. Senators in the
early 1980's.

   Ideally, your instructor will discuss the major findings
which you and your classmates come up with as you test the other
hypotheses, and you will see precisely how well each of them
stands up under detailed examination.

At the end of all this work you will know some specific information which you didn't know before about U.S. Senators. Will you at this point be able to say that a given hypothesis is true? Surprise! The answer is an emphatic, "No!" It is time for the bad news: you can never say that a given hypothesis is true. Once you grasp this point, you will have gone a long way toward understanding what the scientific method is all about.

How is it, you ask, that we can never prove hypotheses true? Well, for a statement to be "true," it must work all the time under all conditions. But if you think about it, we can never have enough evidence to cover all time frames and all possible conditions where a hypothesis might apply. Hence, we can never be finally certain that new evidence won't appear to undermine the hypothesis.

Ultimately, all we can do with hypotheses is to falsify them or fail to falsify them. When we find evidence that runs counter to what the hypothesis predicts, then obviously the hypothesis is false. When we find evidence in the direction predicted by a hypothesis, then we have failed to falsify it (or you could say, as we frequently have done, that the evidence "supports" the hypothesis). But the mere fact that we have found some evidence to support the hypothesis does not mean that evidence to falsify it does not exist. It just means that we haven't yet stumbled onto it.

Remember that "true" means always and in all conditions. Until we test a hypothesis "always and in all conditions," we can't be sure it is true. And since technically, we have no hope of ever testing any hypothesis under all possible conditions, we must give up any attempt to say that we have verified a hypothesis. We have simply failed to refute it yet. Of course, if a number of different studies of one hypothesis all support it, we can say that "we are increasingly confident that the hypothesis works" (that is, it predicts outcomes correctly). We can talk about the "degree of confidence" we have in various hypotheses. And some hypotheses which are supported time and again in a variety of settings and eras (such as the hypothesis that political participation is positively correlated with level of education) almost come to take on the characteristic of scientific "laws." But we must always bear in the back of our mind that lingering doubt, that nagging suspicion, that each principle, which we think we know, is merely a tentative supposition—one which we must be ready to ditch, dry-eyed, at the first solid experiment which refutes it.

The scientific method, truly understood, must promote an open mind and a willingness to look hard facts in the face. One must never become so wedded to a theory that it becomes impossible to give it up when confronted with undeniable evidence which undermines it. The seventeenth-century Catholic prelates who forced

Galileo to recant his theories typify the obverse of the scientific mind.[*] Emotionally clinging to pet theories, refusing to accept clear evidence, even using force to hide facts from the world: all these actions illustrate the closed, narrow, defensive mind at work. At its best science represents something vastly different—an open-ended, questing search for truth. As such, the true scientist is the enemy of oppressive, authority-laden systems which would stifle the free flow of information.

The true scientist also retains an open mind about his own theories. He is painfully aware that new discoveries can throw past bodies of knowledge into disrepute. Any serious researcher has found time and again that pet ideas fail utterly to pan out upon extensive examination. And the history of science is a history of theories "everyone knew" to be true which turned out to be false or misleading. (Ptolemy's theories gave way to Newton's, which later were subsumed by Einstein's.) The scientist concludes that he must never be satisfied with early, rapidly-arrived-at conclusions. He continues to look for new evidence and ingenious new ways to test his hypotheses. He remains forever dissatisfied with the existing state of knowledge on any scientifically-researchable subject.

These are grandiose ideals. We have tried to measure up to them in the methods employed throughout this chapter. We went back and forth several times from observation to hypothesis and back to observation, having no hesitation about changing the hypothesis when a given observation ran counter to it. We kept an open mind about each hypothesis as new evidence came before us. Now, even at the "end" of our labors we must caution you to keep an open mind about each of the hypotheses—no matter how well supported some of them may have been. We must remain skeptical of even a hypothesis as strongly supported by our data as H-13 (liberalism correlates with support for labor). Think after all, about how much evidence we used to test this hypothesis compared to the totality of possible evidence we could have used. We tested it by using the voting records of a mere 100 political leaders in one country over the course of one year. Throughout recorded history there have been millions of political leaders, thousands of countries, and thousands of years. Clearly, if we spent the rest of our lives, we could never gather all the evidence necessary fully to test this one hypothesis (or any other). Do you wonder, now, why we say that no hypothesis can ever be shown to be true?

---

[*]   Stalin provides a similar example, closer to our own time, of power forcing science to renounce a well-supported theory in favor of an erroneous one. For a time all biologists in the Soviet Union had to discard Darwinism for the crackpot theories of Trofim Denisovich Lysenko, Stalin's favorite scientist. Not unnaturally, Soviet biology suffered a dramatic decline in quality during this period.

Throughout this chapter we have taken you by the hand as we examined some data about U.S. Senators and then developed and tested hypotheses relating to that data. It is time for you to venture forth on your own. Your job is to develop and test some hypotheses from a new set of data. Once again, we have done preliminary work for you: we have already gathered the data. (In the next chapter you will learn how to gather data on your own.) Look at Appendix 2. There you will find information on five different variables as they apply to each of the 50 American states. These variables include:

  a. The wealth of each state, measured by per capita income;
  b. Crime rates in each state, measured by number of prisoners behind bars in a given year;
  c. Support for feminism in each state, measured by the number of women holding public office per 100,000 inhabitants;
  d. Degree of participation in politics by the citizens in each state, measured by voting turnout at a recent election;
  e. Political tendencies in each state, measured by the Democratic percent of the two-party vote in a recent election.

These variables were chosen more or less haphazardly as we browsed through the _1980 Statistical Abstract of the United States_. We would like you to start looking at the data in Appendix 2 in the same way that we started looking at the first simple summary of data on U.S. Senators on page 60. What hypotheses occur to you as you peruse the table? Formally, we ask you to do the following:

  A. Write out 5 hypotheses which occur to you as you casually look over the information in Appendix 2. Be sure the hypotheses are phrased correctly according to the rules enunciated in Chapter 3.

  B. Test one of the hypotheses you wrote in section A, above. Follow the format presented in Table IV-1, page 96. In testing your hypotheses you may use as your average the national mean, which we supply in the table.

  C. Just to keep you in practice, calculate the _median_ for at least one of the five variables.

The point of this exercise is to induce you to apply what you have learned in this chapter to an entirely new set of ideas and numbers. If you have followed us systematically up to this point, the exercise should not be difficult (though perhaps time-consuming). If you find you have trouble with this assignment, go back and review what you have read, then consult the instructor. You will find it essential to have this material under your belt before moving on to the next chapters.

FOOTNOTES TO CHAPTER IV

1. See the discussions of this point in Seymour Martin Lipset, Political Man: The Social Bases of Politics (Garden City, N.Y.: Anchor Books, 1963), pp. 38-45; and in Daniel Lerner, The Passing of Traditional Society: Modernizing the Middle East (New York: The Free Press, 1958), pp. 43-75.

2. See, for instance, Robert S. Gilmour and Robert B. Lamb, Political Alienation in Contemporary America (New York: St. Martin's Press, 1975), pp. 37-44. See also Gabriel A. Almond and Sidney Verba, The Civic Culture: Political Attitudes and Democracy in Five Nations (Boston: Little Brown and Company, 1963), p. 68, and the discussion in Sidney Verba and Norman H. Nie, Participation in America: Political Democracy and Social Equality (New York: Harper & Row, Publishers, 1972), pp. 125-37. Note, however, that Alan C. Elms suggests that levels of alienation (i.e., distrust of government) have reached such high levels recently that the traditional distinctions between classes on this variable no longer show up. See Elms, Personality in Politics (New York: Harcourt Brace Jovanovich, Inc., 1976), pp. 19-21.

3. All studies of authoritarianism have found this relationship. For a summary of the findings, see William F. Stone, The Psychology of Politics (New York: The Free Press, 1974), pp. 151-2. See also Roger Brown, Social Psychology (New York: The Free Press, 1965), pp. 518-23, and Gertrude Selznick and Stephen Steinberg, The Tenacity of Prejudice (New York: Harper and Row, 1969), pp. 135-69. For a criticism of the concept of "authoritarianism" precisely on the grounds that it may simply be a measure of educational level rather than of personality, see Herbert H. Hyman and Paul B. Sheatsley, "The Authoritarian Personality: A Methodological Critique," in Richard Christie and Marie Jahoda, eds., Studies in the Scope and Methods of the Authoritarian Personality (Glencoe, Ill.: The Free Press, 1954), pp. 50-122. The original, classic study of authoritarianism is, of course, Theodor W. Adorno, Else Frenkel-Brunswick, Daniel J. Levinson, and R. Nevitt Sanford, The Authoritarian Personality (New York: Harper & Row, 1950).

4. See the summary of studies on the relationship between education and political participation in Lester W. Milbrath and M. L. Goel, Political Participation: How and Why do People Get Involved in Politics? 2nd ed. (Chicago: Rand McNally College Publishing Company, 1977), pp. 98-102.

5. James D. Barber, The Presidential Character: Predicting Performance in the White House (Englewood Cliffs, N. J.: Prentice-Hall, Inc., 1972).

6. For a brief summary of this study by David Olson of the University of Minnesota, see The New York Times, January 12, 1981, p. B4.

7. See Robert Freed Bales, Personality and Interpersonal Behavior (New York: Holt, Rinehart and Winston, 1970).

8. (Washington: Congressional Quarterly, Inc., 1981).

9. Michael Barone and Grant Ujifusa, eds., (New York: E. P. Dutton, 1982).

10. (Washington: United States Government Printing Office, 1981).

11. See Bill Keller, "Congressional Rating Game is Hard to Win," Congressional Quarterly 39 (March 21, 1981): pp. 507-22. The information used to construct the ADA and AFL-CIO rating systems is found on pp. 518-20.

12. Christopher Buchanan, "Youth is on the Right in House Freshman Class," Congressional Quarterly 39 (January 3, 1981), pp. 3-4.

13. Dean Jaros calls this phenomenon "nonsubstantive conservatism." See his discussion in Socialization to Politics (New York: Praeger Publishers, 1973), pp. 73-76.

CHAPTER V

GATHERING THE DATA

Having the previous chapters under your belt, you've made a
major step toward a scientific understanding of the world. In particular, you've mastered the process of going from casual observation to formal generalization about the way people and nations behave. The next step follows logically. You must see whether a
generalization holds up when you test it against data that you collect systematically. This chapter describes how to go about collecting the information that will lead you to retain or reject your
hypothesis.

Defining the variables
Before you can begin gathering any data, you must define your
variables. (Remember that you will have two variables for each hypothesis you wish to test.) Defining variables is not as easy as
it might sound. Furthermore, it is one of the central steps in the
research process. So let us approach the matter carefully.

For each variable we wish to examine, we must first have a
general idea of what it means and then we must say specifically
what steps we will take to identify the real-world events which
that variable refers to. To put this another way, we must first
have a conceptual definition of our variable and then an operational definition. A conceptual definition is, essentially, a dictionary definition. It is broad and general. It provides a basic idea
of what your variable refers to, but nothing more. An operational
definition is a precise set of instructions. It tells you how to
recognize what you described in your dictionary definition when it
appears in the real world.

Let's take a simple example to illustrate these terms. In the
hypothesis, "being a doctor is correlated with membership in the
Republican Party," we would need conceptual and operational definitions for both terms—"being a doctor" and "membership in the Republican Party." Let's begin with conceptual definitions. We must
first decide what our terms, in this particular research project,
are going to mean. For example, what do we have in mind when we
say that someone is a doctor? It turns out that both authors of
this book are doctors—doctors of philosophy, or Ph.D.'s. Are we
to be included in this hypothetical study of doctors? Is a "doctor" a physician, or is he anyone who has received a doctor's degree from a university (lawyers, ministers, educators, etc.)?

Now you see why you need a conceptual definition. Until you
provide a general idea of what your term means, you cannot even say
what your study is all about. In this case you could do two completely different studies—one of "doctors," meaning physicians, or

one of "doctors," meaning highly educated people. A conceptual definition choosing between one of these two possibilities is essential.

Let's say you decide to restrict your hypothetical assertion to physicians, since that's the group you really wish to study. Question: what is a physician? Answer: one who practices medicine. This is a dictionary, or conceptual, definition. We now have a broad idea of what one of the terms in our hypothesis means. Simple, isn't it?

We run into more difficulty with the other term in our hypothesis—"membership in the Republican Party." Exactly what is a Republican Party member? When you stop to think about it, there are at least three possibilities. He could be

1) (in legal terms) an officially enrolled or registered member of the Republican Party;
2) (in behavioral terms) someone who habitually votes for Republican candidates; or
3) (in psychological terms) someone who thinks of himself as a Republican, no matter how he is enrolled or votes.

These distinctions aren't trivial. There's often quite a discrepancy between an individual's official party enrollment and his voting behavior. Every Representative sent to the Maine State Legislature by the city of Portland has, for more than a decade, been a Democrat. Portland sends ten Representatives to the Legislature, and the score for the last ten years is: Democrats 50 - Republicans 0. Yet Republicans enjoyed a slight numerical majority over Democrats, during most of those years, among officially enrolled voters.

Does this mean that Portland's Board of Voter Registrars was playing fast and loose with registration figures? Or that Portland Democrats were taking seriously the election day exhortation to Democratic Party workers of the late Chicago mayor, Richard Daley ("Vote early and vote often")—tying up traffic in downtown Portland with "mobile voter units?" Maybe. But neither of these explanations is likely. Instead, the situation is a bit more complicated.

For most of its history Maine was a one-party Republican state. This meant that if an individual wanted a choice in elections for Governor, Congressman and Senator, he would have to vote in the Republican primary election, because whatever Republican candidate emerged from the primary was sure to win the general election in the fall. To vote in the Republican primary, one had to enroll as a Republican. So a number of voters who thought of themselves as Democrats (or independents) registered as Republicans so they could have some input into state politics where it really counted—in the Republican primary. Of course, these people could then vote for Democratic candidates in the fall, if they wanted to make a futile gesture, but they were still registered as Republicans.

In recent years Maine has become a two-party state. Real alternatives are presented to the voters in November. Democrats no longer have to participate in Republican primaries to have some impact on state government. Since Democratic candidates now have a good chance of being elected in general elections, the "rational" Democratic voter can return to his party and vote in Democratic primaries, knowing that he is making a serious choice among candidates who might actually get elected to office in November.

Yet not all voters are perfectly rational, as political scientists would have them. Many in Portland who regard themselves as Democrats, but voted in Republican primaries in the past, have simply not gone to the bother of going down to City Hall to change their enrollment to Democratic. So the Republican proportion of enrolled voters in Portland, Maine, is a misleading guide to real Republican voting strength in that city.

Another factor explains the bloated Republican registration figures. Not only the state of Maine but the city of Portland used to be under Republican control. In those days, getting city services depended on being in the right party. Areas with heavy Democratic majorities simply didn't get their streets cleaned as often, didn't get new school buildings as frequently, and didn't receive the same amount of police protection as those areas where Republicans predominated. Many voters decided that discretion was the better part of valor and enrolled as Republicans. Signing up for the wrong party was a minor irritant compared to the major one of not having your streets cleared of the seventy inches of snow that falls in a typical winter.

Clearly, choosing your conceptual definition for a term is a crucial stage in the research process. You will get different results depending on how you define the variables. You must decide early how you conceive of the variable you are exploring, and you must state clearly what your conception of it is. Note also that your conceptual definition of a term must not deviate very far from widely-accepted or conventional usages of the term. Any of the three definitions we gave earlier would be satisfactory as conceptual definitions for "membership in the Republican Party." However, defining a Republican as

4) someone who is stupid, stubborn, old-fashioned, and militaristic would be unacceptable. Except for ardent Democrats, this is not what people generally have in mind when they use the term

"Republican." Your conceptual definition would be hotly disputed by most serious researchers, who would consequently reject your findings as well. Make sure your conception of a term lies within the range of definitions normally used by people familiar with that term.

Picking your conceptual definition of a variable clearly involves choice. It is not just a matter of going to a dictionary. Often one must choose between several definitions or alter existing definitions to fit the concept one has. The "simple" hypothesis listed above--"being a doctor is correlated with membership in the Republican Party"--could actually have one of six different meanings.

1. Highly educated people are usually enrolled as Republicans.
2. Highly educated people usually vote for Republican candidates.
3. Highly educated people usually think of themselves as Republicans.
4. Those who practice medicine are usually enrolled as Republicans.
5. Those who practice medicine usually vote for Republican candidates.
6. Those who practice medicine usually think of themselves as Republicans.

Your research on this hypothesis could go in any of six different directions. Needless to say, if you start working with more complex hypotheses (say, "Alienation is correlated with political instability"), the number of possible meanings for each statement becomes legion. Now do you see why choosing clear conceptual definitions at the outset is important?

Let's say that in our doctor-Republican hypothesis, what we wish to assert is that one who practices medicine is likely to think of himself as a Republican. We would then choose meaning number 6 for our hypothesis. Later on, perhaps, we might test the hypothesis on voting behavior (#5). For the moment, however, we will deal strictly with the self-image of medical doctors. Our conceptual definition of Republican Party member would therefore be: "A Republican Party member is a person who thinks of himself or herself as a Republican."

As we have seen above, the simplicity of such a conceptual definition is deceptive, since it has followed a set of difficult choices about what we wish to test.

When you alter a commonly accepted dictionary definition of a term or choose between one of several possible definitions, you must make a case in defense of your choice. Our defense might read as follows. Coogan's uncle, who is a doctor, is a dyed-in-the-wool Republican. Hour after hour Coogan has had to listen to his diatribes against the Democrats and his support of all things Republican, including even a torturous defense of former President Nixon's ethics. Coogan has observed that his uncle never misses a chance to see William F. Buckley roast a Democrat on his television show and that those of his patients who admit to being Democrats leave his office complaining about sensitive rear ends and unusually high bills. Oddly enough, this man hasn't voted since the election of 1932. Herbert Hoover, he claims, was the last "real" Republican. Furthermore, Coogan has noted that his uncle's colleagues share his Republicanism and his pattern of non-voting. We wonder, then, whether his views and his behavior pattern are characteristic of most physicians.

Our hypothesis--about doctors being Republican--follows directly from some specific observations of the real world. What we have actually experienced is one, and then several, medical doctors who continually think of themselves as Republicans. Although we state our hypothesis broadly ("being a doctor is correlated with being a Republican"), our conceptual meaning for the hypothesis follows from what we actually saw with our own eyes ("those who practice medicine think of themselves as Republicans"). Notice that if Woshinsky had seen several lawyers and Ph.D. friends voting election after election for Republicans, our conceptual understanding of the hypothesis would have been quite different: highly educated people usually vote for Republican candidates.

An intellectual defense of one's conceptual definitions is usually necessary, as well as a defense based on observations. In the case of our doctor-Republican hypothesis, we prefer for two reasons to think of doctors as physicians rather than holders of a particular degree. First, the most usual meaning which people assign to the word "doctor" is "one who practices medicine." A definition centered on degree-holding would be confusing. Second, there seems to be no intrinsic reason for lumping all doctorate-holders together. While "physicians" would appear to be a reasonably cohesive, clear-cut group of people with many things in common, the same is not true of all holders of doctor's degrees. Those holding doctorates could be physicians, businessmen, high school administrators, college lecturers, research scientists, lawyers, ministers, and so on. What do all these people have in common? They do not even form a clear, undeniable group in the sense of being "the highly educated members of our society." A number of other people (those with M.A.'s, M.S.'s, L.L.B.'s, A.B.D.'s, and so on) would also have to be considered "highly educated." The group of "physicians" clearly stands for "all those who practice medicine." The group of "doctorate-holders" doesn't clearly stand for anything. You can see why we decided to define "doctor" as "one

107

who practices medicine" and not as "one who holds a doctorate."

We also have some good reasons for our conceptual definition of Republican. We feel that enrollment and voting activities are particular manifestations of a broader phenomenon: how one thinks about oneself in relation to politics. Psychologists have long felt that self-image is a key to understanding behavior.[1] How one defines oneself determines how one behaves. Those who are self-confident interact easily and positively with others. Those who are insecure are shy and defensive in the presence of others. In the same way, thinking of yourself as a Republican will affect your political behavior. You will promote the party in informal conversations, you may contribute money to it or work for its candidates, you may enroll as a Republican Party member, you may vote for Republican candidates, you will convince your children that they too are Republicans, and so forth. In short, a host of activities follows from your initial commitment to Republicans.

We believe that this in-depth, psychological attachment is the most important idea behind "Republican Party membership," not a particular act which might follow from that attachment—such as enrollment or voting.[2] It is your emotional commitment that really defines you as a Republican, not how you enroll or vote. Besides, enrolling or voting Republican may reflect ephemeral or idiosyncratic behavior. Our earlier discussion showed the odd reasons people might have for enrolling as Republicans (even when it had no impact on their self-image). And one can even vote Republican while remaining a Democrat at core. Democrats remained the majority party in the 1950's, even while Eisenhower was handily winning two presidential elections. Many Democrats briefly defected from their party simply because they "liked Ike." Self-image is an enduring phenomenon, not easily susceptible to change. It will presumably have a strong impact on people's enduring behavior patterns, and that is why we prefer using it, rather than short-term actions, as the basis for our definition of Republicanism.

Operational instructions - reliability

Now that we have devised and defended conceptual definitions for our terms, let's move on to "operationalize" them. An operational definition is <u>a set of instructions</u> that tell you precisely how to recognize a phenomenon when it occurs in the real world. When you say that a doctor is "one who practices medicine" and a Republican is "one who thinks of himself as a Republican," you have only defined your terms conceptually. You have not really indicated precisely how to recognize someone "who practices medicine" or someone "who thinks of himself as a Republican." You must now discover how to do exactly that.

How do you recognize a doctor? How about using the following set of instructions?

108

1. Get a list of all doctors in your community.
2. All individuals on that list will be defined as "doctors", for the purposes of this study.

The trouble with these instructions is that an individual attempting to carry them out would be faced with several options. She could look under "Physicians" in the Yellow Pages of the telephone book. There she would find a pretty complete list of the doctors in your city. Of course, those who have died or retired within the last year will still be listed, and those who have arrived recently will not be included. Still, the phone book is reasonably accurate.

Local and national medical societies are another potential source for this information. However, communities have rival medical societies, and a researcher would have to make sure she covered them all to complete the listing. And in some areas only a fraction of physicians—sometimes as low as 40%—belong to a medical association.

So one must make a choice about where to get the information. Since the Yellow Pages look like the best bet, a good operational definition of "doctor" would read this way:

1. To get a list of doctors, look in the Yellow Pages of _____ (your city).
2. Everyone whose name is listed under "Physicians" will be included in the list of doctors.

Notice what we've done here. A simple operational definition, such as "Get a list of doctors in this community," is inadequate. That instruction is imprecise. If other researchers tried to duplicate your study to validate the findings, they might come up with different results simply because they used a different list of doctors. In Massachusetts, for example, many doctors belong to the conservative, Republican-oriented local branch of the American Medical Association. An approximately equal number belong to the liberal, Democratically-oriented Massachusetts Medical Association. An individual trying to duplicate your research in the state of Massachusetts by interviewing doctors who were members of the AMA would come up with findings totally at variance from those obtained by someone using the MMA's list.

The moral is clear. If an operational definition is ambiguous, imprecise, or subject to varied interpretations, it is defective. A good operational definition will give instructions so precise that every researcher who follows them will get the same results. This characteristic is known as reliability. It allows others to check on your research and permits the duplication of important research results.

Without a reliable operational definition, your research is meaningless. What if the man who invented penicillin had used the following instructions for his operational definition?

1. To obtain penicillin, take the right kind of mold and filter it.

If he had died of a heart attack immediately after writing those words, the world would be a different place today. It is unlikely that we would have access to penicillin, for how could anyone follow those instructions and get the same substance obtained by the original researcher--that is, penicillin? What is "the right kind of mold?" One could hardly find a more ambiguous, imprecise instruction than that. And what is meant by "filter it?" Filter it through what? with what? at what temperature? Again, we have a very imprecise instruction. And the result of this unreliable operational definition is that the research cannot be duplicated, no one else can obtain penicillin, and the original work all goes for naught.

Precise instructions, then, lie at the core of reliability. In drawing up rules for the operationalization of variables, we would have to start with this point.

Rule #1: You must give precise, specific instructions for the steps to take in order to observe in the real world the phenomenon described by your term.

Two obvious corollaries follow from this rule. First, operational definitions involve a <u>process</u>. They specify a series of actual steps to take to get one's hands on the phenomenon under study. Vagueness must be avoided at all costs in the process. Do not, therefore, define a variable (which is itself a concept) by reference to another concept. If one says that a doctor is "someone who heals people," you still have not told how to identify a person "who heals people." You have defined one concept in terms of another. You have, in short, given a conceptual definition, not an operational definition. Similarly, if you say that "democracy is a system of government by free elections," you have also defined one concept (democracy) in terms of another (free elections). This is a perfectly satisfactory conceptual definition, but it is not an operational definition, because you have not told what steps we would have to take to be sure that some phenomenon we were observing was indeed a "free election."* Be careful, then, to follow our second rule:

---

*We suggest below a way of operationalizing the term "free elections." See pp. 118-119, Democracy Defined.

Rule #2: Don't define one concept in terms of another, but in terms of a process or series of steps to be undertaken.

A second corollary derives from Rule #1. At any point in an operational definition where two different researchers might head in different directions, you must specify which direction to follow. Thus, your instruction for researchers studying doctors in Massachusetts would not say:

1. Get a list of doctors belonging to the medical association.

Remember, there are two important medical associations in Massachusetts, so two different researchers might at this point make two different decisions, end up with two different lists, and obtain two quite different results. (And what kind of "science" is it when two people studying the same phenomenon come up with diametrically opposed conclusions?) No, rather your instructions for researchers on Massachusetts doctors should read as follows:

1. Get a list of all Massachusetts members of the American Medical Association.
2. Get a list of all members of the Massachusetts Medical Association.
3. All people on either of these lists will be included in the list of "Massachusetts doctors."

These instructions insure that at a crucial point in the research process, different observers will head in the same direction and get the same results. This point leads to the next rule.[3]

Rule #3: You must be especially careful to give specific instructions whenever two researchers might follow different procedures.

A fourth rule follows directly from our discussion of lists. If you are going to use a list to provide an operational definition--and this occurs very frequently in social science research-- then you must be sure the list contains all members of the universe you wish to describe. And you must tell exactly what list you used so that others can use the same list in following up your research. These points lead to:

Rule #4: You must clearly describe any list of individuals or entities used in your research, and this list must be as complete as possible.

These rules are fundamental . . . and pretty much a matter of common sense. Many students, however, are impatient to get on with

111

the actual testing of a hypothesis. As a result, they often give minimal attention to these rules. Thus, the credibility of their research is doomed from the outset.

Our discussion of operational definitions up to this point has given us a pretty good idea of how to get our hands on some real live doctors. Now how do we identify people as Republicans? Though this had become an increasingly difficult task in recent years, the election of Ronald Reagan suggests that there are still a few lurking here and there. By what sign shall we know them?

Remember, our conceptual definition of a Republican is "one who thinks of oneself as a Republican." How do we find out how people think of themselves? Since the science of electroencephalography hasn't yet reached the point where we can learn a person's party identification by attaching electrodes to his head, we will have to elicit the information verbally. That is, we will have to get the person to open his or her mouth and tell us in his or her own words.

All this may seem so obvious that you are growing impatient. "Why," you may say, "don't we just ask the person?" You would propose this operational definition for "Republican:"

1. Ask a person what his party identification is.
2. All those who answer "Republican" will be classified as Republicans.

Looks easy enough, doesn't it? But wait. This operational definition violates Rule #3 and probably Rule #1 as well. It just isn't specific enough. Different researchers could "ask a person what his party identification is" in a number of different ways. To avoid any difficulty, we must state precisely what question or questions we are going to ask people in order to define them as Republicans. We now have another rule:

Rule #5: When conducting surveys, state the exact question or questions which will be used to categorize people in the sample.

Now that we know what we must do, let's come up with a question that will separate Republicans from others. How about this?

As you cogitate on the political ramifications of American national party structures, would you asseverate that the Republican Party occupies a strategically important position in your self-concept?

That's a bit too complicated--even for doctors. One can imagine a typical response: "Cut the crap! Don't they teach you any English in college? What is it you're trying to say?" Your respondent might suggest Rules #6 and #7:[4]

Rule #6: In questionnaires, use wording that occurs in everyday conversation; avoid social science jargon.

Rule #7: In questionnaires, avoid long, complex sentence structures; keep sentences short and straightforward.

Let's try again. Will this question identify the Republicans?

Do you think of yourself as a Republican? That is, as one who is in favor of a domestic policy of self-reliance for the poor and who believes that America's national interests must come ahead of its desire to see a global implementation of a human rights policy? Or do you think of yourself as a Democrat--one who supports increased aid for the less-well-off members of society and a decrease in support for authoritarian regimes abroad?

Phew! That's several questions in one. So right away it violates Rule #7. And it poses an impossible choice for one who is in favor of both a domestic policy of self-reliance for the poor and a foreign policy based primarily on fostering human rights. Your respondents must be able to give an answer without going through a contorted internal debate. This sort of problem leads us to formulate Rule #8.

Rule #8: In questionnaires, each short-answer question must pose a simple choice.

For our next effort, we'll avoid trying to set down a list of principles. Let's concentrate instead on the personalities associated with the parties. Here goes.

Do you identify with the Republican Party--the party of William McKinley, Herbert Hoover and Richard Nixon? Or do you identify with the Democratic Party--the party of Thomas Jefferson, Franklin Roosevelt and John Kennedy?

Here we take into account the fact that American focus more on personalities than on issues in reacting to poltiics. And we lend the question historical perspective by citing well-known Presidents of each party; doing so also gives the respondent information to help remind him what each party stands for. Still, isn't there something fishy about the list of Presidents? The Democrats cited are overwhelmingly seen today as successful, the Republicans as failures. The formulators of this question are obviously Democrats! And slanted questions will not produce objective social science. (To introduce Republican bias into the question, you could contrast Democrats Grover Cleveland and Jimmy Carter with Republicans Abraham Lincoln and Dwight Eisenhower.) We conclude that one must not make the respondent feel like a fool for giving a particular response to a question. Therefore, you must observe this rule:

Rule #9: In questionnaires, don't load the questions.

There is an added problem in the two previous questions we have put forth. A number of individuals could not give any answer to either question. These are the numerous people who call themselves independents. Your question must allow them to give an answer also. So . . . the rule which suggests itself at this point is:

Rule #10: In questionnaires, each question must allow all respondents to classify themselves.

How can we phrase a question to satisfy all of these rules? Let's examine this one:

> Generally speaking, when it comes to politics, do you think of yourself as a Democrat, a Republican, an Independent, or what?

Here we have a question that is easy to understand, that poses a simple choice, that is not loaded in favor of one response, and that allows all respondents to classify themselves readily. What more could we want?

It turns out there is one more nice aspect to this question. We happen to know that it works. People are not confused by it, and the number of respondents who classify themselves as "or whats" (Communists, Prohibitionists, etc.) is miniscule. (This is important. You don't want a large percentage of your sample falling in some residual or "Other" category. So in making up questions, it's a good idea to think ahead to the ways people are likely to respond and put all the most likely responses in the question itself, so few will have to say, "But I'm none of those; I'm something else.")

How do we know the question works? Simple: George Gallup has been using it for 40 years! And political scientists have latched onto this question as the basic way of identifying people's party orientations.[5] Is there anything wrong with appropriating someone else's question? Is it plagiarism? Not if you give credit to the originator of the words—or thoughts. And your instructor will be pleased that you took the trouble to look into previous research to see how others handled similar problems.

We now have operational instructions for recognizing "doctors" and "Republicans." Let's try to anticipate what will happen when respondents reply to the question on party identification. Most, to be sure, will classify themselves according to one of the choices provided. But there will be some who don't feel comfortable with the options. They might want to put themselves in between. Take those who say, "Well, I'm an independent, but I lean toward the Republican Party." How would you classify them? It depends on what you are trying to show. Are you saying that doctors are true-blue, dyed-in-the-wool Republicans, or merely that they tend to associate themselves—however weakly—with the Republican Party? The choice is up to you, but you must make it clear, before you administer the questionnaire, exactly how to code such responses. If you don't you will have left open the opportunity to fudge the results after the test is administered, and you will have violated Rule #3, which states that you must specify instructions whenever two researchers might follow different procedures. That rule applies to all steps in the testing of your hypothesis—drawing the sample, phrasing the question, and coding the results.

Sometimes operational definitions can become fairly complex and involve several steps. The complexity of the operational definition depends on the complexity of the variable you are trying to define. With simple variables such as "doctor" and "Republican," we did not need very lengthy operational definitions. But as variables become more abstract, the number of steps needed to operationalize them increases. Let's say we wish to explore the proposition that "well-informed citizens will be deeply involved in politics." Just how do we define "well-informed citizen?"

A well-informed citizen would presumably be someone who knows a lot about politics and government. So we could ask people a question to see what they know. How about this one?

Do you happen to know who is currently President of the United States?

Obviously, this question is no good. Ninety-five to 100 per cent of the American population would get it right and hence be qualified as "well-informed citizens!" Let's try another.

Can you name the Assistant Minority Whip in your state's House of Representatives?

The problem with this question is that almost no one would get it right, and hence we would find almost no "well-informed citizens."

115

Let's get serious about this. Here's a question that should work:

> Can you name the two major candidates who competed
> for a seat in the U.S. House of Representatives from
> this district in the last congressional election?
> If so, please give their names.

We would expect some people to be able to answer this question and others to be stumped by it. It would also appear to distinguish those who are "well-informed" from those who are not. After all, well-informed citizens ought to know who the candidates for Congress were during the last election in their district.

It turns out that this question "works." Precisely 26.5% of the U.S. citizenry can answer it correctly.[6] We are left with an intuitively satisfactory result. About one-quarter of the populace is "well-informed;" three-quarters are not. It would be surprising if a majority turned out to be "well-informed," and it would be appalling if the proportion of informed citizens were much smaller than a quarter.

Are you ready to accept, then, the following operational definition for "well-informed?"

1. To find the well-informed, ask the sample of people
    you are working with this question:
    "Can you name the two major candidates who competed
    for a seat in the U.S. House of Representatives from
    this district in the last congressional election?
    If so, please give their names."
2. All those who correctly identify the two candidates
    will be labeled "well-informed."
3. All others will be labeled "not well-informed."

Is there anything about this operational definition that bothers you? Doesn't it seem a bit presumptuous, a bit hasty, to categorize someone's level of political knowledge on the basis of one simple question? Would you like it if the professor based your entire grade for this course on one question? The point is that a person might be quite well informed about politics and just happen not to remember the name of one of those two candidates in the last election. Despite all his knowledge he would still be labeled "not well-informed" by your definition—clearly an incorrect labeling. How do we avoid this problem?

The mistake we have been making lies in our search for the <u>one</u> question that will separate informed from uninformed among our respondents. In fact, being well-informed means having a lot of information at your disposal. Therefore, it would make sense to ask

you a number of questions to identify the breadth of your knowledge. On the other hand, being well-informed doesn't mean perfectly informed. You can't be expected to know everything. You
could miss a question or two and still be well-informed. Finally,
we must recognize that there are degrees of knowledge. It doesn't
make sense to divide people into geniuses and dummies. There are
gradations, or levels, in between these extremes.

With these points in mind, we suggest the extended operational
definition of "well-informed" which follows:

1. To identify levels of political information, ask the
   sample of people you are working with the following
   questions:
   a. Now I'd like to ask you a few questions that you
      may or may not be able to answer. Do you happen
      to recall whether President Franklin Roosevelt
      was a Republican or a Democrat? (Which?)
   b. Who is the governor of _____ (this state) now?
   c. About how long a term does the governor serve?
   d. What's the county seat of _____ County?
   e. About how many years does a United States Sen-
      ator serve?
   f. Do you happen to know about how many members
      there are on the United States Supreme Court?
      How many?
   g. What were the last two states to come into the
      United States?
2. Those respondents who answer 6 or 7 of the above questions correctly will be labeled "well-informed."
3. Those respondents who answer 3 to 5 of the above questions correctly will be labeled "moderately well-
   informed."
4. Those respondents who answer fewer than 3 questions
   correctly will be labeled "not well-informed."[7]

This operational definition recognizes that there are levels of
political knowledge and that a person doesn't have to know everything to be well-informed. Do you feel that this process would
distinguish those people who are truly knowledgeable from those
only moderately so and those who know very little? We hope so.
Summing up what we have learned here, we suggest our final rule:

Rule #11: In operationalizing complex variables, it
will often be necessary to propose several
ways of identifying the variable, to sum
these steps in some kind of scoring process,
and to invent categories--based on the scores
obtained--which stand for stronger or weaker
degrees of the variable under examination.

This last aspect of operationalization--the use of what social scientists call "multiple indicators" and the development of a method of scoring those indicators--takes practice to master. An exercise is therefore appropriate at this point.

Assignment #11
We suggest above that the well-informed will be more active in politics. Formally, the hypothesis might read:

> *H-V-1: Political participation is positively correlated with political knowledge.*

We have already shown you a way to operationalize political knowledge. Now it's your turn. Write an operational definition for "political participation." Remember, your definition should be based on more than one question, it should contain at least three levels of participation, and it should tell what scores are necessary to fall into each category. Before writing your definition, be sure to review the eleven rules for operationalizing which appear in this chapter.

You are perhaps starting to see that the more abstract or complex the concept, the more difficult it is to operationalize it and the greater the number of steps involved. Imagine operationalizing variables such as "political legitimacy," "economic exploitation," or "individual happiness." Yet these terms are meaningless without operational definitions, so we must try. To give you an idea of how to devise operational definitions for terms of high-level abstraction, we reproduce here an attempt undertaken by Woshinksy a few years ago to define that impossibly ambiguous variable, "democracy." Pay close attention, because we shall ask you some questions about it afterward.

Democracy defined

Conceptual definition:

> At its core democracy implies freedom of expression, competition among political leaders for the right to govern, and the right of the governed to choose their leaders. Periodic free elections insure these outcomes. Hence, for a country (city, province, county) to be democratic, it would have to have periodic free elections. Democracy is therefore defined as the existence within any political unit of a pattern of periodic free elections.

Operational definition:

> To "see" periodic free elections, you would have to do the following.

118

1. You must first specify exactly what area you are examining: Gorham, Maine; New York City; Colorado; Argentina; or whatever.

2. Within that area you would have to see someone speaking on radio, on television, or before groups of people expressing one set of ideas and someone else during the same week speaking in a similar place but expressing quite different ideas. You would have to see this phenomenon of contradictory ideas being freely expressed at least once a week during a normal campaign period (minimum of one month).

3. Speakers and candidates for office would have to represent different political parties. You would have to see followers of at least two parties actively trying to persuade citizens to vote for their party. You would have to see these activities taking place freely—with no interference on the part of police, military, or armed gangs of thugs.

4. On election day you would have to see a large number of people filing into a polling place, picking up ballots on which the names of at least two different candidates for each office were listed. These people must then retire into a closed, private booth, mark their ballots for the candidate(s) of their choice, and drop the ballot into a large box. There must be no way of identifying how anyone voted.

5. At the end of the voting day all the ballots must be removed from the box and counted honestly.

6. For each office the candidate with the most votes must be declared the winner.

7. On a legally prescribed day within three months of the election the winning candidate(s) must take over the office(s) to which they were elected.

8. You would have to see this entire electoral process (steps 2-7) repeated on a regular basis—say, every one, two, four, or five years—for at least 40 years.

9. If, within the area you are examining, steps 2-8 occur, you would label that area "a democracy."

NOTE: If the area under examination is large, many observers—not just one—will be required.

What is your reaction to this operational definition? Do you feel it would have its intended effect--that is, would it identify democracies? How easy would it be to carry out? Your instructor may ask you to answer some of these questions in writing or simply to come to class prepared to discuss them.

Let us get at specific problems with this operational definition. Does it violate any of the eleven rules enunciated earlier? If so, list which ones and tell how it violates them.

The hardest rule to meet is Rule #3: give precise instructions whenever two different researchers might go in different directions. How well does the operational definition of democracy meet the requirements of this rule? Make a list of 3 (or 4 or 5) places where the instructions are not precise enough, where different researchers might act in different ways, and where reliability would therefore not be achieved.

As a final question for thought, how do you think Leonid Brezhnev might react to this definition of democracy? Write out conceptual and operational definitions of democracy which might be proposed by Communist (or Fascist or Socialist) scholars.

If you have followed us to this point, you will now know how to write operational definitions that are reliable. This is an important accomplishment. It means that the instructions you write will be clear enough so that anyone who wishes to duplicate your research will be able to classify the entities or individuals under study in the same way that you did.

The degree of reliability that can be achieved among professional social scientists varies a good deal, depending on what is being studied. High degrees of reliability can be achieved in measuring some variables--sex or age, for example. That is, we expect you could write instructions that could be followed almost perfectly by 10 other people to weed out the males from the females in a group of 100 people, or to separate these people into age groups of "young," "middle-aged," and "old." In other cases reliability is very difficult to achieve--in the classification of personality types, for instance. One famous researcher once proposed dividing all politicians into three types: administrators, agitators, and theorists.[8] Imagine trying to place each U.S. Senator into one of these three categories. Can you think of some instructions you could write which would allow you and ten other people working independently to classify each Senator identically--as either an administrator, an agitator, or a theorist? (Don't worry if you can't. The man who proposed this typology never did, either.)

Operational Instructions - Validity

You can see that reliability is easy to understand, but somewhat more difficult to practice. Reliability is not the only criterion which must be met by an operational definition. The other criterion is known as validity. To be valid, your set of operational instructions must correspond closely to your conceptual definition of the term you are using. Put another way, validity occurs when the thing you actually get your hands on, after following the instructions, corresponds reasonably well to what most people have in mind when they hear your conceptual definition.

Since the distinction between reliability and validity is important to grasp, let's use an extreme example to illustrate the difference. We shall return to our attempt at classifying Republicans and Democrats. First, let's remember these conceptual definitions:

Republican - someone who thinks of himself or herself as a Republican.
Democrat   - someone who thinks of himself or herself as a Democrat.

Then let's offer a set of operational instructions:

1. Ask the subject to stand against the wall.
2. Measure his or her height in inches.
3. Divide this figure by the number of representatives on the city council in the city where he or she resides.
4. We now have height in inches divided by city council members. Anyone whose quotient is 8 or above will be classified as a Republican.
5. Anyone whose quotient is below 8 will be classified as a Democrat.

Now what's wrong with this? The operational definition, believe it or not, is "reliable!" Anyone following your instructions would classify each subject in the same way. But it is not valid. That is, it's obvious that height and city council membership have nothing to do with an individual's party preference. Our conceptual definition stresses that people's party orientation must be learned by finding out how they "think about themselves." Therefore, we would expect the operational instruction to have something to do with asking people how they think about themselves politically. These operational instructions do nothing of the kind. They don't correspond to what most people have in mind when they read the conceptual definition. They are therefore invalid.

Let's take another example, somewhat less absurd.

Operational definition of Republican:
1. Ask respondents the following questions:
   a. Which political leader do you respect most?
      i) Jimmy Carter   ii) Gerald Ford
   b. Which of the following Presidents did a better job for the country?
      i) Dwight Eisenhower   ii) John Kennedy
   c. Assuming that a choice had to be made, which would you say is more important?
      i) reducing inflation ii) reducing unemployment
2. One point will be given for each of the following answers:
   a. (ii); b. (i); and c. (i).
3. Anyone who scores 2 or 3 points will be classified as a Reupblican.

This definition is once again reliable. Each researcher would classify each individual who responded in the same way. But do these responses give a valid description of a Republican? Do they allow you to say that anyone who scores 2 or better "thinks of himself as a Republican?" Very possibly not. A Democrat might be concerned about inflation, dismayed by President Carter's floundering on the issues, and embittered at President Kennedy's policies which led the U. S. toward entry in the Vietnam War. He might, therefore, give the "Republican" answers listed above, yet still think of himself as a Democrat. Again, we have an operational definition which is reliable, but not really on the mark--not valid.

We want an operational definition which is on target and which various researchers can use to get identical results. We can illustrate this point spatially.[9] Using the bull's eye of a target as the symbol of what we want to achieve, we can say that a definition which is both reliable and valid would have the shots clustered at the center.

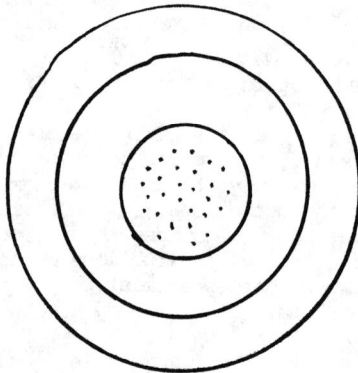

A definition which is reliable, but invalid, would have its shots clustered, but they would be off the mark, like this:

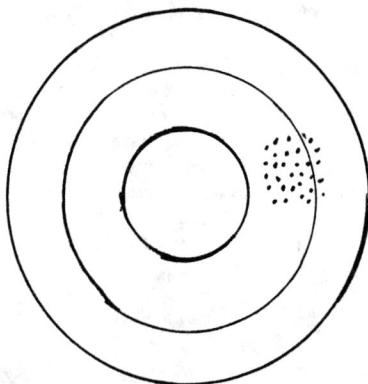

And a definition which is neither reliable nor valid would look like this:

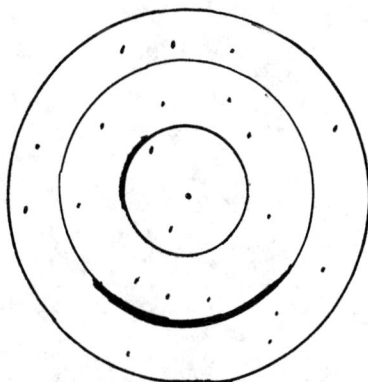

These symbolic representations underline the main point of this section: an operational definition must be both reliable and valid, or it is useless.

Assignment #13

  It is important to be able to recognize acceptable (that is, valid and reliable) operational definitions. Listed below are a number of operational definitions (preceded by conceptual definitions) for several different variables. Tell which set of instructions would be acceptable for a research project and which would not. If an operational definition is unacceptable, tell why—that is, tell which of the eleven rules for operationalizing it violates (more than one possible), or whether it is invalid, and why.

123

1. *Variable; Alienation.*
   Conceptual definition: a sense that the leaders of the country don't care about you or have your welfare at heart.
   Operational definition:
      a. *Ask the respondents in your sample this question: "Have you ascertained that the hegemony enjoyed by the elite elements of our polity in no way corresponds to an inclination on their part to indulge in pursuit of desiderata for the hoi polloi, or not?"*
      b. *All those who answer, "Yes," will be classified as "alienated."*

2. *Variable: Trust in political leadership.*
   Conceptual definition: an inclination to support current political leaders, to assume they are responsible people of integrity trying to make decisions which are good for the country as a whole.
   Operational definition:
      a. *Ask the respondents in your sample these questions:*
        i. *"Do you really believe that an incompetent opportunist like Alexander Haig should have been appointed as Secretary of State?"*
        ii. *"Don't you think a mossback like Warren Burger ought to retire as Chief Justice of the U. S. Supreme Court?"*
        iii. *"Do you think the eight millionaires in our Cabinet can really understand the needs of the common man in this country?"*
      b. *Assign one point for a NO answer to question (i); one point for a YES answer to question (ii); and one point for a NO answer to question (iii).*
      c. *Respondents will be categorized as follows:*
        i. *Those scoring 3 will be classified as "very alienated."*
        ii. *Those scoring 1 or 2 will be classified as "somewhat alienated."*
        iii. *Those scoring 0 will be classified as "not alienated."*

3. *Variable: National Wealth*
   Conceptual definition: the amount of money available to the average citizen in a country.
   Operational definition:
      a. *Using a standard almanac or other similar reference source, look up the "per capita income"*

124

figures for 1982 for all countries which were members of the United Nations in that year.

  b. Find the median per capita income figure for that group of countries.

  c. All countries with a per capita income level above the median will be classified as "wealthier than average;" all countries below the median will be classified as "less wealthy than average."

4. *Variable: Dictatorship*
   Conceptual definition: a system of government in which one, or a small number of people, hold most of the power.
   Operational definition:

   a. Pick a number of countries that strike you as interesting.

   b. Go to the library and read one book on each of these countries.

   c. Determine from this book whether power is held by a small number of people or a large number of people.

   d. All those countries in which power is held by a small number of people will be classified as "dictatorships;" all countries in which a large number of people hold power will be classified as "non-dictatorships."

5. *Variable: Liberalism*
   Conceptual definition: a belief that government ought to be active in helping the disadvantaged of society--poor, elderly, minority groups, etc.
   Operational definition:

   a. Take a sample of people in your city.

   b. Ask each person a number of questions to elicit his attitudes toward the role of government in relation to our socially disadvantaged groups.

   c. All those who think government should do more to help the disadvantaged will be classified as "liberals;" all others will be classified as "non-liberals."

6. *Variable: Publicity-seeking Behavior*
   Conceptual definition: a tendency on the part of some politicians to seek ways of making themselves known to a broad public, usually through: (a) the intense use of speech-making; (b) a habit of making dramatic charges and proposals; and (c) a pronounced tendency to seek widely-recognized higher offices.

Operational definition:

a. Get a list of the 435 members of the U.S. House of Representatives for the current year.

b. Look up the amount of national publicity each member obtained by using the Index to the *New York Times* for the current year. Publicity will be measured by the number of separate stories in which a congressman's name appears in the *New York Times*.

c. Whenever the Index indicates that a Congressman's name appeared in a story in the current year, assign one point to that Congressman.

d. When all names have been checked in the Index, each Congressman will have a point total. These totals will probably range from 0 to several hundred.

e. Find the median number of points.

f. All Congressmen whose point totals are over 150% of the median will be classified as "high publicity-seekers."

g. All Congressmen whose point totals are under 50% of the median will be classified as "low publicity-seekers."

h. All Congressmen whose point totals fall in between these two groups will be labeled as "moderate publicity-seekers."

Assignment #14

The more operational definitions you construct, the better your "feel" for how to do it. In Assignment 11 we asked you to construct an operational definition for political participation. We hope your instructor went over some of your attempts in class and then outlined for you a good set of instructions for measuring participation. Now we suggest a similar assignment which can be useful as a class exercise. This time we expect the class as a whole to produce operational definitions for a number of variables, so that you get a feeling for both the range of possibilities and the general pattern underlying all operational definitions.

Following is a list of 33 variables. Each student should choose (or be assigned) the operationalization of one of these terms.

Working-class status
Political instability
An educated society
Poverty
Authoritarian
Conservative
Communist

Class consciousness
Middle-class
Economic growth
Non-voting
Powerful (as applied to legislators)
Powerful (as applied to heads of state)

126

Urban district	Powerful (as applied to nations)
Legislative effec- tiveness	Governmental legitimacy Citizen apathy
Ethnicity rate (in states or legisla- tive districts)	War Isolationism Self-esteem
Nationalism	Party cohesion and factionalism
Social mobility	Ideologue
Corruption	Coup d'etat
Electoral fraud	Level of bureaucracy (when
Regionalism	comparing states)
Inflation	Party loyalty (among the electorate)

Each student's assignment is to compose a reliable and valid set of operational instructions for recognizing and measuring one of the variables listed above. Let's review the steps involved in data gathering.

Step 1: Compose a clear conceptual definition of the variable. State your reasons for defining it in these terms.

Step 2: Draw up a set of operational instructions for recognizing your variable. You must adhere to the following rules.

Rule #1: You must give precise, specific instructions for the steps to take in order to observe in the real world the phenomenon described by your term.

Rule #2: Don't define one concept in terms of another, but in terms of a process or series of steps to be undertaken.

Rule #3: You must be especially careful to give specific instructions whenever two researchers might follow different procedures.

Rule #4: You must clearly describe any list of individuals or entities used in your research, and this list must be as complete as possible.

Rule #5: When conducting surveys, state the exact question or questions which will be used to categorize people in the sample.

127

Rule #6:   In questionnaires, use wording that
            occurs in everyday conversation; avoid
            social science jargon.

Rule #7:   In questionnaires, avoid long, complex
            sentence structures; keep sentences
            short and straightforward.

Rule #8:   In questionnaires, each short-answer
            question must pose a simple choice.

Rule #9:   In questionnaires, don't load the
            questions.

Rule #10:   In questionnaires, each question must
            allow all respondents to classify
            themselves.

Rule #11:   In operationalizing complex variables,
            it will often be necessary to propose
            several ways of identifying the vari-
            able, to sum these steps in some kind
            of scoring process, and to invent cat-
            egories--based on the scores obtained--
            which stand for stronger or weaker de-
            grees of the variable under question.

Step 3: Assess the reliability and validity of your
         operational instructions.

Step 4: Describe the sources from which you would gather
         data. These could include: a random sample of
         telephone numbers, a sample of every third page
         from a Congressional hearing, a complete enumera-
         tion of states allowing their Governors an item
         veto (taken from The Book of the States), etc.
         To complete this step, it will help to read the
         rest of this chapter.

Carry out Steps 1-4 and bring your results to class. Be on
your toes to defend your operational definitions and to spot problems in those proposed by others. (Get a good night's sleep
beforehand!)

Sampling
    We are almost ready to move into the field and begin to test
a hypothesis. But before we do, we must learn how to select the
individuals or entities we are actually going to examine. What if
we were studying a variable which occurs in a limited number of
cases--nations possessing nuclear weapons, for example? We could

128

easily collect data on each of these nations. Even if we wanted to study a group as large as the French National Assembly, it would be possible (with a lot of effort) to gather data on all its members: 491 Deputies. But if we're dealing with something like an occupational group (Norwegian fishermen), a religious following (Hindus in India), or an ethnic sub-culture (the Basques of Spain, the Kurds of Iran), it's a different story.

When George Gallup or Louis Harris tell us that "58% of the American people think inflation is the most important problem facing their country today," does that mean that they have gone out and interviewed all 225,000,000 Americans to find out what was on their minds? If so, how come they never got to you--or to us? No. At today's prices, it costs $30-$50 for each interview, so what Gallup and Harris do is limit, drastically, the number of people they talk with.

The total number of individual cases you are studying, or wish to generalize about, is known as the universe you are investigating. From what we have said, it should be clear that when the number of cases in your universe rises beyond a certain level, it will become impossible for you to examine each case. The exact point at which this impossibility occurs will differ from project to project, from researcher to researcher. Some people will have more time, energy, and money than others. In a short, college-level research paper a student may be able to gather data on a mere 50 to 100 cities (or countries, or town managers, or whatever). A professional, well-funded research outfit may be able to examine several thousand cases (U.S. citizens, multinational corporations, residents of nursing homes, etc.). But for every research project some numerical limit ultimately exists. Beyond that point the project cannot examine additional cases. This point usually occurs somewhere between a few hundred and a few thousand. It may be possible to interview everyone in a small town of 2,000. It would be a great strain, but possible, to interview everyone in a city of 30,000. It is simply impossible to interview everyone in a city of 500,000. All the more reason why everyone in an entire country can never be interviewed for any research project.

Most serious researchers eventually undertake a study in which the universe they wish to explore is so large that they cannot gather data on all individual cases within it. What do they do? They must take a sample of the cases within their universe. In short, they abandon the hope of studying all the cases and opt for the second-best solution of studying some of them. One of the first decisions you must make as you head into the field to gather data is this one: do I get information on all members of my universe, or only on some of them? To sample or not to sample?

You can usually answer this question quickly. First, find
out how many cases there are in your universe. If the number is
at all large, you will obviously have to sample. If the number is
reasonably small (say, under 100), you can probably deal handily
with the entire universe. But what if you aren't certain? Say
the number turns out to be 265 (the number of members of the
Canadian House of Commons). Should you sample or study the entire
universe? The best way to decide is to gather the infromation you
want on 5 or 10 of the cases in the universe. Then calculate how
long it would take you to do the entire universe, and make your
decision. If you are looking for ages and religious preferences
of U.S. Congressmen, it wouldn't take you long to get the data for
all 435 individuals. But if you are going to do psychological
profiles of these people, you'd better limit yourself to a very
small sample. That sort of thing takes time.

If you decide that you can study an entire universe, the information in the rest of this section is irrelevant to your project. But if you find it necessary to sample, a new problem a-
rises. Just how is sampling done? Which particular members, out
of the entire universe, are chosen for study?

There are several ways to sample (and several good ways not
to), but since we wish to remain at an introductory level in this
book, we will discuss only one way: the best way. In sampling,
you are picking a few cases from an entire universe of cases.
When you write up your results, you will generalize about the universe, but your data will actually be based only on the small part
of it which you gathered information on. So it is crucial that
your sample be as much like the universe as possible. Ideally, the
characteristics of the sample will be very close to that of the
universe, so that your generalizations (based on the sample) will
be valid (to the universe).

You have the best chance of getting a sample similar to your
universe if you draw up a random sample. To many the term "random"
implies haphazard, casual, even slipshod. In fact, a random sample
has an explicit definition and it must be carried out carefully
to insure mathematical randomness. Research findings from samples
which are not random usually cannot be trusted and often should be
ignored altogether. A random sample has this simple but specific
definition: it is one in which each case in the universe has an
equal chance of appearing in the sample. If you follow that guide-
line, you will obtain samples which, most of the time, have characteristics quite close to that of the universes from which they
are drawn.

You can draw random samples in various ways. If your universe
is small enough (say, 100) you could write the name of each case
on a slip of paper, put all the paper in a hat, and remove blind-

folded some of the pieces of paper (say, 10). In this case each member of the universe would have an equal chance (one in ten) of appearing in the sample, and the sample would be random. You must be certain, however, that each piece of paper is exactly the same size as the others, and that no piece is stickier than the others. Larger, stickier pieces of paper would be more likely to be chosen than the others, and therefore randomness would be thrown off.

Dice are sometimes used to generate random numbers, but here you must be careful. When you roll two dice, certain numbers (e.g., 7) are much more likely to appear than others (e.g., 2 or 12)--as craps players know very well. (If you don't believe this, try rolling two dice a hundred times and keep track of the results. While there is only one way for a two to come up--"snake eyes"-- there are six ways for a seven to appear.) The roll of one die will approach pure randomness, but imperfections in construction of the die will usually lead one number to appear slightly more often than others.[10]

In practice, professional researchers do not bother with rolling dice or putting paper into hats. Statisticians have found a way to generate purely random numbers, and computers have been programmed to generate hordes of them. For instance, the Rand Corporation has put out a book entitled A Million Random Digits.[11] Professionals draw on this type of data for their random samples. Or they will go down a list and take every Nth name. If you want a sample of 300 from a telephone book containing 30,000 names, you will go through the book taking every 100th name. If you use a table of random numbers to get your first name (say the 67th person in the book) and then take every 100th name after that, then every person in the book had--from the beginning--an equal chance of appearing in your sample, and it is a random one.

Professional pollsters have to engage in more complicated maneuvers than we can describe here,[12] but they have become sophisticated in working toward ways of approximating a true random sample. Their results show the utility of this approach. George Gallup has been predicting Presidential elections since 1936. Until the 1980 election his predictions were less than 2%, on the average, from the actual results of the national vote. The 1980 election was a little special. A large number of voters apparently made up their minds at the last minute--too late for pollsters to register this shift in the electorate.

As opposed to the scientific random sample, other polls--the haphazard kind--are deficient. We are all familiar with the street corner or shopping center poll. Usually taken during the hours of 9 to 5, these polls do not include people who work during business hours, and therefore produce an unrepresentative or biased sample.

Many of the poll results cited by American politicians to demonstrate public support of their positions are based on biased samples. You have probably seen mail questionnaires which your Senator asks his constituents to return. Those who answer are probably confident that the Senator will pay attention to their opinions. Naturally, they will expect him to pay attention because they are in agreement with him. Why should you bother writing Ted Kennedy to tell him to become more conservative when there is not a ghost of a chance that he will follow your wishes? Likewise, liberals don't write Strom Thurmond asking him to help the poor and the Black. In short, most politicians hear most of the time from a biased sample and if a sample is biased, its results mean absolutely nothing at all. They are simply worthless. Even if the sample is very large. In 1936 the Literary Digest polled five million people. Their prediction: Alf Landon (Alf who?) would beat Franklin Roosevelt in a landslide. Of course, Roosevelt went on to win the greatest Presidential victory in modern American history, and the Literary Digest went broke. How could they be so far off with such a big sample? Easy. The methods used to pick people for the sample insured a collection of upper-middle and upper-class voters, who were mostly Republican supporters.[13] They had a biased sample. These people were simply overwhelmed in the election itself by the millions of poor and working-class voters who liked the way Roosevelt was dealing with the Depression.

It goes without saying that other biased samples—such as letters to the editor, phone-ins to radio or TV stations, or even casual conversations with friends—are utterly worthless as a gauge of representative public opinion. (They do have, to be sure, other uses.) People are often surprised to learn this truth. Pauline Kael, a New Yorker movie critic and member of New York's cultural elite, expressed amazement at President Nixon's landslide re-election in 1972 with the words, "I can't believe it. No one I know voted for Nixon." Of course, if she had paid attention to professional pollsters rather than to the biased sample represented by her liberal circle of friends, she would not have been surprised at all.

Size of the sample

How big a sample must you have to produce accurate results? When people first learn that Gallup predicts correctly most of the time the way tens of millions of Americans will vote, they assume he must have sampled a good percentage of those voters in order to be that close to the mark. In fact, Gallup usually interviews about 1500 people—and never more than 7,000. That is, he interviews perhaps one person for every 100,000 adult Americans, or .001% of the population. (So if you ever get picked to be interviewed in a Gallup Poll, imagine the burden of responsibility you will be shouldering. One hundred thousand people will be making their opinions known through you!)

132

This may seem like a flimsy basis for predicting the opinions or votes of millions of people. But it works! Mathematicians have proven that a random sample (we repeat, random) of 1500 cases will come within 3% of predicting what the actual universe of cases looks like 95 out of 100 times. Note two points here. Five times out of 100--or every 20th time--a sample of 1500 will not accurately predict to the broader universe. How do you know if your sample is that one in twentieth fluke? You don't. You are just taking a chance it isn't. But it's a pretty good risk. Most of us are quite content to have odds of nineteen to one going for us. (Sometimes, by the way, you can suspect your sample of being the one in twenty oddball--when its results are quite different from those of all other samples taken from similar universes.)

Don't forget our second qualification to the accuracy of samples. The pattern they show predicts the pattern within the universe only to within plus or minus 3%. Much of the time this qualification is unimportant. If your sample shows that 81% of his constituents love Senator Blowhorn, it hardly matters whether that number is actually 78% or 84%. The conclusion is clear. Senator Blowhorn should be reelected handily. But what if a poll shows (as many did) that John F. Kennedy is leading Richard M. Nixon by 51% to 49%? Given the plus or minus 3% rule, we know that Kennedy's actual support among voters is somewhere between 48% and 54%, Nixon's somewhere between 46% and 52%. Now the "somewhere" is of vital importance. The fate of the most powerful branch of government in the most powerful nation in the world depended on which of those two men had even one vote over the 50% mark. Polls which said that each was "about" 50% were useless for predicting the final outcome. And in fact no poll can predict an election as close as that of 1960 (or 1968 or 1976). When candidates are within three percentage points of each other, pollsters simply have to say it is "too close to call."

Random sampling, in short, does not give us a perfect picture of the universe. It is the best thing we can do, however, when the universe is too big for practical examination. And most of the time sampling produces results which are close enough to the universe for all practical purposes.

You may still be wondering how sampling can work. Try to imagine it this way. If the classroom in which you take this course were filled with millions of black and white marbles which were all stirred up so that they were distributed randomly, how many marbles do you suppose you'd have to pick out before you had a pretty good idea of the relative proportions in which they were present in the room? Reaching in blindfolded and grabbing ten would probably not help much. You might just by chance get ten black marbles. But by the time you got to 100 you'd be starting to get an idea of the overall distribution in the room. When you

133

got to 500, you'd start to get confident of your results (and tired of counting). When you reach 1500, you'd be damned confident!

You will be happy to know that your instructor will not require you to go out and interview 1500 people. We mention this figure--and the corresponding degree of accuracy it produces--to show what is necessary for good research and to increase your sophistication in assessing research intelligently. When you read newspaper articles about "current public opinion," for example, be sure to find out whether the conclusions are based on a random sample and how many people were actually polled.

Let's try another tack. In order to make the statistics you will learn in the next chapter work well, you need at least 20-25 cases in each box, or "cell," of your table. If you are comparing the party identification of physicians with that of the general public (to test your hypothesis that "being a doctor is correlated with being a Republican"), you'd hope to come up with figures like these (because they support your hypothesis).

		OCCUPATION	
		Physicians	All others
PARTY IDENTIFI-CATION	Republicans	30	20
	Democrats, Independents and Others	20	40

This means that you would have to sample 50 physicians and 60 non-physicians. That's easier than 1500! But suppose there are only 25 physicians in your community. Or your instructor gives you just one week to test your hypothesis. You'll either have to settle for smaller numbers or test the "other" category by taking a non-random sample (say, of your classmates). The important thing is that you understand the procedures and the amount of accuracy they insure. Of course, if you do not sample randomly, your findings can be regarded only as suggestive, pending a full-blown examination of your hypothesis (which you may want to undertake in another course or as an independent study project).

So how large a sample should you aim for? Try to anticipate your results. Guess what your final table will look like, then try to sample enough individuals, or cases, to fill it out. The closer you get to this goal, the more impressive your results will be. And if you can sample randomly, your findings will be even more persuasive. But if you must compromise on either the size or the randomness of the sample, go ahead and do so. What you are doing is a research exercise, not a major paper or project to be written up in a professional journal.

134

The hypothesis as a comparative statement

You will have observed that the preceding table, which illustrated data that might be collected to show that "being a doctor is correlated with being a Republican," included information not only on doctors and Republicans, but also on non-doctors and non-Republicans.

Why do we do this? What would happen if we didn't include this information? Let's say that you took a survey to test the doctor-Republican hypothesis and cited the following data as proof of support for this relationship:

TABLE 1

	Republicans	Non-Republicans
Physicians	30	20

What does this show? That doctors are likely to be Republicans? Yes, but suppose another student came along and presented information from a survey he'd done of the general public (i.e., non-doctors).

TABLE 2

	Republicans	Non-Republicans
General Public	40	10

Now is the original hypothesis supported? In a sense, yes. Doctors are, after all, more likely to be Republicans than not. But so is everyone else. In fact, the hypothesis and the data cited in Table 1 are positively misleading, because the important finding (from Table 2) is that doctors are less likely to be Republican than everyone else. A hypothesis that obscures reality is of no use at all.

When you write a hypothesis in the form "X is correlated with Y," keep in mind that this statement implies that X is particularly strongly correlated with Y—or that X is more strongly correlated with Y than is non-X. So when we say that "being a doctor is correlated with being a Republican," we mean that doctors are more likely to be Republican than people who do other kinds of work.

It follows, then, that in testing the hypothesis in question, you must gather data on the party affiliation not only of doctors but of people in other occupations as well. You can see why this is necessary if you recall the discussion in Chapter 3 of dependent and independent variables. In this example occupation is the independent variable and party identification the dependent one.

135

We are really saying that if we vary occupation, party identification will also vary. When we define occupational status as that
of "physician," we will expect a high level of Republicanism.
When we change occupational status--to farmer, laborer, stunt fly-
er, or more generally "non-physician"--we will expect party identification also to change, specifically to a lower level. So only
by varying the independent variable (physician and non-physician)
will we be able to see whether any change is produced in the dependent variable (high or low levels of support for Republicanism).

       To conclude, data on one variable never mean anything by them-
selves. They take on meaning only when they are compared with data
on something that is not-that-variable. In case you need to be
further convinced, imagine this situation. You return home from a
trip abroad in mid-July and ask a friend of yours, "How're the Sox
doing?" He replies: "Great! They've got a 50 and 29 record."
This information gladdens your heart--for about two seconds. Then
your friend goes on, "The only trouble is, the Yankees have a 59
and 20 record, and the Sox are 9 games out of first place." With
this news you learn once and for all that only comparative statements mean anything. We have to compare the Sox with the non-Sox
before we get a true picture of the world.

Locating data
       Our modern world is characterized by the easy availability of
an enormous amount of information. The data sources at your disposal are legion. If you cannot create your own data (through
some kind of survey or other method), a quick trip to any library
will provide you with more than you could ever need for all your
college research papers. We suggest here a few of the basic
sources you could turn to in developing good political science
research projects.

       1. Public Opinion Surveys. In this chapter we have concen-
trated on public opinion research to illustrate our points. To
find out whether doctors are more likely to be Republicans than
are people in other occupations, it would be necessary to survey
the two groups. You might get a list of doctors from the telephone
directory, call them up, identify yourself and the project you are
doing, and ask them that standard question on party identification
we provided earlier. If you have time, you'd want to do the same
with a random sample of the general public.

       If you don't have time, it would be acceptable for purposes
of a research exercise to survey 50 to 60 of your fellow students.
(Perhaps your instructor would be willing to devote a class period
to the mutual exchange of questionnaires). Or if your variable is
one that has been studied in national surveys, you could use information from those sources. One of the best of these is the
Gallup Opinion Index.[14]   You might compare information from your

own survey of physicians with data gathered by Gallup on the whole population. The information you would present might appear as follows:

OCCUPATION

		Physicians	National Sample
PARTY IDENTIFI-CATION	Republicans	30	312
	Non-Republicans	20	1155

Needless to say, you must give credit to George Gallup for collecting the information on the national sample!

2. <u>Voter Registration List.</u> If you want to test hypotheses on voting behavior or party enrollment, a wealth of information exists in the office of your local board of voter registrars. Suppose you wanted to compare the party enrollment of different ethnic groups. If you hypothesized that voters of Irish descent were more likely to be Democrats than other voters, you could go down to city hall and ask to examine the Registration List. There you would find the voter's name followed by his or her party enrollment. You could then take a random sample of pages, go down each page looking for "Irish" names. (This approach is not 100% reliable. You might call someone "Irish" whom we would not. Still, you can minimize reliability problems by stating at the outset that you would record only voters with particular names as Irish [you'd have to make a list] and that you would not include questionable cases ["Costello," for example] in your sample of "non-Irish" voters.)

You can also use the registration lists to find out who is likely to vote. Most lists contain notations beside an individual's name indicating whether he or she voted in recent elections. Thus, you could test propositions such as "Franco-Americans (or Hispanic-Americans) vote less frequently than Anglo-Americans."

3. <u>Newspapers and magazines.</u> Press coverage is very important to a politician, to political parties, and to interest groups. Your library is likely to have the New York Times and your local community's paper available on microfilm. In addition, national magazines such as <u>Time</u> and <u>Newsweek</u> provide a good mirror of what is being said and how much is being said about people and issues.

A good place to start finding out who and what is being covered is the <u>New York Times Index.</u> There you will find notations such as these:

Bayh, Birch. A.28, 77, p. 3; S. 19, 77, p. 1; S. 22, 77, p. 1.
Referenda. Atomic Power, O. 9, 78, p. 13.

These notations tell you that articles on Birch Bayh appear on page 3 of the August 28, 1977, issue of the New York Times, as well as on page 1 of the September 19 and 22 issues. Coverage of an atomic power referendum appears on page 13 of the October 9, 1978 issue.

4. Other sources of information. There are many collections of data and information which can be invaluable to anyone undertaking serious research in political science. We list here only the most useful and readily available to students of American politics. Most of these will be on the reference shelf in any decent library. (If they aren't, ask your librarian why not.)

a. The Almanac of American Politics.[15] This is probably the most useful single source of information on American politics. It is updated every two years, and you should own a copy if you are at all serious about the study or practice of public affairs. It presents a vast array of information about each Senator, Governor and Congressman. This includes voting scores for congressmen as determined by a variety of national interest groups; demographic and economic information about each state and congressional district in the nation; short well-written profiles about each political leader and the politics of that leader's state or district; the amount of money which each department of the federal government spends in each state and district; and so forth.

Similar data can be found in the "Avis" of political almanacs, Politics in America.[16]

b. Congressional Quarterly.[17] This magazine centers on the doings of Congress. It comes out every week with a host of information on what has been occurring in Congress (down to the subcommittee level) and many good, analytical articles about developing patterns in our national legislature. It also presents a CQ Almanac[18] packed with data and articles summarizing the legislative and political history of the previous year. The Congressional Quarterly outfit also publishes many other vital reference works, which most college libraries obtain.

c. Sessional Index to the Congressional Record.[19] This reference work lists each Congressman, the number of times he or she speaks on the floor of House or Senate, and the subjects addressed. It could provide useful data for testing a number of hypotheses about the behavior of congressmen.

d. Congressional District Data Book.[20] Here is a rich source of information on Congressional districts in the United States. It includes various information about the residents of each district, such as their age; their educational levels; their income levels; employment and occupation data; race; and the way they voted in recent elections. Further, detailed maps are pro-

vided of each Congressional district (helpful if you want to see
whom you share your Congressman with, and for other purposes).

e. Congressional Directory.[21] This book, published
every year, lists personal information about every Senator and
Congressman: date of birth, where born, past career and positions
held, present committees, etc. It also provides a great deal of
information about how Congress and the other two branches of
American government are structured.

f. American Votes (vols. 1-14).[22] This series contains
election returns for every county, in every year, for all major
state and national elections since 1952.

g. The Book of the States.[23] This is a useful source of
information on state politics. It includes comparative information
on the powers of governors, services provided in the various
states, trends in state legislation and so forth. It is updated
every two years.

h. Blue Books, Registers, Legislative Manuals. Each
state publishes a series with a title similar to one of those
indicated here. These works contain information on towns and cities in the state, forms of government, names of state and local
officials, population sizes, votes in gubernatorial elections, and
(sometimes, but not always) a summary of the laws enacted by the
legislature in the past session.

i. City Directories. These are published in almost
every moderate to large-sized city in the United States. They
contain census-type data on each household (number of residents,
ages, occupations, marital statuses) as well as a business directory and a "reversed telephone book" (numbers first).

j. U.S. Census Reports.[24] These are based on data collected by the Bureau of the Census in the U.S. Department of
Commerce. They provide information similar to that included in
city directories. However, the information is presented in terms
of averages for geographical and political units (city blocks or
counties, for example) rather than by individual households. The
Census Reports contain, in addition, a great deal of information
about local government: e.g., clientele served, services provided, number of officials, forms of political organization, etc.

5. Bibliographic guides to other reference materials. We
have touched here on just a few of the most common and useful
sources of data. Many more abound. Luckily, other scholars have
taken the trouble to write entire books telling you about possible
reference materials for political science research. Perusal in
the following three books will provide you with more research leads

than you could ever follow up in a lifetime.

Holler, Frederick. The Information Sources of Politi-
cal Science, 2d rev. ed., 5 vols. (Santa Barbara,
Cal.: ABC-Clio Press, 1971).
Kalvelage, Carl and Morley Segal. Research Guide in
Political Science, (Morristown, N.J.: General
Learning Press, 1976).
Merritt, Richard and Gloria Pyseka. The Student Po-
litical Scientist's Handbook. (Cambridge, Mass.:
Schenkman Publishing Co., 1969).

6. Your library's reference librarian. A very important, and
often neglected, source of information is the reference librarian
in your local or college library. This individual is intimately
familiar with data sources and reference materials of every kind
and can usually tell you quickly whether something you want exists
and where to find it. His or her specialty is locating information that students and faculty members can't discover on their
own. Use this person!

Assignment #15
*We will be less specific in this assignment and leave the de-
tails to your instructor. It is useful for students to get an idea
of the many kinds of information and data which exist. The more
familiar you are with data sources, the easier it will be to develop hypotheses. Students are often stymied when it comes to
thinking of hypotheses. Part of the problem is that you just don't
know what information is available on which you could do research.
It may never have occurred to you that you can discover both the
average income and the rate of participation in recent elections
for every county in this country. Once you see this information
before you, it may occur to you that poorer people might vote in
lower numbers than richer ones. Using the information we mentioned, you could go ahead and test the hypothesis, "Wealth is positively correlated with voting participation."*

*To help familiarize you with data sources, we would like to
encourage your instructor to develop, in class, three or four hypotheses, send everyone to the library to gather small amounts of
data on each one, and then put all the data together and test the
hypothesis at the next class session. We, for instance, have
tested in this way propositions such as, "More powerful Senators
will get more publicity than less powerful ones." (Formally
stated: "Among political leaders, power is correlated with the
attainment of publicity.") In a class of twenty, we might have
each student responsible for gathering data on five Senators. For
each Senator the student would have to determine whether he was
powerful or not (by checking in the Almanac of American Politics
or the Congressional Directory for the offices he holds) and how*

much publicity he gets (by counting the number of times he is listed in the *New York Times Index*). Other hypotheses get students to use other library sources. Once you actually have a look at some of the available materials, you will have a much better idea of how to use them for your own projects. And as you gather the data for your class assignment, you will probably see many other kinds of data in the same source. Some of these should give you ideas for research projects.

We have found this a useful exercise for our students and hope your instructor will follow up on it also. But if he doesn't, there is nothing to stop you from going to the library on your own and browsing through some of the sources we listed. We cannot exaggerate the importance of becoming familiar with these reference materials.

1. For instance, see the discussions in these two basic text-
books: Theodore M. Newcomb, Ralph H. Turner, and Philip E. Con-
verse, <u>Social Psychology: The Study of Human Interaction</u> (New
York: Holt, Rinehart and Winston, Inc., 1965), pp. 47-79 ("The
Nature of Attitudes"); and Roger Brown, <u>Social Psychology</u> (New
York: The Free Press, 1965), pp. 647-53.

2. We take our lead in this regard from that seminal study of
voting—Angus Campbell, Philip E. Converse, Warren E. Miller, and
Donald E. Stokes, <u>The American Voter</u> (New York: John Wiley & Sons,
Inc., 1960). See their chapter on "The Impact of Party Identification," pp. 120-45. Note in particular this passage (p. 121):
"Only in the exceptional case does the sense of individual attachment to party reflect a formal membership or an active connection
with a party apparatus. Nor does it simply denote a voting record,
although the influence of party allegiance on electoral behavior
is strong. Generally this tie is a phychological identification,
which can persist without legal recognition or evidence of formal
membership and even without a consistent record of party support.
Most Americans have this sense of attachment with one party or the
other. And for the individual who does, the strength and direction
of party identification are facts of central importance in account-
ing for attitude and behavior."

3. This rule is suggested by the discussion in James L. Payne
<u>Foundations of Empirical Political Analysis</u> (Chicago: Markham
Publishing Co., 1973), pp. 26-28.

4. These rules, and Rule #8, are suggested in James L. Payne,
"Will Mr. Harris Ever Learn?" <u>National Review</u> 26 (June 21, 1974),
pp. 701-02.

5. See the discussion in <u>The American Voter</u>, op. cit., pp.
121-28, and in particular pp. 122-3, including footnote 1.

6. Calculated from data in Table 4 (p. 130) of Stanley R.
Freedman, "The Salience of Party and Candidate in Congressional
Elections: A Comparison of 1958 and 1970," in Norman R. Luttbeg,
ed., <u>Public Opinion and Public Policy: Models of Political Link-
age</u>, rev. ed. (Homewood, Ill.: The Dorsey Press, 1974), pp. 126-
31.

7. The questions (a) through (g) in this operational defini-
tion derive from the "Political Information Scale" used by Donald
R. Matthews and James W. Prothro in their study, <u>Negroes and the
New Southern Politics</u> (New York: Harcourt, Brace & World, 1966).
Questions (a) and (g) seem dated now, and Question (d) would not
seem a good question for states with weak county governments, so

that a person wanting to use this scale today outside the South might want to use slightly different questions. The categories devised in steps 2-4 of our operational definition are slight variations on those proposed by Matthews and Prothro.

8. This famous typology was proposed by Harold D. Lasswell in Psychopathology and Politics (Chicago: University of Chicago Press, 1930).

9. The spatial illustrations in this paragraph are derived from the presentation in Jimmy R. Amos, Foster Lloyd Brown, and Oscar Mink, Statistical Concepts: A Basic Program (New York: Harper & Row, Publishers, 1965), p. 65.

10. For good introductions to the science of sampling, see Charles Backstrom and Gerald Hursh-César, Survey Research, 2nd ed. (New York: John Wiley and Sons, 1981) and Seymour Sudman, Applied Sampling (New York: Academic Press, 1976).

11. The Rand Corporation, A Million Random Digits (Glencoe, Ill.: The Free Press, 1955).

12. Backstrom and Hursh-César, op. cit., ch. 2, "Drawing Samples."

13. Those polled included subscribers to the Literary Digest, automobile owners and those who had a telephone in their homes-- all relatively wealthy people during the Depression.

14. (Princeton, N. J.: The Gallup Poll), monthly.

15. Michael Barone and Grant Ujifusa, The Almanac of American Politics, 1982 (Washington, D.C.: Barone and Co., 1981).

16. Alan Ehrenhalt, ed., Politics in America: Members of Congress in Washington and at Home (Washington , D.C.: Congressional Quarterly, Inc., 1981).

17. (Washington, D.C.: Congressional Quarterly, Inc.), weekly.

18. (Washington, D.C.: Congressional Quarterly, Inc.), annually.

19. (Washington, D.C.: Government Printing Office), annually.

20. 2nd ed., (Washington, D.C.: Congressional Quarterly, Inc. 1974).

21. (Washington, D.C.: Government Printing Office), annually.

22. (Washington, D.C.: Elections Research Center).

23. (Lexington, Ky.: Council of State Governments), biennially.

24. (Washington, D.C.: Government Printing Office).

CHAPTER VI

EVALUATING THE DATA

You have now reached the most exciting stage in any research project. You are ready to put things together to see what you have discovered.

You have, by this point, enunciated a theory, developed one or more hypotheses, and gone out and gathered the data needed to test those hypotheses. Now what do all those data tell you about the hypotheses?

It turns out, unfortunately, to be untrue that "facts speak for themselves." Rather, they just sit there, waiting for manipulation and interpretation. If you don't believe this, take a look right now at Appendices I and II. There you will see an enormous number of facts about U.S. Senators and American states. Now what do those facts mean?

Obviously, neither you nor we can say just by looking at those columns of numbers. We must "do something" with those numbers and interpret the results before any meaning can be derived from these facts. In this chapter we suggest a few of the "somethings" you can "do" with numbers once you have gathered a quantity of them. Or to put it formally, we shall propose some statistical manipulations you can use to make clear what your data show. And we shall suggest ways to interpret the results of your statistical calculations. Researchers often call this process "playing with the data" or "number crunching." The purpose of the endeavor is simple: you are trying to learn whether your data support, or fail to support, your original hypotheses.

Causation vs. correlation

Before we discuss how to make sense of our data, we must first explore a theoretical issue touched on earlier in Chapter III. There we described two types of hypotheses. One outlines a causal relationship: X causes Y. In the latter version one is not postulating a direct causal relationship. One is simply observing that where a lot of X is found, so too will there be a lot of Y. Conversely, as X decreases, Y will also. But one is not saying that X causes Y. In fact, one could interpret the statement, "X is correlated with Y," in several ways, including these:

1. X and Y co-vary, but are both caused by a third variable, Z. One might, for instance, find a relationship between traffic jams and height of buildings—as buildings get taller, the number of traffic jams increases. But one does not cause the other. Both are probably caused by a third variable, urbanization. (As cities get bigger, buildings get taller and traffic jams increase.)

145

2. X and Y co-vary, because X causes Z which in turn causes Y. One might find that an increase in industrialization correlates with an increase in attempts to curb pollution. But the reason for this relationship might be that industrialization causes pollution which in turn causes attempts to control pollution. Industrialization by itself did not cause the anti-pollution activities.

3. X and Y co-vary, but we are uncertain yet whether X causes Y or Y causes X, so we retain the more ambiguous wording ("X is correlated with Y"), pending additional research on the two variables. An example of this circumstance is the hypothesis, "Interest in politics is correlated with knowledge about politics."[1] Here we really aren't sure which variable causes the other. Does one first become interested in politics and then go out of one's way to learn about it? Or does one first learn something about politics, and from that knowledge develop an interest in it? Until elaborate exploration of this hypothesis has been undertaken, we aren't able to specify the direction of the causal relationship, so we content ourselves with the correlational statement.

4. X and Y co-vary, but this relationship occurs purely by chance and has nothing to do with a cause-and-effect process. Some researchers have noted a relationship between the outcome of the baseball World Series and U.S. presidential elections. When the National League team wins the World Series in an election year, Democrats usually win the Presidency. If the American League team wins, a Republican becomes President. But no one is seriously suggesting that Democrats win the election because the National League team won the World Series. These are simply two unrelated events, which by chance show a relationship. Note that with the trillions of events which occur in the world, a certain number of phenomena will co-vary purely by coincidence. Superstitions, astrology and other irrational beliefs derive from this fact. Some events will, occasionally, correlate with other events for no particular reason other than chance. Those who need to believe in supernatural explanations will latch on to these non-related covariations to justify their irrational beliefs. For instance, carrying a rabbit's foot will, once in a great while, by chance be followed by good luck. The superstitious person will use this coincidental relationship to justify his belief that "carrying a rabbit's foot causes good luck."

Testing correlational statements is easier than testing causal ones. To test a correlational statement, you need merely show that X and Y "go together." Where you find one, you find the other. Where you get less of one, you get less of the other. Where you find a lot of alienation in a society, you also find a lot of political violence. When you don't see much violence, you won't see much alienation either. It is not hard to find ways of testing the correlational type of hypothetical statement. You must check to see what value Y has when X is high and what value Y has when

146

X is low. Then you draw the appropriate conclusions.

Testing a causal statement is more involved than testing a correlational statement. To conclude that "X causes Y," you need to show 1) that X preceded Y, 2) that you have good reasons (a theory) for believing that Y must follow from X, 3) that other possible causes of Y (P, Q, Z, etc.) do not account for the apparent relationship between X and Y, and 4) that a statistical correlation exists between X and Y. Let us discuss each point in detail.

1. Time order A cause must always precede its effect. If we hypothesize that the production of vast amounts of propaganda against a perceived enemy causes war, we must be prepared to show that these materials were published before the war began. This is nothing but simple common sense. However, researchers aren't always as careful to take this step as they should be.

In the preceding chapter, we considered the hypothesis, "Being a doctor is correlated with being a Republican." To test this assertion, we merely had to show high levels of Republican sympathy among doctors and lower levels of Republican sympathy among non-doctors. Suppose, however, that we wish to make a more emphatic statement. We are convinced that there is a causal relationship between being a doctor and being a Republican. Something in the medical-school experience, we believe, convinces many students to adopt Republican values. We assert, therefore, that "being a doctor causes Republican party membership." How would we go about testing this hypothesis?

It is now no longer sufficient merely to show statistical correlation. One must also show that the process by which one becomes a doctor (the medical-school experience—including internship and residency) occurred before one became a Republican. After all, it is quite possible that many people who are now both doctors and Republicans were already Republicans before entering medical school. If this is the case, then being a doctor did not cause them to become Republicans. In fact, it is likely that going to medical school and becoming a Republican are both caused by a third variable: family wealth. Wealthier people are more likely to be Republicans and also more likely to send their children to medical school. If this were the case, the doctor-Republican correlation would represent a spurious relationship rather than a causal one. The true causal relationships would be: wealthy families cause children to become Republicans; and wealthy families cause children to embark on high-status professional careers.

Now how can we test to see whether it is indeed the medical-school experience, and not family wealth, that causes Republicanism? There are two alternatives, and the first is preferable. We could interview a sample of incoming medical school students, asking them—simply—what their party identification is. One could then wait until they have become full-fledged doctors. Once they have hung a shingle outside an office, they have presumably been exposed to the pressures and socialization experiences which, we postulate, will turn them into Republicans. At this point we interview them again. A second survey done a few years after the first would establish whether or not a significant change in party identification had occurred. This type of research is called a "longitudinal study," and is carried out by social scientists only occasionally. (It is done only on occasion because it takes so long. One has to wait years, sometimes decades, before the research is completed.)

The alternative is to sample a group of incoming medical students and compare their party orientations with that of a sample of practicing physicians. If the party identifications of the two groups were significantly different from each other, you could infer that something is happening in the medical-school experience and in the occupational encounters of the first years following medical school to induce people to become Republicans.

This approach—comparing two groups of people who are at different stages in their lives—is often used as a substitute for the longitudinal study. Nevertheless, it has some drawbacks. When we compare the same people at different stages in their lives, we are holding one crucial variable constant: their early socialization experiences. When we compare two groups of people at different life stages, this variable is not constant. Any differences we find between the two groups might not be the result of the years separating the two groups and the experiences connected to those years (which, remember, we are hypothesizing as the independent variable). The differences between the two groups might rather spring from different childhood, adolescent, or early adulthood experiences which occurred before the adult events we are postulating as the crucial variable.

Our hypothetical case of doctors becoming Republicans illustrates this point. If we sample current medical-school freshmen and current adult physicians and find the latter are more Republican, we can not necessarily attribute the Republicanism to medical-school experiences. It may be that earlier graduates of medical schools came primarily from Republican family backgrounds, while the current crop of incoming students reflect independent or Democratic backgrounds as a result of scholarships, affirmative action programs, and the like.

In short, the longitudinal approach produces more persuasive data. It should be employed whenever possible. Frequently, this approach is practical, even for students writing papers over a few short weeks. There exists a good deal of historical data, which allows researchers to follow events or processes over extended

148

periods of time. For instance, what causes wars? Ideological dis-
agreements? Production of vast amounts of propaganda against an
enemy? Assassination of political leaders? Economic conditions?
"Fortunately," the twentieth century is full of examples of wars
that were well covered in periodicals easily available to students
of political science. Use of these materials could produce a longitudinal study on the fascinating question of why wars take place.

Often one can show that cause preceded effect without resort-
ing to before and after measurements. If you were testing the hypothesis, "Parents' party identification causes children's party
identification," you could argue persuasively that the probability
of the first variable occurring before the second is very high.
Most parents will have developed a party identification before
their children do, and the influence of parent on child is usually
greater than the influence of child on parent in such matters as
political opinions. Hence, if we find a relationship between party
affiliations of parents and children, we would be on safe ground in
assuming that the parents caused the children's orientations, rather than the other way around.

It is sometimes hard to determine which variable precedes the
other. We have already suggested the example, "Interest in politics is correlated with knowledge of politics." In testing a theory that one of these variables caused the other, one must proceed
carefully to determine which one "came first." You might ask a
group of people this question: "What is your earliest memory of
politics?" Some might answer this way:

> From my earliest days I remember my parents and their
> friends excitedly discussing politics. I was fascin-
> ated by the fun and the competition they were involved
> in, so as I got older I decided to learn more about
> politics and get involved too.

These people would be classified as those whose "interest in politics came before and caused knowledge." Others might give this
type of answer:

> I first encountered politics when I started learning
> about all the Presidents in 6th-grade history class.
> Then we had to learn who our city councillors were,
> and the more I learned, the more fascinated I became
> by the subject.

Individuals responding in this manner would be classified as those
whose "knowledge of politics came before and caused interest."
Pursuing this particular research project would hardly be easy.
The two responses we quoted here are clear and simple to categorize. Most would be ambiguous, inconsistent, difficult to follow.

149

Reliability problems in such a study would be enormous. Different researchers would classify the same respondents in different categories. We are not saying that the study would be impossible. But we do wish to suggest that separating cause and effect—deciding which came first—is not always the straightforward matter it might appear to be at first glance.

2. **Theory.** When you find a statistical correlation between X and Y, you have not shown that one variable causes the other. This is true for two reasons. First, many statistical correlations represent spurious relationships, as we suggested earlier. Such is the case with the statistical correlation between the number of inhabitants in China and the number of cars bought by residents of California (there is a long-term upward trend in both variables). This type of relationship is clearly unimportant for research purposes and should be ignored. The underlying reason for ignoring correlations such as these will be explained shortly.

A second reason why statistical correlations don't always represent causal relationships derives from our earlier point about the validity of samples. If you are working with samples, remember that a certain number of them will not be true reflections of the universes from which they are drawn. Usually, samples are drawn in such a way that there is a nineteen in twenty chance that they will represent the universe accurately (to within plus or minus 3%, remember). That is to say, however, that there is a one in twenty chance that statistical correlations shown in your sample would not be valid for the universe you wish to generalize to. (In other words, the correlation would disappear if the entire universe were studied.) This point is usually written in the following way in research reports, articles, or books: "The probability that the relationship between the two variables is due to chance is .05." And the same point is made in condensed form in the small print under a table: "p < .05." (For some samples you can say that "p < .01" or even "p < .001.")

A statement that "p < .05" means that there is a five per cent chance that the relationship between two variables appears, not because it is real, but simply because this particular sample, rather than another random sample from the same universe, was drawn. That is a pretty low probability. It does mean, however, that one in twenty statistical correlations you find will not be "real."

Statistical correlations may not represent causal relationships, then, either because they are spurious or because they result from unrepresentative samples. You can eliminate most doubt about a given correlation, however, if you have previously predict-ed the correlation. And to predict it, you need to offer a theo-ry—a set of reasons—that enable you to make the prediction. This is why we emphasized the theoretical section of your paper. If you predict, in your theory, that X will cause Y, and then you show, through your data, a strong correlation between X and Y (and you also show that X precedes Y), then you are on pretty safe ground for retaining your theory and believing that X does indeed cause Y.

Remember, there are two types of theory that can be cited as the basis for a hypothesis. If you are making a causal statement, you must state your reasons for believing that the independent variable causes a change in the dependent variable. If you are making a correlation statement, you must explain why a third variable causes simultaneous changes in two other variables. To make this point clear, let's look again at the diagrams offered in Chapter III. ("————→" represents causality.)

Causal relationship   Correlational relationship

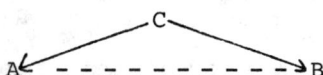

A————————→B

C
A ← - - - - - - - - - →B

In both cases, you must offer reasons for believing that a causal relationship exists where there are arrows in the diagram. In the correlational relationship you must also offer reasons for believing that there will be a statistical relationship between A and B.

3. Elimination of other variables. When we assert that X causes Y, we are also implying that other variables do not cause Y. One way to show that X causes Y is to show that no other variable does. If other variables are eliminated as causes of Y and only X is left, then X must be the causal factor. (But of course, this is true only if the other three conditions for causality are met: X precedes Y, you have a theory to explain why X causes Y, and you find a strong statistical correlation between X and Y.)

Now the "elimination of other variables" is not exactly an easy thing to do. In the strictest sense, it can never be done. There are billions of possible variables, and we will never know enough about the world to be sure that some distant—and seemingly far-fetched—variable might not actually be the cause of Y. For instance, why do people participate in politics? In studying this question, political scientists have isolated educational level, social background, and family political involvement as strong causal factors influencing the dependent variable, participation. They have eliminated other variables—such as a psychological need for power or intense feelings of alienation—as possible causes of participation. And yet they have not tested, and could not possibly test, all possible causes of political involvement. We may some day find that variations in body metabolism, humidity level, or IQ scores cause variations in participation and "wipe out" (as

151

statisticians say) the correlations between participation and the other variables we mentioned, such as education.

How does one deal with this real problem: the inability to eliminate all other potential causes of Y except X? We suggest four intellectual strategies. First, we can adopt Robert Dahl's axiom, "there is no 'action at a distance.'"[2] We expect causes to be fairly close, in time and place, to the effects they produce—or we expect, at least, to see a fairly clear connection between one and the other. This does not have to be so, but most of human experience suggests that it is. Therefore, we are dubious of "causes" far removed in time, space, and logic from the effects they are supposed to produce. When we try to explain an event like the American Civil War, we look at factors close to the time and place of that war: slavery, economic differences between North and South, conflicting cultural values. We do not look at factors such as "the amount of bread consumed in Poland in 1821." These points lead us to enunciate the following rule:

> Rule #1: In considering the potential causes of a vari-
> able (Y), eliminate all farfetched possibili-
> ties—those well removed in time, space, or
> logical reasoning from the variable.

A second way of dealing with the problem of "other variables" has already been suggested. You must propose and defend a theory for the cause you believe to be the correct one. But in this theory you must also propose reasons why other likely variables are not causes of your dependent variable. Your audience is much more likely to accept X as the cause of Y if you can argue convincingly that A, P, and Z could not possibly cause Y. So if you are conducting research to test your belief that poverty causes crime, it would be important in the introductory section of your paper to show reasons why other factors often presumed to cause crime—broken homes, for example—are deficient as causal explanations of this variable. The rule suggested here is:

> Rule #2: In considering the potential causes of a vari-
> able (Y), you must propose theoretical reasons
> for the variable(s) you believe cause Y and also
> reasons against other variables often presumed
> to cause Y.

How many other variables do you have to consider in the theoretical justification of your hypothesis? We can propose no simple rule, but ordinarily the number will be small: say, three to six. It depends on the subject. For any dependent variable you can imagine studying, more than one cause for that variable has probably been proposed by different scholars. For some variables only two or three causes will have been proposed. A dozen or more may have

152

been proposed for others (such as the causes of revolution). A solid research effort will usually discuss, and eliminate, at least three potential causes of variable Y before arguing for one or more variables as the causal factor(s). (These elminated causes usually sound reasonable--obeying Rule #1--and will usually have been put forth by serious scholars in other research efforts). In a student research exercise we suggest that you consider, and eliminate, at least one other potential cause of your dependent variable in the theoretical section of your paper.

A third intellectual strategy for dealing with the "other variable" problem is to test for statistical correlations between those variables and the dependent variable, Y, you are trying to explain. What you essentially wish to see is whether these third variables (A, P, Z, or whatever) will "wash out," or cause to disappear, the relationship which you find to exist between Y and the cause you believe to be the real one, X. You do this by holding X constant and varying the other factors, one at a time. If one or more of them cause extensive variation in Y, you can conclude that they are a more important cause of Y than X. If they do not cause much variation in Y, then you can retain your faith that the variation in Y caused by X is "real." That is, X is actually the cause of Y and not the other variables. The following rule sums up this idea:

> Rule #3: In considering the potential causes of a variable (Y), you must test for the effect of "other variables" on Y, while holding constant the factor (X) which you believe in fact causes Y.

In this short book we will not show you specifically how to test for the effect of third variables on X-Y relationships. This task is an essential one, however, in any serious scientific study. Books on statistics spend a good deal of time on this problem, and your particular instructor may introduce you to some statistical devices which we do not have time enough to consider here. Whether she does or not, however, you should be aware that most causal theories are regarded as unconvincing until extended tests for "other variables" have been undertaken and shown to bear no fruit.

A fourth way of dealing with the "other variable" problem is simply to remember our point in the final section of Chapter IV. Science is an open-ended process. You can never ultimately "prove" that your variable, X, causes Y, as opposed to the multitude of possible variables (A through Z, and beyond). You simply do the best job you can of eliminating the most obvious competing variables which could be argued to cause Y, and then keep an open mind about other possibilities which might arise in the future. You can retain your confidence in X, while realizing that future studies could well uncover a better explanatory variable (say, Q) which supersedes X as the cause of Y. Thus, any conclusions you draw about the causes of Y, based on your "other variable" explorations, must be regarded as tentative. This leads to our final rule for examining the potential causes of a variable:

> Rule #4: In considering the potential causes of a variable (Y), remember that you can never examine all reasonable causes; be prepared for the possibility that future research will uncover variables which provide better explanations of, and correlate more strongly with, Y than the variable (X) you currently postulate as the cause of Y.

4. Statistical correlation. Let us review briefly. To suggest that one variable causes another, you must first show that it precedes the other variable; you must then propose a theory as to why that variable should cause the other; and you should then go on to show that other likely factors do not, in fact, cause your dependent variable. In addition to these points, there is one other crucial element in the case for a causal relationship. You must show some degree of statistical correlation between your two variables.* Naturally, if the variables do not correlate, there can be no causal relationship between them. If Y does not change when X does, then X can not possibly be a cause of Y.

How do we show statistical correlation? Luckily, you are already familiar with some basic methods for doing this. One of these is the use of percentages. We use percentages in a way that follows logically from the point our hypothesis is making. When we say that X is correlated with (or causes) Y, we mean that where we find a lot of X, we will find a lot of Y; with a small amount of X, we get only a little Y. We earlier hypothesized that where we found doctors, we would also find Republicans; conversely, among non-doctors we expected to find fewer Republicans. What this would mean, in terms of percentages, is that we would expect to find a greater percentage of Republicans among doctors than among non-doctors. Our independent variable is "being a doctor." We must separate those who have "a lot of" this variable (who are indeed doctors) from those who don't have it at all (non-doctors). Once we have these two groups, our hypothesis says that group A (doctors) will have more of variable Y (Republicanism) than group B

---

* The precise degree of correlation depends on a variety of factors: your own degree of intellectual rigor, for example, and various conventions widely accepted in the social science disciplines. We deal with this problem at several points in the remainder of this chapter.

(non-doctors). And we test this prediction by seeing whether
doctors have a greater percentage of Republicans in their midst
than do non-doctors.

One indicator, then, of the degree to which the data support
your hypothesis is the difference between the percentages of the
two groups having the property that you hypothesized to be particularly strongly associated with one group.

We have already discussed another common measure used to test
correlations: averages. Let's say you wished to test the hypothesis, "Among nations, wealth causes high levels of literacy." You
would take a sample of countries and for each gather two statis-
tics--say, income per capita and national literacy rate. Then you
would divide the countries into "wealthy" and "non-wealthy"--that
is, into those with more or less of your independent variable,
wealth. You would then calculate the average literacy rate in
each of the two groups of countries. If your hypothesis is working, you should find more of the dependent variable (literacy)
among the wealthy countries than among the non-wealthy ones. To
be specific, wealthy countries should display a higher average
literacy rate than non-wealthy ones.

When you are calculating averages, don't forget that there are
two ways to do this. The mean is usually acceptable, but be sure
to use the median if there are a few extreme cases that distort the
total picture. A comparison of the mean with the median (as we
showed in Chapter IV) can lead to some interesting conclusions
about the distribution of a property within a particular group. To
see for yourself that the mean-median distinction is not simply a
matter of dry statistical theory, try the following exercise.

Assignment #16
   *Study the data below. What conclusions do you draw from these
figures?*

Country	Median family income	Mean family income
Kuwait	$ 800	$29,000
U. S.	$20,800	$26,200
France	$14,800	$21,900
W. Germany	$21,700	$23,100
England	$11,900	$12,100
Sweden	$21,000	$21,200

Though you are not likely to have encountered it before, there
is another figure that is more useful than a percentage or an average in telling you how strongly two variables are related to one
another. That is the correlation coefficient. A correlation coefficient is simply a number between 0 and 1 that expresses the
strength of a relationship. If the number is close to 0, it means
that there is no relationship. If it close to .5, it means that

there is a moderate relationship. When two variables show a correlation coefficient below .3, we generally conclude that there is not much of a relationship between them.

To show you how this works, let's pick up our old chestnut--the doctor-Republican hypothesis. The correlation between these two variables for the hypothetical data presented on page 134 is .50. The relationship between occupation and party identification, in this case, is of moderate strength.

Knowing the value of a correlation coefficient can be particularly important in explaining complex phenomena. If you have a sample of people and you want to see what variables correlate with their party identifications, it would be useful to calculate correlation coefficients for the relationship between different independent variables and your dependent variable--party identification. You could present the data in this way:

Correlation coefficient between an individual's
party identification and his or her

Father's party identification	.70
Occupation	.53
Religion	.46
Ethnic group membership	.37
Educational level	.21
Age	.09
Sex	.03

Such a presentation allows us to compare the relative importance of several independent variables, each of which plays a role in determining an individual's party identification. Notice, also, that it is a more economical way to summarize the relative importance of a number of variables than it would be to make a series of statements such as the following:

-82% of children share their father's party identification.
-57% of doctors are Republicans, while only 34% of non-doctors are Republicans.
-62% of Jews, 51% of Catholics, and 36% of Protestens are Democrats.
-And so forth.

A correlation coefficient can also be expressed as a negative number. In this case, it simply means that the relationship between two variables is opposite to that which was hypothesized. We might test the hypothesis that "being wealthy is correlated with being a Democrat," and find that the correlation coefficient between wealth and Democratic party identification is -.38. What does this mean? That there is a moderate to weak inverse or negative relationship between income and identification with the Democratic Party. In other words, contrary to my original expectations, if you are wealthy, you are somewhat more likely to be a Republican than a Democrat.

A correlation coefficient tells us two things, then. Its size tells us how strong the relationship is. Its sign tells us whether the relationship between the two variables is in accord with, or opposite to, the direction that we originally hypothesized. Let's try interpreting a few correlation coefficients, just to get the hang of it.

Assignment #17
What would you conclude from the following correlation coefficients? Make sure you take both the size and the sign into account. And note these two points about phrasing:

1. A negative correlation coefficient is preceded by a minus (-) sign. A positive coefficient is not preceded by any sign.

2. It is understood that the correlation is between increasing amounts of a property. In example (e), the correlation coefficient refers to the degree to which higher social class is correlated with greater voter turnout.

> a. *The correlation coefficient between Republican party identification and political conservatism is .15.*
>
> b. *The correlation coefficient between minority group membership and voter turnout is -.70.*
>
> c. *The correlation between a father's and a son's party identification is .70.*
>
> d. *The correlation between a child's positive evaluation of the Presidency and his positive evaluation of his father is -.13.*
>
> e. *The correlation coefficient between social class and voter turnout is .43 in the U.S., .38 in India, .31 in Nigeria, .30 in Great Britain, .28 in Italy, .24 in Mexico, .18 in West Germany, and .10 in Austria.*

How do you calculate a correlation coefficient? Unfortunately, there are lots of ways. Books on statistics can take several chapters to present them all. For our purposes—which are merely to provide a brief introduction to the calculation and use of these figures—we will concentrate primarily on one type of cor-

157

relation coefficient, called gamma (written γ). And we will "tor-
ture" our data so that we can use gamma on it. Let's take as an
example the following data, which have been collected to show the
relationship between individual income and the strength of an
individual's party identification.

| | | Strength of Party Identification | | |
Individual	Yearly Income	Independent	Weak. Party ID	Strong Party ID
Jones	$ 6,000	X		
Smith	8,000		X	
Harold	12,000		X	
Thomas	13,000	X		
Farquhar	19,000			X
Egbert	21,000	X		
Semple	26,000			X
Stackhouse	26,000			X
McGillicuddy	31,000			X
Day	31,000	X		

To find out how strongly the variables, "income" and "strength
of party identification," correlate with each other, we must first
compose a rather elongated table, as shown below. We shall place
the independent variable on the left side and the dependent variable on top, although some authorities urge just the opposite. And
please note this important point: always set your tables up so
that the strongest values of the two variables that you expect to
associate with one another appear in the upper-left-hand corner.
In this case we hypothesize that the richer you are, the stronger
your party identification will be. The richest person should
therefore have the strongest level of party identification. If
this were indeed the case, then he (she) would appear in the upper-
left-hand corner of the table. The converse of this pattern is
the lower-right-hand corner. In this case, if the poorest person
had the weakest level possible of party identification, she (he)
would appear in the lower-right-hand corner of this table. The
table is set up correctly as follows:

| | | Strength of Party Identification | | |
High		Strong	Weak	Independent
	31,000	1	0	1
	26,000	2	0	0
	21,000	0	1	0
Income	19,000	1	0	0
	13,000	0	0	1
	12,000	0	1	0
	8,000	0	1	0
	6,000	0	0	1
Low				

158

The next step is the calculation of a figure called P_s. It is simple, if a bit tedious. Here's how to do it. Take the number in the uppermost left-hand corner and multiply it by the total of everything that is both below and to the right of it.

```
1   01
2 ┌─────
0 │ 00
1 │ 10
0 │ 00
0 │ 01
0 │ 10
0 │ 10
0 │ 01
```

This gies us 1 x (5) = 5. Save this 5!

The next step is to move down to the next row, take the number appearing in that cell, and multiply it by the total of everything below and to the right of it.

```
1   01
2   00
0 ┌─────
1 │ 10
0 │ 00
0 │ 01
0 │ 10
0 │ 10
0 │ 01
```

This gives us 2 x (5) = 10. Save this 10!

Continue the same procedure on down through this column. (In this example, there's only one more figure to calculate.) Then move on to the second column and, beginning at the top, go through the same procedure. When you have completed your calculations, add up all your numbers.

QUESTION: P_s for this exercise is _____.

Now we need to calculate a second number, known as P_d. To do this, we simply reverse the procedure used for calculating P_s. Begin this time in the upper-right-hand corner and multiply the number appearing there by the total of everything that is both below and to the left of it.

```
        10 ┐ 1
        20 │ 0
        01 │ 0
        10 │ 0
        00 │ 1
        01 │ 0
        01 │ 0
        00   1
```

This gives us 1 x (6) = 6. Continue down the row, performing a calculation for each number. When you have finished with that column, move to the middle column and go through the same procedure. Add all the numbers obtained from your calculations.

QUESTION: P_d for this excercise is _____.

Now we are ready to calculate gamma. The formula for gamma is simple:

$$\text{gamma } (\gamma) = \frac{P_s - P_d}{P_s + P_d}$$

QUESTION: What is the value of gamma for the preceding data?

_____

QUESTION: Based upon this figure, what can you say about the relationship between income and strength of party identification among the ten individuals surveyed?

Now let's take some other data that don't fit the assumptions upon which gamma is based and see whether we can't do some fast and fancy footwork to allow us to use gamma with them. Suppose we want to test the hypothesis, "Sex is correlated with enrollment in a political party," and we gather the following data:

Sex	Party Enrollment			
	Democrat	Republican	Independent	Other
Male	45	28	36	1
Female	36	30	44	0

Gamma, strictly speaking, can be used only when the values of both variables are ordinal. This means that the values of each variable can be arranged in an ascending order based on some quantity. Income is such a variable. $20,000 is more than $10,000, which in turn is more than $3,000, etc. Strength of attachment to party is another. A strong party identifier has a greater amount of pro-party attachment than a weak party identifier, who in turn has more than an independent. Therefore, we were perfectly justified in using gamma to test our previous hypothesis, "Individual income is correlated with strength of party identification."

Sex and party enrollment, however, are another matter. They are called nominal variables. The distinction between a man and a woman, or a Republican and a Democrat, is based not on a quantity, but on a conceptual or legal definition. Nominal variables employ names (man, woman) to distinguish units of the variable from each other. Ordinal variables can employ degrees of a quantity to distinguish units in the variable from each other. The ability to work with degress allows us to rank units within an ordinal system; thus:

160

<u>Strength of party identification</u>
Strong

Weak

Nil (the independent)

(<u>Interval</u> measures allow us to say <u>precisely how much distance</u>
there is between units within a variable--as with IQ scores, where
we can not only distinguish degrees (genius, average, moron), but
also precise distances between units (a "genius" score of 162 is
precisely 64 points higher than an "average" score of 98.)

If we want to use gamma to test our sex-party hypothesis, the
problem boils down to a way of turning our nominal variables into
ordinal ones. Statistical purists may squawk, but let's see what
we can do anyway. Suppose that what we are trying to show is that
men are more likely than women to be Democrats. We must make each
of the variables in some sense ordinal. That is, instead of just
distinguishing men from women, we must say that men are "more"
something than women. But what does a man have more of than a
woman? Maleness! Voila! And what does a Democrat have more of
than a Republican, an independent, or an adherent of some other
party? Good sense? Perhaps, but remember that we can't let values
distort our scientific research. No, the answer is Democratic party identification. The Democrat has "more" of it than do any of
the others.

What can we do with the data, then, to allow us to calculate
gamma? We "collapse" the table, dividing it into categories in
which all those who possess one characteristic are grouped into
one row or column and all those who don't have that trait are
grouped in the other. We would do it as follows:

<u>Sex</u>	Party Enrollment	
	Democrat	Other (Republican, independent, other)
<u>Male</u>	45	65
<u>Female</u>	36	74

Now we can go ahead and calculate gamma, which in this case is
rather simple.

QUESTION: What is the value of gamma for the preceding data?

*QUESTION: Based upon this figure, what can you say about the
relationship between sex and party identification among individuals
surveyed above?*

The table presented above represents the most common way of

presenting data in the social sciences. It is called a 2 x 2 table, and each of the four numerical values in the table stand in what are called cells. Cells are identified in the following way:

a   b

c   d

Gamma for a 2 x 2 table is often called Yule's Q (after its inventor, G. Udney Yule), and its simple formula is:

$$Q = \frac{ad - bc}{ad + bc}$$

Two-by-two tables are often used when working with nominal variables. Let's illustrate by going back to Hypothesis H-12 from Chapter IV: "Among political leaders in the U.S., representation of a Southern district is positively correlated with the holding of top power positions." What this tells us to do is divide all U.S. political leaders into Southern and non-Southern, and then see which group is powerful (as opposed to non-powerful). The 2 x 2 table we would set up to test this hypothesis looks like this:

		Political Power	
		Powerful	Non-powerful
Region	Southern	a	b
	Non-Southern	c	d

Notice that we have been careful to set the table up so that the values we expect to correlate with each other (Southern-powerful) appear in the upper-left-hand cell, or cell a.

We can now use this 2 x 2 table and Yule's Q to test our hypothesis that Southerners are more powerful than non-Southerners. For this purpose we shall employ the data in Appendix I on all 100 U.S. Senators. What we need to do is take each individual Senator and place him in one of the four cells of the table. We begin with Alabama's Senator Heflin. He represents a Southern state, but he does not have power in the Senate, so we place him in cell b, like this:

		Political Power	
		Powerful	Non-Powerful
Region	Southern		Heflin
	Non-Southern		

As we go down the list of Senators, placing each in the appropriate cell, we would shortly encounter Alaska's Senator Stevens. He is

162

a non-Southerner who happens to be powerful, so he would fall into cell c:

		Political Power	
		Powerful	Non-Powerful
Region	Southern		Heflin
	Non-Southern	Stevens	

Continue through the list of Senators until all of them are classified into one of the four cells. (Note that you don't actually have to write each individual's name in the table. Just record the number of individuals who appear in each cell.)

Assignment #18
   Complete building the table which we began in the last paragraph. When you finish, you should have four different numbers (one each in cells a, b, c, and d) which add up to 100. Now calculate Yule's Q for this table. Based upon this figure, what can you say about the relationship between "being Southern" and "being powerful" in the United States?

Other common tables used in the social sciences take the 2 x 3 or 3 x 3 forms. They look like this:

a	b	c		a	b	c
---	---	---		---	---	---
d	e	f		d	e	f
				g	h	i

You can, of course, calculate gamma from these tables in the regular way (going down each row, and so forth). With the number of cells reduced in this manner, it is also possible to create formulas for gamma for these particular cases. For instance:

Gamma for a 2 x 3 table

$$\gamma = \frac{[a(e + f) + bf] - [c(d + e) + bd]}{[a(e + f) + bf] + [c(d + e) + bd]}$$

And:

Gamma for a 3 x 3 table

$$\gamma = \frac{[a(e + f + h + i) + d(h + i) + b(f + i) + ei] - [c(d + e + g + h) + f(g + h) + b(d + g) + eg]}{[a(e + f + h + i) + d(h + i) + b(f + i) + ei] + [c(d + e + g + h) + f(g + h) + b(d + g) + eg]}$$

As you can see, once the number of cells advances even a little beyond the level of a 2 x 2 table, it becomes easier to calculate gamma the way we originally showed you rather than try to plug numbers into lengthy formulas.

Returning to our hypotheses on Senators, we could set up a 2 x 3 table to test Hypothesis H-5, "Among political leaders in the U.S., there is no correlation between age and party." The party variable produces two cells (Democrat and Republican). The age variable could produce three cells (young, middle-aged, and old). (You would, of course, have to provide operational definitions for each of these three terms.) The table to set up would look like this:

		Young	Age Middle-Aged	Old
Party	Democrat	a	b	c
	Republican	d	e	f

Note that it makes no difference whether we place "Democrat" in the upper row or "Republican," since in this hypothesis we are postulating no correlation and hence don't expect values to cluster in the upper-left-hand cell, as we usually do.

Assignment #19
Using the data on all 100 U.S. Senators, in Appendix I, calculate gamma for the above table. What operational definitions did you use for Young, Middle-aged, and Old? Based upon your gamma figure, what can you say about the relationship between age and party among American political leaders?

Making further use of the data on Senators, we can easily set up a 3 x 3 table. Let's take Hypothesis H-1, "Among political leaders, age is negatively correlated with liberalism." You have already divided age into three categories. You should also be able to divide Senators into three categories based on their ideology: liberal, moderate, or conservative. The rest is easy.

Assignment #20
Set up a 3 x 3 table which will allow you to test Hypothesis H-1. State the operational definitions for your terms. Calculate gamma. (Remember that the table should be set up in such a way that gamma will be negative if the hypothesis is being supported.) Based upon your calculation for gamma, what can you say about the relationship between age and liberalism among political leaders?

Assignment #21
Test three other hypotheses, using a 2 x 2 table, a 2 x 3 table, and a 3 x 3 table, calculating Yule's Q or gamma, and making use of the data in Appendices I and II for your hypotheses.

*At least two of these hypotheses should derive from the Appendix
II data. Be sure to state your operational definitions and to set
your tables up correctly. Your instructor may assign additional
hypotheses. Or he may assign specific hypotheses to various students in the class, in such a way that all possible hypotheses will
be tested by the class as a whole.*

At this point you should be thoroughly familiar with the calculation of a correlation coefficient. Before moving on, we pause
to stress the value of this statistic. It is a wonderfully simple,
elegant way of summarizing a great deal of data about the relationship between two variables. For instance, Yule's Q (or gamma) for
the relationship between "being Southern" and "having power" (Hypothesis H-12) is exactly .03. We derive this one figure after examining two individual pieces of information (the region he represents and the degree of power he holds) for each of 100 U.S. Senators. All the data condense into this one figure, and that figure
instantly tells us all we need to know about the hypothesis. In
this case, .03 tells us that there is no correlation at all between
the region a political figure represents and the likelihood that he
will hold political power in the national legislature. In short,
it tells us at a glance that Hypothesis H-12 has been falsified.

The correlation coefficient is a marvelous tool for putting
your findings into perspective. It tells you in brief summary
form the strength and the direction of a relationship between two
variables. You have just picked up an important device to put in
your bag of scientific tools.

Let's move on to one last tool useful for showing the strength
and direction of correlations between variables. Up to this point
each statistical device we have presented has had the effect of
condensing, reducing, or consolidating information. This can be
extremely useful, as we have just suggested. But some reductions
or consolidations of data produce artificial results which distort
the picture we are trying to form about our evidence. For instance, the mean can be thrown off by a few extreme cases. And the
tables we have constructed often force quite disparate units into
the same cells. If we constructed a 2 x 2 table to test the hypothesis that older Senators are more conservative, we might have
to place in the same cell Senator A with an ADA score of 41 and an
age of 59 and Senator B with an ADA score of 3 and an age of 81.
Both Senators are "old" and "conservative," but Senator A just
barely falls into each category, while Senator B is a prime representative of each. Calling them the same type of Senator twists
reality rather than illuminating it for us.

To prevent this problem, one would like to find statistical
devices which preserve <u>all</u> relevant information about the cases
under examination. There are such devices. Many are sophisticated
and complex. A full discussion of them lies beyond the scope of

this book. But a brief introduction to one of them is both possible and useful in this introductory text.

The simplest device which utilizes all relevant information in the testing of a hypothesis is the scatter diagram or scattergram. The scattergram dramatically illustrates the correlational principle underlying any hypothesis: that the more one finds of variable X, the more one will find of variable Y, if the hypothesis is working. If you hypothesize a correlation between age and wealth, you expect to find that the older people are, the more money they will have. While 25-year-olds might be making $15,000 a year, 40-year-olds will be earning $25,000, and 58-year-olds raking in $40,000. The more you have of one variable (age), the more you have of the other (wealth).

The principle behind the scattergram is to transfer all our information to a graph which, in a clear snapshot of the data, will show instantly whether the expected correlation is occurring. A graph always has two axes. The vertical axis runs "up and down" and the horizontal axis runs "across." Each axis represents one

THE BASIC COMPONENTS OF A GRAPH

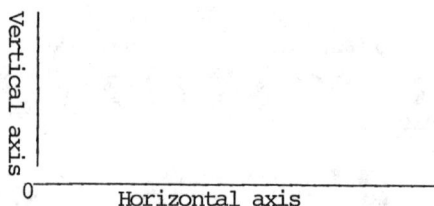

of the two variables that form the hypothesis being tested. Points along the axis represent units of measurement for that variable. If we were using the graph above to test our age-wealth hypothesis, each point on the vertical axis might represent 10 years of a person's life, while each point on the horizontal axis might stand for $10,000 worth of yearly income. The point where the axes meet is designated as the lowest value for both variables (usually zero). Note that only numbers can be plotted on a graph, so we cannot use the scattergram unless both variables in the hypothesis can be expressed in interval measurement.

To construct a graph, you take each variable at a time and begin at the zero point. Moving to the right on the horizontal axis, or upward on the vertical axis, you designate a given length of line as standing for a particular numerical value. Each additional, identical length of line along that axis represents that quantity again, so that the numbers mount in value systematically as one proceeds along the axis. The exact value imparted to each measurement point depends entirely on the data you are working with.

If you are measuring number of children per family, the numbers
will not go very high. You might in this case designate each one-
half inch as representing one child. But if you are measuring IQ,
which can reach 200, you might decide to have each one-half inch
on your axis represent 10, 15, or even 20 IQ points (depending on
the size of your graph paper). And of course, if you are working
with the population of countries, you might have to have each one-
half inch represent 50,000,000 people or more.

To understand scattergrams, pictures are more useful than
words. Below you will see the outline of a graph designed to illustrate the correlation between SAT scores and grade-point averages for students in American universities. The hypothesis being
tested would probably state: "For American college students,
scores on SAT tests taken before entering college are positively
correlated with grade-point averages during the college years."
To test this hypothesis, we will say that the vertical axis on our
graph represents values of the SAT score (which range from 200 to
800). The horizontal axis will be used to designate grade-point-
average values (these run from 0 to 4). As you see on the graph,
grade-point averages increase as one goes from left to right on the
horizontal axis; SAT scores increase as one goes from bottom to
top on the vertical axis.

BASIC FORMAT FOR A GRAPH CORRELATING
SAT SCORES AND GRADE-POINT AVERAGES

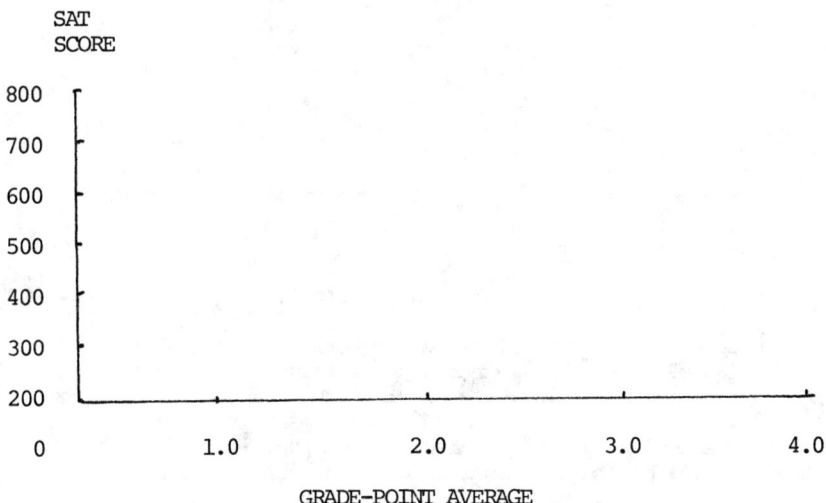

Now let's imagine what kind of pattern we would get if our hypothesis were being supported by the data. Someone with a rather
low SAT score of 350 ought to be having real trouble in college—

167

let's say he ekes out a 1.0 grade-point average in his first year. Someone with an SAT score of 480 (close to average) ought to do about average work in college and end up with a 2.0 grade-point average. The bright student with a 625 SAT score should get at least a 3.0 grade-point average, while the genius (790 SAT) ought to have close to a perfect 4.0 grade-point average. The graph below represents the pattern we have just described. Points A, B, C, and D represent our four students. Their scores lie along a line which represents a perfect correlation between our two variables. Each movement along the line represents an increase in the SAT-score value and an increase in the grade-point-average value-- exactly as the hypothesis predicts. When we move from point A to point B, we move from the student with a 350 SAT score and a 1.0 grade-point average to the student with the 480 SAT score and the 2.0 grade-point average. And so on.

BASIC FORMAT FOR A GRAPH CORRELATING
SAT SCORES AND GRADE-POINT AVERAGES

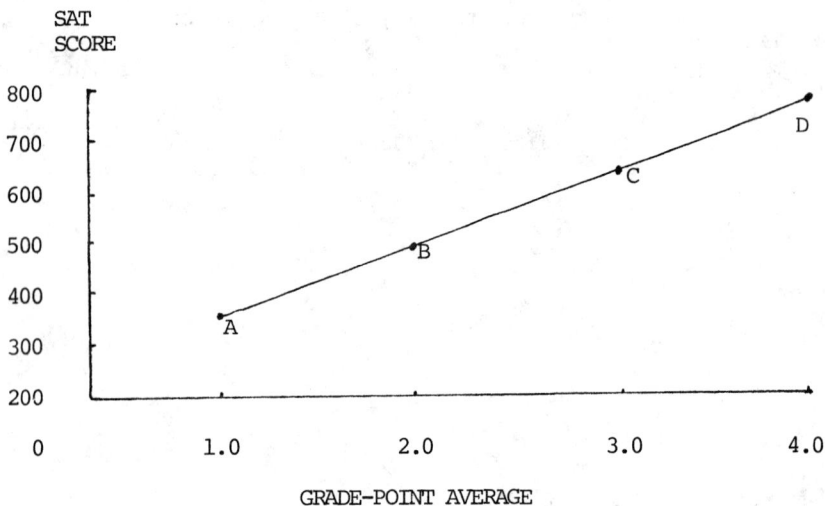

SAT
SCORE

800
700
600
500
400
300
200

0   1.0   2.0   3.0   4.0

GRADE-POINT AVERAGE

In short, the way to illustrate a perfect relationship between two variables on a graph is through a straight line running upward and to the right from the base point of the graph. This is known as a "line with a positive slope." The closer your specific data come to resembling a straight line with a positive slope, the stronger will be the relationship between your two variables.

So far we have remained in the realm of theory. Let us now get practical. How do we actually get our own particular data onto the graph? Nothing could be simpler. For each unit we are investigating (whether it be counties, committees, or congressmen), we have two numerical pieces of information. We merely use these two numbers to place each unit on the graph. Let us illustrate.

Let's say we believe that the more education a person has, the more active he or she will be in politics. We wish, in short, to test the hypothesis that "education is correlated with political activity." Being short of funds, we take a random sample of only 25 from the town in which we reside. We glean two pieces of information from these respondents. We find out how many years of education they have completed and how many political activities they have engaged in during the past year. (This second piece of information is often gained by showing people a card with a variety of political activities written on it—writing your congressman, attending a political rally, contributing money to a candidate, etc. —and asking them to tell which ones they have engaged in during the past year.) Our survey might produce the following data:

Respondent	Years of education completed	Number of political activities engaged in during past year
Brown	14	4
Smith	8	0
Jones	20	7
White	11	3
Black	13	1
Sawyer	9	6
Thompson	13	4
Johnson	6	0
Green	15	5
Williams	10	1
Jackson	11	2
Conway	17	0
Anderson	17	6
Edwards	18	6
Matthews	17	5
O'Brien	8	1
Hanson	9	2
Porter	21	8
Ross	12	4
Wheeler	19	7
Gardiner	20	1
Emerson	14	5
Lamb	6	5
Carr	9	1
Tucker	15	4

As you see, we have two numerical facts about each respondent. We have, say the humanists, reduced people to the status of numbers. We are going to do worse! Each respondent will shortly be reduced to the status of a dot. Watch.

169

First, let us set up our graph. We will use the vertical axis to stand for years of education, while designating the horizontal axis as our measure of political activity. Before doing any work, we would set the graph up, as follows:

Graph 1A

The Relationship Between Education and Political Activity

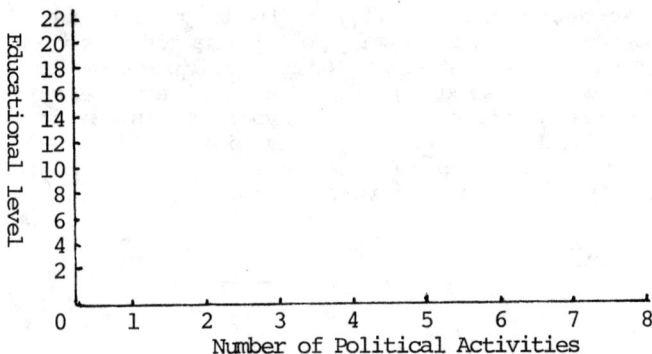

It is important to set the graph up properly. Note these points:

1. Label the graph clearly ("Graph 1," "Graph 2," etc.). In the body of your text you often have to refer to "Table 3," "Graph 5," and so forth. If they are clearly marked, the reader will have no trouble locating them.

2. Always give graphs (and tables) titles which tell as clearly as possible what they are about. The reader can then see at a glance what you are trying to do.

3. Use all of the graph paper available to you. The horizontal axis should run most of the way across the paper. The vertical axis should go most of the way up and down the paper. This way whatever pattern you produce will be clear. If the graph lies shriveled up in a small corner of the graph paper, the data will be all scrunched together, and it will be hard to see just what you have.

4. Always label both axes clearly, so that the reader knows precisely what variable is being illustrated by each axis.

5. Always write the numbers in clearly so that the reader can see the values possessed by each variable.

170

With the graph set up, we begin to put our data on it. For
each person in our sample, we have two numerical pieces of information which correspond to values on the two axes of the graph.
What we must do for each person is to find the point on the graph
where those two values intersect and mark that point with a dot.
We begin with the first respondent, Brown. He has completed 14
years of schooling and engaged in 4 types of political activity
during the past year. To place Brown on the graph, we go up the
vertical axis (which measures education level) to number 14. We
then move to the right until we reach point 4 on the horizontal
axis (which measures number of political activities). At the
point where 14 vertical) and 4 (horizontal) intersect on the graph,
we place a dot. Voila!

Graph 1B

The Relationship Between Education and Political Activity

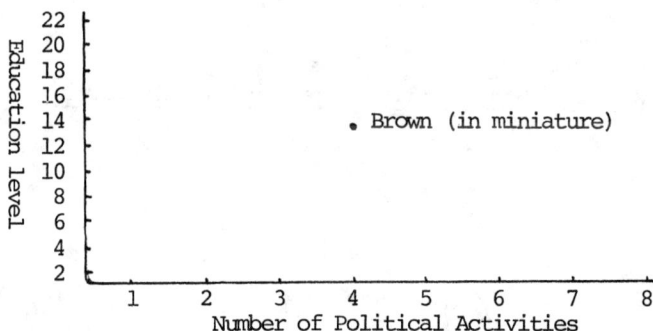

Having survived this intellectual challenge, we move down our
list of respondents to Smith. Smith never got beyond 8th grade and
(as our theory predicts) was totally inactive in politics last year.
To represent him, we go up the vertical axis to 8 and stay right
there, since his score on the horizontal axis is zero. Our graph
now looks like this: (see Graph 1C next page)

Let's try one more respondent to make sure you have the idea.
The next person on the list is the highly-educated Jones. She may
have a Ph.D. (20 years of education completed) and engaged in 7
kinds of political activity last year. Our theory is looking good,
so far. To place Dr. Jones on the graph, we go up to 20 on the
vertical axis and over to 7 on the horizontal one. We now have the
following result: (see Graph 1D next page)

Are you starting to get the picture? And yes, we did intend
the double meaning. You should by now see how to place all the
respondents onto the graph. You should also be starting to see a

171

The Relationship Between Education and Political Activity

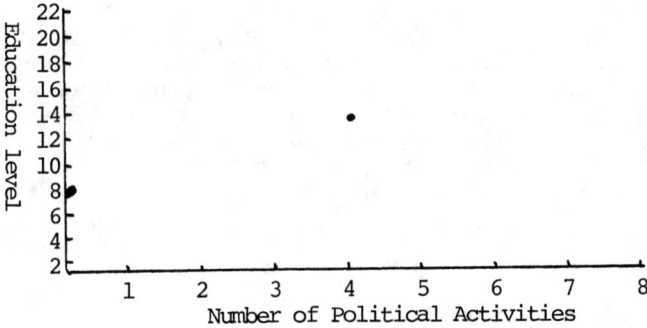

The Relationship Between Education and Political Activity
(Education level vs. Number of Political Activities)

The Relationship Between Education and Political Activity

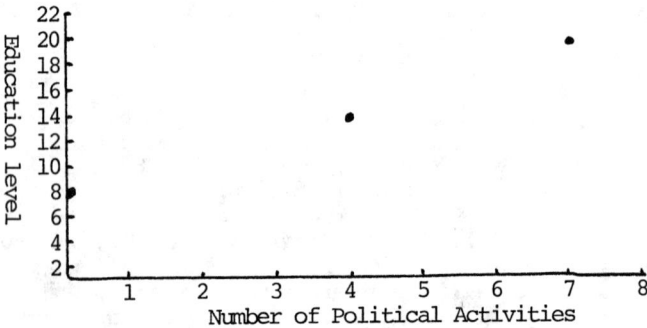

The Relationship Between Education and Political Activity
(Education level vs. Number of Political Activities)

pattern forming, precisely that pattern predicted by our hypothe-
sis--that is, a straight line with a positive slope. (Of course,
the line is not perfectly straight, but one never finds perfect
correlations in the social sciences.) Just because the first
three cases form the pattern needed to support our hypothesis, however, doesn't mean that the rest will. Let's see what the totality
of the data show us.

Assignment #22
    *Take a piece of graph paper and set it up as we have done for
this hypothesis. (Be sure to use the entire page of paper; don't
scrunch things down in a corner.) Then complete the scattergram
which we have begun on these pages. That is, place every respondent
in our fictitious sample onto the graph. Be sure to do this before*

172

turning the page. You will have to master this technique and use it in other exercises, so it is preferable to have done it on your own once before comparing it with our results. When you have completed the exercise, turn the page and see whether your graph looks like ours.

How did you do? If you were unable to produce a graph which looks something like ours, then you need to go back and review the previous pages and try again. If you are really having trouble, check with the instructor for some personal assistance.

Let's assume that you have now mastered the technique of the scattergram. What does this device do for us? Look again at our completed Graph 1E. This graph contains every single piece of information we have on our 25 respondents relevant to the two variables whose relationship we are investigating. Nothing is consolidated, reduced, or thrown away. More than that, it provides us with an instant picture of how well those two variables correlate with each other. In this case it is quite clear that we have a good correlation. The dots form a definite pattern, and that pattern suggests a straight line with a positive slope. What we have here is excellent support for our hypothesis that education is correlated with political activity.

Note one thing we did in this graph. We have clearly labeled the deviant cases. Lamb and Sawyer are two activists who are participating in politics more than we would expect from their levels of education. Conway and Gardiner are well-educated people who are much less active than the theory predicts. Exceptions to the rule always tell us something. You should always examine deviations from a pattern and try to explain what causes them. In this sample the independent variable, education, predicts the value of the dependent variable, political activity, for all but these four cases. Why are these men different? An in-depth look at them might suggest other factors which cause or deter participation in politics, and since that is what we obviously want to explain, it is important to conduct that examination.

You might, for instance, find that Lamb and Sawyer, although poorly educated, came from extremely active families. This finding would lead you to a new hypothesis: "Family political activism causes political activism in family offspring." It may turn out that both Conway and Gardiner have had histories of mental problems. You might conclude that "mental instability correlates negatively with political activism." Both these hypotheses would, of course, have to be tested fully in additional research. The point is, your examination of the deviant cases has led you to think more deeply about the roots of political participation and to enunciate two interesting hypotheses which are clearly worth further study. Any research worth its salt generates more questions than it answers.

Graph 1E

The Relationship Between Education and Political Activity

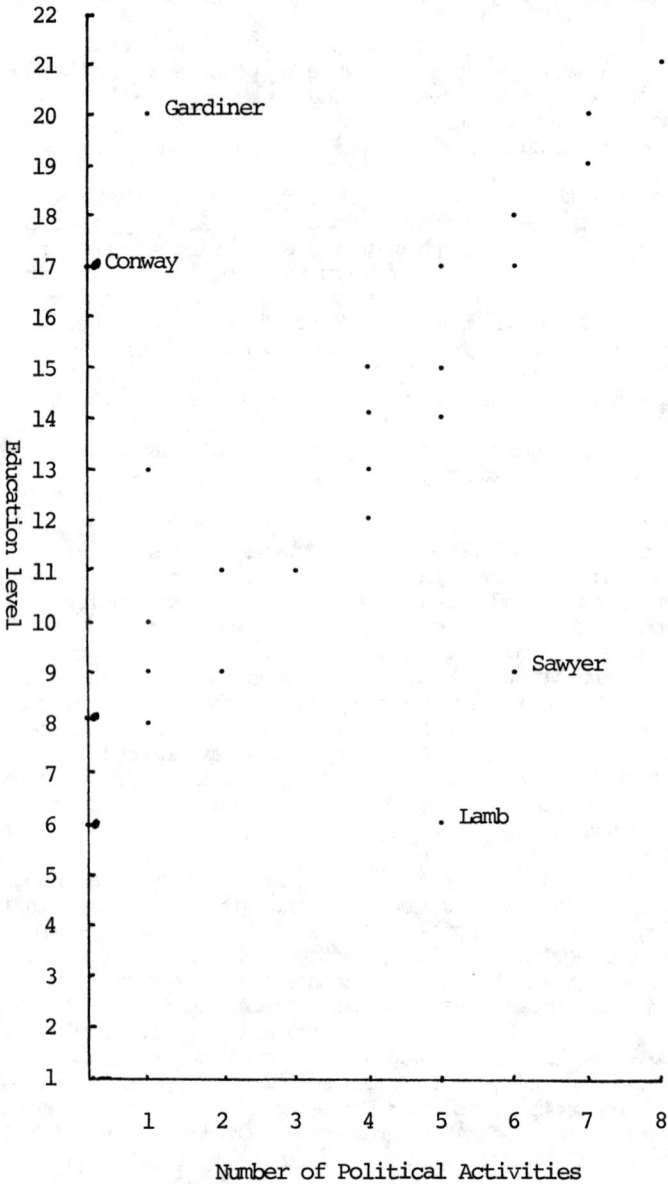

Let us return to the scattergram. We did, of course, rig things by providing you with data which support the hypothesis so nicely. We wanted to be sure you could visualize what "support for the hypothesis" looks like in a scattergram. In the real world, scattergrams which show as strong a correlation as ours does are rare. You sometimes have to squint your eyes pretty carefully to find a pattern. Although we cannot go into detail here, it turns out that if you can see even a hint of those dots forming around a straight line with a positive slope, there is some support for the hypothesis. But you should be careful not to talk yourself into seeing a pattern which isn't there, just because you want your hypothesis to "come out right."

The pattern of dots in a scattergram could take an infinite number of forms. Generally speaking, however, there are four major possibilities. The first we have already illustrated. The pattern could suggest a straight line with a positive slope and thereby provide support for the hypothesis. The second possibility is a pattern suggesting a straight line with a negative slope. Here the dots cluster around an imaginary line moving from the upper left to the lower right. They illustrate the inverse of the relationship posited by the hypothesis. That is, as you get more of variable X, you get less of variable Y (contrary to your prediction).

The third possibility is no pattern at all. The dots are just spread around all over the graph with no apparent picture emerging. In this case you have no relationship, no support for the hypothesis.

Finally, you might get a curvilinear pattern. For example, the dots might suggest a straight line with a positive slope for a while, but, when they reach a certain point, curve downward and finally form a straight line with a negative slope. Or the curve could take other forms. A curvilinear pattern suggests a complex reality, one more complex than we can explain in this text. To explore this topic, you must turn to advanced statistics texts. If you happen to find a curvilinear scattergram in your own research project, we suggest you turn to your instructor for guidance in interpreting the relationship between your variables.

You should also know that in more advanced statistics texts you could learn how to draw the line which best "fits" between all those dots, and you could also learn a statistic (r) which summarizes the correlation between your two variables, based on the numerical values represented in the scattergram. These topics also lie beyond the scope of our present work.

We conclude that the scattergram, by itself, is a valuable visual device for outlining the pattern formed by the totality of your data. You should use it whenever you have interval data on two variables which you believe correlate with each other. To make sure you have the scattergram well under your belt, try this next exercise.

Assignment #23

You have already used the data in Appendices I and II to test a variety of hypotheses about U.S. Senators and American states. Take any one of those previously-formed hypotheses and test it again with those data, this time through the use of a scattergram. Obviously, you can use only variables for which interval data exist. (There is no way to plot "Democrat" or "Southern" on a scattergram, so your choice of hypotheses is somewhat reduced.) Be sure to set your graph up correctly before you begin. When you have completed the exercise, write out your conclusions (one to three sentences). What pattern did you find and what does it show about the hypothesis? Once again, we suggest that the instructor assign each possible hypothesis to at least one student in the class, so that the group as a whole may learn how well the various hypotheses stand up under rigorous testing.

Statistical significance

To complete this introduction to statistics, we must deal with one last concept: statistical significance. When you work from samples, it is not enough to show a relationship between your variables. You do not rush into print the minute you find a moderate to strong correlation coefficient. You must also show that your finding is statistically significant. This expression does not mean that your finding is "important." It means that your finding was unlikely to have occurred by chance just because your particular sample, and not some other, was drawn from the universe you are generalizing to.

Let's make this point another way. Let's say that you hypothesize a relationship between A and B in a universe of 100,000 units. You draw a random sample of 2000 units and find a strong correlation coefficient of .68 between A and B. So your hypothesized relationship appears in the sample you drew. But what you really want to know is: does it appear in the universe? Of course, we can never be sure it appears in the universe short of studying the entire universe. But we can answer another question: what are the chances that this particular sample will reflect the universe accurately? Luckily, we can answer this question. We can often say that "samples such as the one we drew will accurately reflect the universe from which they are drawn nineteen times out of twenty." We then decide whether we wish to bet on odds which are in our favor 95 to 5. Most social scientists are willing to accept these odds.

Let's go into more detail. Look at the following data:

Table VI-1

| | | Party Identification | |
		Democrat	Non-Democrat
Religion	Catholic	80	15
	Protestant	60	50

Gamma for this table is .63. This indicates we have found a relationship of moderate strength (and therefore worth reporting) between being a Catholic and being a Democrat.

But would we feel secure in generalizing to the entire voting population of the United States from a sample of 205 people? It seems unlikely. We would feel much more confident, had we sampled ten times as many people and obtained these data:

Table VI-2

| | | Party Identification | |
		Democrat	Non-Democrat
Religion	Catholic	800	150
	Protestant	600	500

This increase in confidence would occur, despite the fact that the correlation coefficient for both tables is identical. Why would we feel more confident? As we noted in Chapter V, the larger the sample, the greater the likelihood that it will reflect the universe accurately. Or to put it another way, the larger the sample, the less is the likelihood that our findings result from the fact that we studied these particular units from the universe, rather than some others.

So, sample size is crucial in determining the amount of confidence we place in our findings. But the shape of those findings also helps determine how much confidence we will have in them. The findings in Table VI-1 derived from a sample of 205 people. What if those 205 people had produced results like these?

Table VI-3

| | | Party Identification | |
		Democrat	Non-Democrat
Religion	Catholic	94	1
	Protestant	60	50

Now the value of gamma is .99. Here we have discovered a relationship so strikingly strong that the likelihood of its having been produced by the fact of having sampled these 205 people, rather than some other 205 people, is virtually nil. No matter how many additional samples of 205 people we drew, we would still expect each of them to show that Catholics are overwhelmingly Democratic. Or to put it another way, we are very confident that the relationship we found in the sample would also be found in the universe it was drawn from.

To know how much confidence to place in our findings, then, we must know not only sample size but also strength of the relationship. We would like a statistic which takes both size and strength into account, one that tells us exactly how likely it is that a relationship found in a particular sample would reappear if we could study the entire universe. Such a statistic exists. It is known as chi-square and is written χ^2. Once you have calculated it, you will be able to say, "Given the size of my sample and the distribution of the data, the probability of my making a mistake when I assert a significant relationship between the variables is less than 5% (or 1% or .1%)." Expressions such as "p<.05" or "p<.01" are shorthand ways to express this complex idea. You frequently see abbreviations such as these in social science literature. They are usually placed at the bottom of a table, and they instantly tell other researchers what the odds are that the findings reported in the table reflect the real relationship in the universe one wants to generalize about.

Chi-square is based on the principle that the greater the difference between the relationship of the two variables in your sample and what you would expect to find if there were no relationship between the variables in the universe, the more likely it is that the relationship you found in the sample accurately reflects the relationship in the universe. In other words, if the difference is large between the actual data and the result you would expect, assuming no relationship, then the chances are good that the relationship between variables which you found in the sample would show up in the universe, if you were ever able to study that large a number of cases.

Let's see how one actually calculates statistical significance. The formula for chi-square is:

$$\chi^2 = \Sigma \ \frac{f_o^2}{f_e} - N$$

Don't let that frighten you. We'll take it one step at a time, The symbol, Σ, means to add up a series of numbers. In this case it means to carry out the $\frac{f_o^2}{f_e}$

operation for as many times as your data require and then to add together all the results of those different calculations. The term, f_o, refers simply to the values you <u>observe</u> in each cell of the table--that is, to the real data you have collected. The term, f_e, refers to the values you would <u>expect</u> in each cell of the table if the hypothesis had been disproven--that is, if there were no relationship at all between the variables. And N refers to the total number of people in the sample.

We are now ready to conduct a test of statistical significance for the data displayed in Table VI-3. The table is reproduced here, with the cells labeled in the familiar a, b, c, d, pattern.

Table VI-3

		Party Identification	
		Democrat	Non-Democrat
Religion	Catholic	94 (a)	1 (b)
	Protestant	60 (c)	50 (d)

f_o, or the observed frequency for the actual data, for cell a is 94.

f_o for cell b is 1.
f_o for cell c is 60.
f_o for cell d is 50.

That's simple enough. What about f_e?

To find f_e for each cell, we must figure out what number we would find in each cell if there were no relationship between the variables. For cell a we have to calculate how many Catholic Democrats we would find if there were no relationship between being Catholic and being Democrat. For the whole population sampled--that is, for Catholics and Protestants--the proportion who are Catholic is 75%. How did we calculate this figure? The total number of Democrats is 154 (a + c), and the total number of individuals surveyed is 205 (a + b + c + d). The proportion, therefore, who are Democrats is 154 ÷ 205 $(\frac{a + b}{a + b + c + d})$, or 75%. Similarly, the proportion who are non-Democratic is 25% (51 ÷ 205) or $(\frac{a + b}{a + b + c + d})$.

If there were absolutely no difference between the proportion of Catholics who are Democrats and the proportion of Protestants who are Democrats (if religion, in other words, had nothing to do with party identification), then we would expect 75% of both groups (Catholics and Protestants) to be Democrats. Seventy-five per cent of 95 is .75 x 95 = 71.25. This is f_e--the expected frequency of Catholic Democrats--for cell a. ("Catholic Democrat .25" is a very short fellow, but we are going to have to count him for statistical purposes.)

How many Catholics would be non-Democrats, if there were no relationship between the two variables? We would expect 25% of the total number of Catholics to be something other than Democrats. Twenty-five per cent of 95 equals .25 x 95 = 23.75. This is f_e for cell b.

Moving on to the Protestants, we can perform the same type of calculation. We expect 75% of them to be Democrats. There are a total of 110 Protestants. So if no relationship held between the variables, 75% of the 110 Protestants should be Democrats. This figure (.75 x 110 = 82.5) is f_e for cell c. And we expect 25% of Protestants to be non-Democrats (or .25 x 110 = 27.5). This is f_e for cell d.

Now that we have the f_o and f_e figures for each cell, we must go back to the formula and do some simple subtraction and division. For each cell, we need to calculate $f_o^2 \div f_e$. Then we need to add the figures for all four cells together and subtract N. That will give us chi-square. It is easiest at this point to set up a table, such as the following:

cell	f_o	f_e	f_o^2	$f_o^2 \div f_e$
a	94	71.25		
b	1	23.75		
c	60	82.5		
d	50	27.5		

To get f_o^2 we multiply f_o by itself. For cell a this equals 94 x 94 = 8836. For cell b, f_o^2 is 1 (1 x 1 = 1). For cell c, the figure is 60 x 60, or 3600, and for cell d it is 2500 (50 x 50).

Now we divide f_o^2 by f_e for each cell. For cell a it is 8836 ÷ 71.25, or 124.01. For cell b it is 1 ÷ 23.75, or .04. For cell c it is 3600 ÷ 82.5, or 43.63. For cell d it is 2500 ÷ 27.5, or 90.91.

Next, we add these four numbers together:

$$\begin{array}{r} 124.01 \\ .04 \\ 43.63 \\ \underline{90.91} \\ 258.59 \end{array}$$

Finally, we subtract N (the total number of individuals in the sample). This will give us chi-square.

$$\begin{array}{r} 258.59 \\ -\ \underline{205} \\ 53.59 \end{array}$$

180

The final table should look like this:

cell	f_o	f_e	f_o^2	$f_o^2 - f_e$
a	94	71.25	8836	124.01
b	1	23.75	1	.04
c	60	82.5	3600	43.63
d	50	27.5	2500	90.91
				258.59
		(minus N)		− 205
				53.59

At last we know what chi-square is for the data in Table VI-3. But this number, by itself, has little meaning. Our original question was, "How much confidence can I have that my results are not due to chance?" To answer that question, we must look up the value of chi-square in a Table of Significance. Here is one:

Table of Significance (1)

If chi-square is greater than	The probability that the relationship is not statistically significant is less than	
1.64	20%	(frequently written .20)
2.71	10%	(.10)
3.84	5%	(.05)
5.41	2%	(.02)
6.64	1%	(.01)
10.83	0.1%	(.001)

We see that our value of 49.59 is much greater than 1.64 or 2.71, or even 10.83. We can say, therefore, that our results are "significant to at least the .001 level." To put it differently, "the probability of getting our results purely by chance (the probability, in other words, of there being no relationship between the variables) is less than one-tenth of one per cent." Those are pretty good odds. We end up being extremely confident that in the universe from which our sample is drawn a very strong relationship exists between being a Catholic and being a Democrat.

You now know how to determine the statistical significance of your findings. Before leaving chi-square, we must make several additional points. First, the Table of Significance shown above can be used only for data from two-by-two tables. For reasons we need not go into here, the numbers in a table of significance will vary, depending on the number of cells in the table where you present your data. Most students undertaking the initial research exercise likely to evolve from the reading of this text will be working with simple tables: two-by-two, two-by-three, and three-by-three. We have already supplied significance levels for the two-

by-two table. Our second Table of Significance shows significance
levels for a two-by-three table. And our third Table of Significance gives significance levels for a three-by-three table. Students working with another kind of table will have to consult their
instructor or an advanced statistics text.

Table of Significance II (for a 2 x 3 table)

If chi-square is greater than	The probability that the relationship is not statistically significant is less than	
3.22	20%	(frequently written .20)
4.60	10%	(.10)
5.99	5%	(.05)
7.82	2%	(.02)
9.21	1%	(.01)
13.82	0.1%	(.001)

Table of Significance III (for a 3 x 3 table)

If chi-square is greater than	The probability that the relationship is not statistically significant is less than	
5.99	20%	(frequently written .20)
7.78	10%	(.10)
9.49	5%	(.05)
11.67	2%	(.02)
13.28	1%	(.01)
18.46	0.1%	(.001)

Another point to stress is that statistical significance cannot be calculated unless your data derive from a random sample
taken from a broader universe. Two corollaries follow from this
point. First, you cannot use chi-square on data taken from a non-
random sample. In other words, if you don't have a random sample,
you cannot tell how likely it is that your results represent the
actual pattern in the universe. Once again, the importance of
relying on random samples becomes evident. The second point is
that chi-square cannot be used--indeed, makes no sense--if you are
studying an entire universe rather than just a sample. We turn to
chi-square to tell us how likely it is that our findings duplicate
those in the universe we are studying. But if we have data on all
cases in that universe (and not just a sample of it), then we <u>know</u>
what the findings are for that universe. We don't need to speculate about what they might be. When we calculate relationships
among variables using data on all 100 U.S. Senators, then we know
what the pattern is among those variables in the Senate. Statistical significance is unnecessary--and in fact meaningless--when

you have the data for an entire universe.

One final point. Notice how the concept of statistical significance again demonstrates the open-mindedness induced by the scientific method. When working with a sample, we can never be absolutely certain that our findings are valid. It is always possible that this particular sample is wholly unrepresentative of the universe from which it was drawn. If we are lucky, that possibility is quite slim. We can say that there is only a one in 20, or one in 100, or one in 1000, chance that our sample is unrepresentative. But still, we do not know for sure. What we do, with statistical significance, is to take bets with ourselves. When we find that "p < .001," we are essentially saying this: "There is a 999 to 1 chance that the findings in our sample would reappear if we could study the universe as a whole; we will accept these odds and report the findings as if they were real for the universe."

Now whether you report certain findings or not depends on how conservative a bettor you are. Almost all researchers will accept odds of 999 to 1 and report findings when p < .001. Most researchers are also pretty happy with odds of 99 to 1; hence, they have no problem reporting findings when p < .01. And a good number are content to accept 19 to 1 odds. Not all researchers will do so, but many will report findings when p < .05. Below that level few researchers will go. Most scholars are conservative. If you find some results where p < .1, it means that there is a one in ten chance that your findings are worthless. Given the general uncertainties of social science research anyway, most scholars feel that that's a pretty big risk to take. Generally speaking, we can say that a consensus has developed around the .05 figure. Findings which are not statistically significant to at least that level are judged dubious and usually not reported.

Our recommendation is that you adopt the .05 level as a rough rule of thumb for determining the statistical significance of your results. If your chi-square figure is not large enough to reach this level, you should conclude that you can not generalize the results in your sample to the universe.

Assignment #24

Let's see whether you can handle chi-square on your own. Remember, as you work on this assignment, that the Table of Significance you use depends on the number of cells in your data table.

The general theory you wish to test posits that the more "scientific" the discipline a student majors in, the more she/he will support President Reagan. Or in precise terms, the "scientificness" of a student's major is correlated with his/her rating of approval of President Reagan. Using a random sample of students in two disciplines, you originally collect these data:

| | | Attitude toward President Reagan | |
		Approval	Disapproval
Major	Physics	19	3
	English literature	36	45

Calculate gamma and chi-square, and tell what conclusions you draw.

Let's make this a bit more complex. You conduct a new survey, adding this time a random sample of students from an "intermediate" discipline, Political Science. Your new results line up this way:

| | | Attitude toward President Reagan | |
		Approval	Disapproval
Scientific Content of Major	High (Physics)	19	3
	Moderate (Political Science)	28	16
	Low (English Literature)	36	45

Again, calculate gamma and chi-square, and tell what conclusions you draw.

After conducting your study, let's say you realize that the simple "Approve-Disapprove" dichotomy makes categorization of relatively neutral respondents impossible. You decide to enhance the sophistication of your findings by re-reading interview responses and re-classifying some respondents into a "Neutral" category. This process produces your final table:

| | | Attitude toward President Reagan | | |
		Approval	Neutral	Disapproval
Scientific Content of Major	High (Physics)	15	5	2
	Moderate (Political Science)	23	10	11
	Low (English literature)	28	14	39

Once, more, calculate gamma and chi-square and draw the proper conclusions.

FOOTNOTES TO CHAPTER VI

1. We are indebted to James L. Payne, Foundations of Empirical Political Analysis (Chicago: Markham Publishing Company, 1973), pp. 137-8, for suggesting this hypothesis.

2. See Robert A. Dahl, "The Concept of Power," Behavorial Science 2 (July, 1957), p. 204.

CHAPTER VII

PUTTING IT ALL TOGETHER

You are ready to enter a new and important phase of your research project. It is time to answer two related questions. What
does your study show? And what does all this mean? The questions
sound alike but are not identical. The first refers to the specific findings of your research. Precisely what did you learn, overall? Did the data support the hypothesis and, if so, how well?
What else did the data demonstrate as you played with the findings?
In short, you need to make a thorough evaluation and summary of
your evidence as it bears on your initial theory and hypotheses.

Beyond this, you have another task. What are the theoretical
implications of your findings? In the concluding section of any
research report you must discuss in as broad and creative a way as
possible the way your research bears on (even illuminates) important, interesting questions of direct interest to most scholars in
the field. Of course, you cannot reach this goal unless you developed a creative theory or began with an interesting question.

The final section of your paper must, then, do two things:
summarize the research and put it into theoretical perspective. We
shall now elaborate on both of these points.

Summarizing the findings
     By the time you reach the concluding section you know a lot
about your data. You have twisted and manipulated the evidence in
various ways. You have used percentages, averages, and tables.
You have calculated gamma or Yule's Q. You may also have calculated chi-square and set up a scattergram.

     After all these proceedings you should have a pretty good idea
of how well the evidence you gathered supports your original theory. Generally speaking, you could come up with one of four conclusions about the way your findings support a given hypothesis.

     1. There may be no support at all for the hypothesis. This
result could occur for one of two reasons (or both):
     a. There may be no correlation between the two variables.
You had hypothesized that A and B would correlate with each other,
yet the correlation coefficient ends up well under .3. Hence, the
hypothesis must be rejected. (In some cases you may have hypothesized no correlation between two variables, and yet found one.
In this case results are the same--rejection of the hypothesis.)
     b. You may have to reject the hypothesis for another
reason. If you are working with a sample, you may find a correlation between A and B, yet find--after calculating chi-square--that

187

this correlation is <u>not statistically significant</u>. That is, it is quite likely that the correlation you found appeared by chance in your particular sample and does not reflect reality in the universe from which the sample was drawn. Lacking statistical significance, your hypothesis must be regarded as not supported by the evidence.

2. <u>The hypothesis may be clearly supported</u>. Manipulations of the data show moderate to strong correlations between the two variables, and these correlations turn out to be statistically significant. Ideally, you will also have held constant every other variable you can think of which might influence your dependent variable and still found a correlation between X and Y, as hypothesized. This type of finding leads you to accept provisionally, or not to reject, your initial hypothesis. (Remember, you have not "proven" it to be correct.)

3. <u>In some unusual cases you may find precisely the opposite of what you originally expected</u>. That is, your calculations show negative correlations between A and B, contrary to the positive correlations you had hypothesized, and these correlations turn out to be statistically significant. (They might, of course, show positive correlations where you had hypothesized negative ones. You are still finding the opposite of what you expected.)

In these cases you have a lot of explaining to do in your final section. How could your predictions be so far away from reality? Yet this type of case often provides the most fascinating and significant results. Major scientific breakthroughs have often come when researchers uncovered evidence leading in exactly the opposite direction from that they expected. So take heart. If you find strong, statistically significant, negative correlations between your variables, it may not mean that you began with a shallow theoretical understanding of the phenomenon under study. (That is, however, a clear possibility!) It may mean that you have discovered something important. You should, therefore, make a special effort to explain theoretically how these results could have come about.

4. <u>The evidence may be mixed, ambiguous, marginally supportive of the hypothesis, or susceptible to interpretation</u>. Unfortunately, this result occurs more frequently than the others. Social life is complex, and the data we work with are often subject to error and slippage. As a result, we are frequently unable to make the strong, positive statements about our evidence that we would like to. More often than not, our results are muddy. We might find a difference of 16% between two groups for a given variable (remember, we posited 20% as the point where a difference makes a difference); we might find a gamma correlation of .28; and we might see only a hint of a trend when we plot our two variables on a scattergram (and yet, by God, there <u>is</u> something there!). This type of evidence hardly gives us great confidence in the hy-

pothesis we started with. Yet something seems to be happening--
and in the predicted direction too. What do we do in these
circumstances?

Ideally, you would check on the relationship between your
two variables under a variety of conditions, holding other variables constant. Perhaps a third variable would cause the weak
correlation between X and Y to disappear altogether. But let us
assume that the feeble correlation holds up under all circumstances
you have time to test for. What then?

The major conclusion is simple. X and Y are correlated, but
not strongly. What this means is that the dependent variable, Y,
will change its value somewhat when X, the independent variable,
changes its value, but the change which X can bring about in Y is
not dramatic and does not occur all the time. That's easy enough.
What does this mean in terms of your theory and your conclusions?

It depends a little on what your theory said to begin with.
If you made an aggressive case in the introduction to your paper
that X was a definite, and perhaps the only, cause of Y, then your
theory has clearly not been substantiated. You must acknowledge
that failure in your conclusion. But if the theory you advanced
held that Y was an extremely complex phenomenon and that X was one
of a number of factors which helped bring it about, then in a sense
you have found evidence to support the theory. X does have some
impact on Y. And you have already explained why X won't be Y's
only cause.

This leads to a final point. Multi-causal explanations are
probably essential for most intricate social processes. Poverty,
war, the formation of a political party: these events are not
caused by one single factor, but by several. The task of social
science is to show exactly how much effect each independent variable has on the dependent variable. Some independent variables
will have a major impact and produce correlations of .5 or better
with the dependent variable. Other independent variables will
have a less powerful effect. They may produce correlations of
only .3 with the dependent variables. They do affect the dependent
variable, but not a lot.

When you find this type of result, you know that you are a
long way from explaining variations in the dependent variable. To
explain variations in Y, you must turn to independent variables
other than your originally hypothesized X. You do this in two ways.
If you have time, you speculate about other causes of Y and then
test to see how well those other variables correlate with Y. But
this option will frequently be impossible for readers of this book.
You will discover, only at the conclusion of a short research exercise, the weak correlation between X and Y. A paper is due the
next day. You clearly have no time for additional gathering and

sifting of evidence.

All you can do in this case is to speculate. Try to figure
out just why X, which you thought caused Y, had little effect on
it. And try to figure out what other variable(s), which you may
originally have omitted from your theory, in fact have a bigger
impact on Y than you once thought. You can't prove anything by
these speculations. But if they are sound, they may lay the
groundwork for additional research on this topic. The next person
(perhaps you) who investigates causes of Y will hold X constant and
check for the influence of the other variables you suggest: P, Q,
N, or whatever.

These speculations can be significant. By the end of your research, you should have gained a thorough knowledge of the variable
Y. Who would be better able to speculate on the factors which
cause it than you? Therefore, your thoughts on this subject are
important. You may be able to suggest avenues for research which
have not occurred to other scholars. All research builds on previous work. Even if your own research led to less than wholly
satisfying results, it could open new doors for others (or for you)
in the future. So don't be discouraged. Let your mind flow freely
in thinking of reasons for the occurrence of Y. These creative
conjecturings may one day bear fruit. And remember, at the very
least you have discovered something: X is not as important a cause
of Y as you (and others) once thought.

Discussing the implications
Once you have presented your data and interpreted their meaning, you are left with one final question. What is the significance of your research findings? How do your data help us understand anything about how the political world operates? We have
come full circle now. We are back at the "So what?" question. So
you found that X correlates (or does not correlate) with Y. What
of it? What difference does this make for our understanding of
politics? Where do we go from here with that knowledge?

These are awesome questions. They underscore the importance
we placed in Chapter II on choosing an interesting research topic
at the beginning. If the topic you have been working on has significant implications for political behavior, then it should not be
difficult to illustrate how your findings enrich our understanding
of politics. But if your original topic was shallow or frivolous,
then you are going to be in trouble trying to show the "broad significance" of your findings.

This section, along with your introduction, calls for the use
of creativity and insight. We cannot provide a formula for discussing the implications of your research in a profound and pro-
vocative way. But if you have learned the habit of clear thinking,
if you have followed us conscientiously to this point, and if you

have thoroughly absorbed the readings in this and other political science courses, you should be able to complete this section of the paper with competence (or even distinction).

The following suggestions, although far from comprehensive, may give you some guidance as you work to draw your research project to a conclusion.

1. Discuss how your research findings are related to variables, processes, consequences or events beyond the research variables themselves. If you have shown that education level is correlated with tolerance—so that, specifically, well educated people are more supportive of civil liberties than less educated people—then an important implication of this finding is that more educated countries are more likely to be democratic than less educated ones. This follows from our notion that "democratic" implies tolerance for (allowing civil liberties to) others, even those we disagree with. So your study has far-reaching implications beyond the findings themselves. You have used your data to suggest one cause of a major type of political system in the world today. Further, you have gone on to suggest new, and eminently testable, hypotheses (e.g., education causes support for democracy; democracies are correlated with high levels of support for education). Research which leads to new research is always the most fruitful and satisfying kind.

2. You can hardly go wrong by showing how your findings bear on questions which social science scholars think about, or study, a lot. Showing how your findings help predict the number of babies a politician will kiss per day will not impress many scholars. But if you suggest that your findings explain the rise of a third-party movement, the growth of political alienation, or an increase in international arms sales, readers will perk up and pay attention. These are important issues. If you have some data which illuminate them, the world will beat a path to your door.

3. This point follows from the second. To know what issues are important, it helps to be familiar with scholarly writings in the area you are examining. Of course, everything is relative. If you are asked to write a 5-page research exercise in an introductory course, you naturally can't be expected to know the literature of political science inside and out. At the least, however, you should be thoroughly familiar with the readings assigned you in that course. Those alone should suggest some broader topics which your findings might shed light on. On the other hand, if you are engaged in a major project—a term paper, an honors thesis, or even a full-scale article—you must read deeply on the subject matter of your research.

For any topic one usually finds a consensus of scholarly opinion around the key issues which research on that topic is expected to shed light on. If you are familiar with this range of issues, then you have a pretty good idea how your research findings can answer some important questions. Following the lead of other researchers is usually a good idea--until you attain a level of scholarly maturity yourself.

4. Finally, give free rein to your imagination. At many points in a scientific research project you have to follow guidelines pretty carefully. There are definite rules--in formulating hypotheses, in drawing up random samples, in determining gamma or chi-square--which must be obeyed, whether you are Albert Einstein or a first-year sociology student. But with your research complete you are free to speculate as broadly, as creatively, as you wish-- all in an effort to show the ramifications and implications of your findings.

No one will hold you to any exact rules at this point. Indeed, the reader is waiting to see what you make of your results, to learn why it was worth going to all that trouble just to show how and in what way X and Y are correlated with each other. This is not the time for narrow thinking. It is understood that you will not be held immediately accountable for your speculations. In the future these speculations should be thoroughly examined and tested--by you and by others, if they are excited by your proposals. But at the conclusion of a research project you are not expected, nor are you able, to dive back in and test the theories you are spinning out. If they are stimulating, you can be sure that they will be tested soon enough. Let yourself go, and tell us how your research explains some important questions which have long intrigued the minds of intelligent thinkers. Remember what one of the great thinkers of our century, Einstein, had to say about the role of imagination in the scientific process:

> Imagination is more important than knowledge. Knowledge is limited; imagination embraces the world, stimulating progress, giving birth to evolution.

We admit it is easier to give this advice than to follow it. It will take some effort on your part to write a satisfying conclusion. We have one more suggestion that may help. Look at examples written by other researchers for models of what the concluding section of a research report should look like. Most social science articles you read have concluding sections. Most social science books have concluding sections at the end of each chapter. And finally, we supply a full-scale, model student research paper in Appendix III. Examine these pieces of evidence carefully. Once you see what is expected (or what is often done) in the concluding section of a research paper, you will have a better feel for how to do your own.

Finally, however, be aware that there is no absolute model for this process. Each research project will have its own conclusion. All depends on what the research uncovered; on what topics the research deals with; and, primarily, on the creativity and insightfulness of the researcher.

The research process is a fascinating blend of conformity to rules and independent reasoning. In the end the excitement of working with the scientific method lies in the new worlds which it opens up to the dedicated researcher. The student who bothers to master the rules imposed by this method will find that he can eventually go beyond the rules to uncover new concepts and even invent new rules. We wish you well as you embark on what is--for us and, we hope, for you--an exciting adventure--the scientific exploration of important research questions.

Assignment #25

You have finally arrived. Having mastered each individual step in the scientific method, you are now ready to put them all together. Your final exercise is to write your own short research paper. Remember that there are five major steps in the research process. We strongly recommend that you organize your paper into five sections: one for each of these steps.

1. Conceptualization. You must describe a problem and show why it is interesting and important. Summarize any findings of others that you are aware of and present a theory that leads to the statement of one or more hypotheses.

2. Statement of the hypotheses. These should be in the proper format. Review the rules for correct formulation of hypotheses. Each hypothesis takes up one sentence only. They should be set aside in a special section to emphasize their centrality in the scientific process. For some short research exercises only one hypothesis may be required by your instructor.

3. Description of the data-gathering phase. Tell the reader specifically and in detail the precise steps you took to obtain your evidence. You should include conceptual definitions and precise operational instructions for each of your variables. Footnote any library sources you may have used. If you took a sample, tell exactly how you did it--step by step. If you took a poll, include the questionnaire in an Appendix. And be sure to assess the validity and reliability of your operational definitions.

4. Presentation of the evidence. This section should include a short recapitulation of the theory, an examination of time order (in the case of a causal hypothesis), and a presentation of the statistical evidence that supports or refutes the hypothesis. This evidence should take these forms:

a. *Percentages;*
   b. *Averages (either mean or median);*
   c. *Tables, accompanied by a correlation coef-*
      ficient and a significance test;
   d. *A scattergram (if you are using interval data);*
   e. *Any other statistical devices which you know*
      and which may prove useful in showing whether
      the data support or refute the hypothesis.

   5. *Discussion. What, overall, did your data show? And what*
is the broad significance of these findings? How do your results
fit into, or alter, our general understanding of how politics
works? Remember, in this section, everything goes. Be as pro-
found, creative, and original as you know how in discussing the
ultimate meaning of your research results.

   6. *Appendices. You may want to attach certain kinds of mate-*
rial--such as a questionnaire--to the research report. These
should be placed at the end in the form of an appendix. We strong-
ly recommend (indeed, require for our own students) that you attach
another document to the research report as an appendix: one or
more sheets containing the raw data from which you derived your
basic research conclusions. Appendices I and II in this book il-
lustrate tables of raw data. Essentially, they consist of the
basic pieces of information about each unit (voter, Senator, state,
nation) you investigated in your sample.

   There are three reasons why we recommend your creating and
attaching an appendix of raw data. First, you will find it helpful
to have your information in this systematic form, rather than on a
hundred different 3 x 5 cards or scribbled on the back of your
notebook. Second, you should get in the habit of letting other
researchers check your evidence. This is standard operating pro-
cedure among professionals. When we read student papers and notice
a finding that seems unusual, we often turn to the table of raw
data to check the evidence for ourselves. Scholars do the same (if
they can) when reading the research reports of other scholars.
Sometimes important errors are found which throw someone's research
findings into doubt. At other times startling new findings are
confirmed by other researchers when they check the original evi-
dence. In both cases the cause of scientific knowledge is advanc-
ed. Presenting your evidence for a check by others is an integral
step in the scientific process.

   Finally, presenting your raw data allows other researchers
(in this case, probably your instructor) to fiddle around with
your data in ways you may not have thought of. We have often dis-
covered interesting patterns in a student's data which the student
herself did not notice. At the scholarly level this process is
called "secondary analysis of data." One researcher will re-ex-
amine the data originally gathered and analyzed by another. Often

194

*the second scholar--by looking at the data with different eyes,
asking different questions, and using different statistical manip-
ulations--will come up with interesting discoveries overlooked by
the first scholar. Once again, the ultimate result of presenting
your data-set for public display is to advance the dissemination
of scientific knowledge.*

*How long should the paper be? This depends entirely on the
instructor's wishes. We have found that assigning a paper of
approximately 10 pages works well in an introductory political
science course. It makes the project a serious one and gives
students enough time to delve into the subject without making it
the major event of their semester. In advanced courses we assign
papers, based on the model presented in this book, of 20 to 30
pages. For the 10-page paper we would suggest the following division of labor:*

1. *Conceptualization section. 2-3 pages.*
2. *Hypothesis section. One sentence per hypothesis.*
3. *Data-gathering section. 2-3 pages.*
4. *Presentation of evidence section. 2-3 pages of
   writing, plus a virtually unlimited amount of
   space for tables, graphs, and other visual pre-
   sentations of the evidence.*
5. *Discussion section. 2-3 pages.*
6. *Appendices. No space limit; as much room as it
   takes to supply the required material.*

*These suggestions can be adapted for papers of longer or shorter
length. Naturally, the specific length of each section will vary,
depending on the research project and the particular student writing it up.*

*That's it. You are now ready to undertake original research
on your own. We wish you luck as you begin this fascinating endeavor. And most of all, we hope that you enjoy yourself
thoroughly!*

APPENDIX 1
Selected data on U.S. Senators, 1980

State	Senator	Party	Age, 1 Jan. 1980	ADA rating, 1980	AFL-CIO rating, 1980	Committee Chairman?
Alabama	Heflin	Dem.	59	39	63	No
	Stewart	Dem.	40	61	67	No
Alaska	Gravel	Dem.	50	39	69	No
	Stevens	Rep.	56	39	50	Min. Whip
Arizona	DeConcini	Dem.	43	67	67	No
	Goldwater	Rep.	71	0	18	No
Arkansas	Bumpers	Dem.	54	56	56	No
	Pryor	Dem.	45	44	42	No
California	Cranston	Dem.	66	83	83	Maj. Whip
	Hayakawa	Rep.	73	22	22	No
Colorado	Hart	Dem.	42	61	47	No
	Armstrong	Rep.	43	17	5	No
Connecticut	Ribicoff	Dem.	70	56	77	Yes
	Weicker	Rep.	49	72	81	No
Delaware	Biden	Dem.	37	67	76	No
	Roth	Rep.	58	22	21	No
Florida	Chiles	Dem.	50	50	53	Yes
	Stone	Dem.	51	33	53	No
Georgia	Nunn	Dem.	41	56	26	No
	Talmadge	Dem.	66	33	58	Yes
Hawaii	Inouye	Dem.	55	67	75	No
	Matsunaga	Dem.	63	78	83	No
Idaho	Church	Dem.	55	50	71	Yes
	McClure	Rep.	55	17	12	No
Illinois	Stevenson	Dem.	49	61	67	Yes
	Percy	Rep.	60	39	41	No

APPENDIX 1
Selected data on U.S. Senators, 1980 (continued)

State	Senator	Party	Age, 1 Jan. 1980	ADA rating, 1980	AFL-CIO rating, 1980	Committee Chairman?
Indiana	Bayh	Dem.	52	61	100	Yes
	Lugar	Rep.	48	17	11	No
Iowa	Culver	Dem.	47	78	89	No
	Jepsen	Rep.	51	22	17	No
Kansas	Dole	Rep.	56	22	28	No
	Kassebaum	Rep.	47	44	25	No
Kentucky	Ford	Dem.	55	78	74	No
	Huddleston	Dem.	54	44	61	No
Louisiana	Johnston	Dem.	48	33	41	No
	Long	Dem.	61	28	50	Yes
Maine	Mitchell	Dem.	46	67	78	No
	Cohen	Rep.	39	33	22	No
Maryland	Sarbanes	Dem.	47	83	95	No
	Mathias	Rep.	57	72	100	No
Massachusetts	Kennedy	Dem.	48	33	100	Yes
	Tsongas	Dem.	39	89	84	No
Michigan	Levin	Dem.	47	94	95	No
	Riegle	Dem.	42	83	100	No
Minnesota	Boschwitz	Rep.	50	28	11	No
	Durenberger	Rep.	45	44	33	No
Mississippi	Stennis	Dem.	78	17	38	Yes
	Cochran	Rep.	42	22	17	No
Missouri	Eagleton	Dem.	50	78	89	No
	Danforth	Rep.	43	50	39	No
Montana	Baucus	Dem.	38	72	82	No
	Melcher	Dem.	55	50	88	No

198

APPENDIX 1
Selected data on U.S. Senators, 1980 (continued)

State	Senator	Party	Age, 1 Jan. 1980	ADA rating, 1980	AFL-CIO rating, 1980	Committee Chairman?
Nebraska	Exon	Dem.	58	39	37	No
	Zorinsky	Dem.	51	22	32	No
Nevada	Cannon	Dem.	68	33	41	Yes
	Laxalt	Rep.	57	11	5	No
New Hampshire	Durkin	Dem.	44	50	94	No
	Humphrey	Rep.	39	6	6	No
New Jersey	Bradley	Dem.	36	72	100	No
	Williams	Dem.	60	72	94	Yes
New Mexico	Domenici	Rep.	48	17	22	No
	Schmitt	Rep.	44	17	24	No
New York	Moynihan	Dem.	53	72	100	No
	Javits	Rep.	76	61	100	No
North Carolina	Morgan	Dem.	54	22	32	No
	Helms	Rep.	58	11	5	No
North Dakota	Burdick	Dem.	72	78	84	No
	Young	Rep.	82	11	20	No
Ohio	Glenn	Dem.	58	67	72	No
	Metzenbaum	Dem.	63	83	94	No
Oklahoma	Boren	Dem.	39	23	37	No
	Bellmon	Rep.	58	28	12	No
Oregon	Hatfield	Rep.	57	50	47	No
	Packwood	Rep.	47	56	44	No
Pennsylvania	Heinz	Rep.	41	50	67	No
	Schweiker	Rep.	54	17	37	No
Rhode Island	Pell	Dem.	61	78	94	Yes
	Chafee	Rep.	57	72	63	No

APPENDIX 1
Selected data on U.S. Senators, 1980 (continued)

State	Senator	Party	Age, 1 Jan. 1980	ADA rating, 1980	AFL-CIO rating, 1980	Committee Chairman?
South Carolina	Hollings	Dem.	58	39	22	No
	Thurmond	Rep.	76	17	11	No
South Dakota	McGovern	Dem.	57	56	88	No
	Pressler	Rep.	38	17	21	No
Tennessee	Sasser	Dem.	43	67	68	No
	Baker	Rep.	54	17	8	Min. Leader
Texas	Bentsen	Dem.	59	39	41	No
	Tower	Rep.	54	6	13	No
Utah	Garn	Rep.	47	17	11	No
	Hatch	Rep.	46	17	11	No
Vermont	Leahy	Dem.	40	83	83	No
	Stafford	Rep.	66	61	58	No
Virginia	Byrd	Ind.	65	22	21	No
	Warner	Rep.	53	22	21	No
Washington	Jackson	Dem.	68	72	84	Yes
	Magnuson	Dem.	75	72	89	Yes
West Virginia	Byrd	Dem.	62	56	58	Maj. Leader
	Randolph	Dem.	78	72	89	Yes
Wisconsin	Nelson	Dem.	64	89	100	No
	Proxmire	Dem.	64	56	53	Yes
Wyoming	Simpson	Rep.	48	17	6	No
	Wallop	Rep.	47	22	6	No
MEAN			53.8	46.3	52.8	
TOTALS		58 Dem., 41 Rep., 1 Ind.				20 Power-holders.

APPENDIX 2

Social and Political Patterns in the United States: Selected Data

State	Wealth: Personal income per capita, 1979	Political tendency: % vote for Dem. Congressmen, 1978	Feminism: Women in office 1979 per 100,000 inhabitants	Participation: % voting for President, 1980	Crime rate: prisoners per 100,000 inhabitants 1979
United States	8,706	53.5	6.3	51.8	132.9
Alabama	6,976	68.4	6.0	47.5	137.4
Alaska	11,252	44.6	49.2	41.2	132.8
Arizona	8,305	50.4	3.5	47.3	128.0
Arkansas	6,785	33.4	12.0	52.6	126.9
California	9,913	51.1	1.4	48.5	89.8
Colorado	8,945	48.8	9.8	56.1	87.2
Connecticut	9,959	58.0	7.7	59.4	68.8
Delaware	9,557	41.8	9.2	56.0	182.8
Florida	8,532	58.5	3.4	50.6	203.2
Georgia	7,515	80.2	3.3	42.3	213.3
Hawaii	9,353	80.1	1.6	45.4	53.9

APPENDIX 2

Social and Political Patterns in the United States: Selected Data (continued)

State	Wealth: Personal income per capita, 1979	Political tendency: % vote for Dem. congressmen, 1978	Feminism: Women in office 1979 per 100,000 inhabitants	Participation: % voting for President, 1980	Crime rate: prisoners per 100,000 inhabitants 1979
Idaho	7,446	41.4	12.4	67.4	87.9
Illinois	9,823	48.2	5.0	57.6	94.5
Indiana	8,686	51.9	3.8	56.5	96.0
Iowa	8,589	49.9	18.4	62.1	71.7
Kansas	9,055	34.8	8.4	54.4	96.9
Kentucky	7,342	55.5	7.8	50.0	100.8
Louisiana	7,477	50.1	4.6	55.0	181.2
Maine	7,057	43.5	21.4	64.8	57.0
Maryland	9,150	65.4	3.7	48.6	186.4
Massachusetts	8,844	69.0	3.4	57.8	50.1
Michigan	9,269	56.8	25.3	54.7	162.0
Minnesota	8,760	51.1	10.8	63.8	51.4

Social and Political Patterns in the United States: Selected Data (continued)

State	Wealth: Personal income per capita, 1979	Political tendency: % vote for Dem. con-gressmen, 1978	Feminism: Women in office 1979 per 100,000 inhabitants	Participa-tion: % voting for President, 1980	Crime rate: prisoners per 100,000 inhabitants 1979
Mississippi	6,167	48.5	6.2	53.4	133.9
Missouri	8,132	62.5	8.1	57.4	113.0
Montana	7,412	50.6	13.9	58.8	97.2
Nebraska	8,341	37.2	10.6	54.7	72.8
Nevada	10,204	69.5	2.3	44.8	195.9
New Hampshire	8,231	48.3	19.9	57.8	34.3
New Jersey	9,702	54.0	5.5	52.8	75.2
New Mexico	7,294	58.5	7.0	50.4	112.1
New York	9,098	51.9	3.6	45.4	120.5
North Carolina	7,359	59.5	3.1	45.4	229.1
North Dakota	7,774	32.9	23.9	56.9	20.8
Ohio	8,775	47.1	8.2	54.6	123.7

Social and Political Patterns in the United States: Selected Data (continued)

State	Wealth: Personal income per capita, 1979	Political tendency: % vote for Dem. congressmen, 1978	Feminism: Women in office 1979 per 100,000 inhabitants	Participation: % voting for President, 1980	Crime rate: prisoners per 100,000 inhabitants 1979
Oklahoma	8,226	56.2	7.4	52.6	140.5
Oregon	8,842	67.2	11.5	58.2	120.4
Pennsylvania	8,559	51.0	5.4	51.7	65.7
Rhode Island	8,266	56.6	4.1	56.3	59.5
South Carolina	7,027	65.6	3.9	42.6	228.1
South Dakota	7,334	47.0	21.3	66.6	89.8
Tennessee	7,299	54.7	3.5	50.1	144.4
Texas	8,649	58.9	4.2	44.7	186.4
Utah	7,185	45.5	5.8	65.4	65.5
Vermont	7,280	24.7	22.5	57.7	60.8
Virginia	8,605	43.7	3.4	47.6	153.4
Washington	9,435	51.8	6.6	50.8	109.2

APPENDIX 2

Social and Political Patterns in the United States: Selected Data (continued)

State	Wealth: Personal income per capita, 1979	Political tendency: % vote for Dem. congressmen, 1978	Feminism: Women in office 1979 per 100,000 inhabitants	Participation: % voting for President, 1980	Crime rate: prisoners per 100,000 inhabitants 1979
West Virginia	7,470	65.7	9.0	52.4	64.2
Wisconsin	8,419	53.0	3.0	64.9	73.0
Wyoming	9,657	41.4	12.5	51.3	101.3

APPENDIX 3

A Model Student Research Paper

The perfect research paper does not exist. Every piece of
writing has some defects, could undergo some improvements. Further, there is no one model for a research paper. How one writes
a paper depends partly on what the subject is, partly on what the
findings showed, and partly on idiosyncratic traits of the writer.
So it is with some trepidation that we offer an example of a good
student research paper. We would feel more comfortable offering
five or ten model papers. Students would then see both the variety
of possibilities, as well as the constant factors which must be
retained in any social science research report.

We offer only one paper for reasons of space. We offer a paper at all because students continually ask us what a good research
paper looks like. Most students completing this book have never
undertaken this type of exercise. We believe (and they usually do
too) that reading a top-level research report will give them ideas
about how to proceed with their own work.

The paper is not perfect, nor could it be. A discussion in
class of its strong and weak points should be helpful to those
about to embark on a research paper of their own. We also recommend that instructors place some of their best recent student papers on reserve in the college library for those who wish to read
more than the one example we provide here.

A few comments about the paper which follows are in order. We
must admit cheating on the following assignment. It is not, in
fact, a "real" student paper. It does derive from a student paper,
but we actually wrote it ourselves. In doing so, we drew on two
basic sources for data and ideas:

James L. Payne, "Show Horses and Work Horses in the
U.S. House of Representatives," Polity 12 (Spring, 1980):
pp. 428-56.
Michael Martin, "Are 'Show Horses' Really Different
from 'Work Horses'?" Paper submitted for a course on the
American Congress, University of Southern Maine, May, 1979.

We also admit that both of us have conducted research on the same
subject matter (incentives) as that dealt with in the paper. The
end result is that the quality of the paper, and probably its
length, are beyond what can normally be expected of students in a
first-year political science course.

This should not lead you to be discouraged. We are trying to
present a model you can strive toward, not one you can easily sur-
pass. After all, "A man's reach should exceed his grasp, or what's

a heaven for?" We are also convinced that some students can produce work at this level, and we encourage you to try to reach it.
Our goal was to show what a good, short research report looks like.
Your own work may not be as long or as detailed. It will probably
tackle very different subjects. Your data may not "work" as nicely
as ours did. Still, your basic structure should bear some resem-
blance to that of our paper. And our discussion of the data will
give you some idea of how to present your own findings.

In the end we do not want you to duplicate our presentation
in your own work. We want you to make creative use of this example. If we achieve our end, it will help you think about the best
way of writing up your own research report.

Model Student Research Paper

Incentives and Behavior Among American Congressmen

Section 1: Conceptualization

Why do political leaders behave as they do? This question
raises a fundamental issue for the understanding of politics. If
we know the causes of an individual's political behavior, we can
explain why he acts as he does and eventually predict what he will
do in a variety of political settings. Further, if we can explain
the behavior of individuals within a political institution, we can
build toward an explanation of aggregate patterns within that body.
So searching for the roots of individual behavior could produce
important payoffs—ultimately, a deeper understanding of political
life.

There are two ways to explain individual behavior. One is to
focus on events and situations external to the actor. The other
is to examine the internal motives which induce people to behave as
they do. In recent years a number of studies have suggested that
real-life behavior springs from attempts to satisfy deep-seated,
psychological needs.[1] One particular set of studies focuses on
what the authors call "incentives for political behavior."[2] Politicians, they hold, enter and remain in politics to satisfy one of
a small number of underlying drives. Without political activity
political leaders would find these drives blocked and their lives
unfulfilled. Politics, for them, brings satisfaction of a profound
and basic human need.

Since the need is strong, many of the actions of political
leaders are centered on ways to fulfill it. Thus, a significant
amount of their behavior can be explained (and ultimately predicted) by their attempts (usually unconscious) to gain the psychological satisfaction which led them into politics in the first place.

Several types of political leaders can be distinguished, based on the particular need (incentive) most responsible for their continuing political commitment. Of these, two in particular merit extended study. One need is a drive for status. The status-type politician is preoccupied with social standing, prestige, and fame. He is in politics to be somebody, to make a name for himself, even to go down in history. Status participants are concerned with their "image," with making a good impression. They pay careful attention to the tactics of personal advancement, to publicity techniques, to the development of public speaking skills.

A second need has been labeled the program incentive. This type differs dramatically from the status participant. Program-oriented political leaders enjoy working on specific policy problems. While the status type will say little about particular policies (rarely going beyond popular cliches), the program type plunges into detailed (and often boring) analyses of specific problems. The program participant is relatively uninterested in the mechanics of getting elected and is not a particularly astute manipulator of other individuals—or of large groups, such as voters.

One of the most powerful political institutions in the world today is the U.S. Congress. If our knowledge of these two types of politicians can help shed light on the behavior of congressmen, it would represent an important explanatory tool for the social scientist. Let us assume that we can identify program and status types among U.S. congressmen. How might their behavior differ from each other? For one thing, the status type should be clearly superior to the program type in self-promotion. Skilled at image-manipulation and zealous at promoting their own careers, they should out-perform the more stolid, workaday program types in attracting the public eye, gaining votes, and reaching higher office.

The program type, who spends his time on the mundane study of specific policy problems, is unlikely to attract the kind of attention which helps the status type boost his career. Besides, the status type works at career-enhancement. The program type does not. Speech-making, television interviews, weekends impressing constituents: these activities take time from what the program type considers central to his work—the study of policy. The status type, who cultivates the skills which will impress a broad public, should fare better than the program type when the public gets its chance to judge these men (in elections).

We would also expect two other differences between these types. The status type should be more prone to seek higher office. For those concerned with prestige and recognition, higher offices convey more of the status they entered politics for in the first place. The program type's focus is on policy manipulation. One can work on policy at any level of government. Presumably, this

problem-solving need would not impel one to seek higher office as
quickly as would a status-seeking need.

Finally, one would expect status types to be more blatant
about using forms of self-promotion than would program types. The
status drive is a relatively ego-oriented one. The focus is on
one's own career enhancement. The program drive (while undeniably
fulfilling a _personal_ need) still focuses outward--away from the
ego and toward general problems in the objective, external world.
One expects, therefore, that written materials emanating from congressional offices will reflect the different incentives of the
member. Status types should be issuing materials markedly more
centered on self-promotion than materials coming from program-type
congressional offices.

These reflections lead to a number of hypotheses.

Section 2: Hypotheses

H-1: Among political leaders, incentives cause varying
      levels of political success, specifically:
      H-1a: The status incentive causes high levels of
            political success.
      H-1b: The program incentive causes only moderate
            or poor levels of political success.

H-2: Among political leaders, incentives cause varying
      levels of political ambition, specifically:
      H-2a: The status incentive causes a high level of
            political ambition.
      H-2b: The program incentive causes moderate to low
            levels of political ambition.

H-3: Among political leaders, incentives cause varying
      levels of ego-reference in materials written for
      a public audience, specifically:
      H-3a: The status incentive causes high levels of
            ego-reference in materials written for a
            public audience.
      H-3b: The program incentive causes moderate to low
            levels of ego-reference in materials written
            for a public audience.

Section 3: Data-gathering

Since we wish to explain congressional behavior, let us focus
on members of the U.S. House of Representatives. Our first task
lies in distinguishing status and program type congressmen. How do
we know them when we see them? In past studies, incentives have

210

been determined from lengthy, in-depth interviews. Such interviews are clearly out of the question for this project. How, then, could one tell whether a congressman is a status type, a program type, or neither?

First, we need a conceptual definition of these two types. It would appear from what we have said that the status type is someone who does not work hard at policy matters but does strive to make a name for himself. The program type would appear just the opposite. He would spend his time on the examination of policy details but minimize publicity-gathering activities. So conceptually, we arrive at these definitions:

> Status type: someone who slights policy work in favor of publicity-seeking.
> Program type: someone who shuns publicity-seeking for policy work.

Now we need to get down to specifics and operationalize these terms. In doing so, we base our operational definitions on the following points. It is well known that the real work of Congress is done in its committees and sub-committees. The congressman truly concerned with influencing policy will show up day after day for the dozens of meetings, where committee members have a chance to question expert witnesses and discuss among themselves the nitty-gritty details of legislation which are so important in shaping the actual policy to be implemented by a given bill. It would seem logical that program types would more likely show up for these meetings and take part in them than would status types. For a person anxious to become known to a broad public, the average committee meeting—unattended and unreported--would seem a dreary waste of time.

The status type, rather than attend committee meetings, finds other activities--such as making speeches, making trips around the country, and meeting reporters--which help him get better known. We would indeed expect him, therefore, to be better known.

We now see how to build an operational definition of the status type. It is someone who does less-than-average work in committee but gets more-than-average amounts of publicity. The program type's characteristics are exactly opposite to this pattern. He does more-than-average committee work but gets less-than-average public coverage. We can now get specific.

Operational definitions of program and status types:
1. Choose two committees at random from the 1971-72 session of the U.S. House of Representatives. In this case we chose the House Committee on Banking and Currency and the House Committee on Public Works.

211

2. Gather all the printed hearings of each committee and all its subcommittees for this two-year period. Break each hearing down into separate (morning or afternoon) sessions and determine the duration in minutes of each session.

3. Inspect 10 live hearing pages in the middle of each session (inserted material does not count).

4. Any congressman saying anything during these 10 pages is credited with participating in committee work the total number of minutes which that session lasted.

5. Find, for each member of both committees, the total number of minutes for which they participated in committee sessions during this two-year period. Those who score above the average will be considered "more hard-working than average." The average (mean) is 2,591 minutes.

6. To determine publicity levels, check the number of times each of these congressmen's names was listed in the Index to the New York Times in 1972.* All congressmen who scored above the average number of listings will be considered "high in publicity-gaining ability." The average (mean) number of listings is 23.6.

7. All congressmen who scored above average on "publicity-gaining ability" and below average on "hard-workingness" will be classified as status types.

8. All congressmen who scored below average on "publicity-gaining ability" and above average on "hard-workingness" will be classified as program types.

9. All other congressmen will be given no incentive classification.

We can now divide all congressmen in our sample into a program, status, or "other" category. The "others" will be mostly ignored in this study. Appendix 1 to this paper lists each congressman, the number of minutes he participated in committee work during 1971-72, the amount of publicity he received in 1972, and his eventual classification based on this information.

Now that we know who the program and status types are, we will move on to find ways of measuring their "political success." One

---

* In the acutal study by Payne which provides the data on publicity used in this paper, a somewhat more involved measure of publicity than simply the New York Times Index was used. To see precisely how the publicity scores in Appendix 1 to this paper were obtained, see the Payne article cited in the remarks introducing this model paper.

measure of political success is increasing popularity. This will be our conceptual definition. Now how do we define this operationally? Let's do it this way.

Operational definition of "increasing political success":
1. Take all congressmen who have been classified as either program or status types.

2. Find the percentage of the vote which they received in the congressional election of 1970. (Since we are dealing with the 1971-72 session of Congress, we know they all had to be winning candidates for the House in the 1970 election.) This information can be obtained from The Almanac of American Politics, America Votes, Congressional District Data Book, and a number of other sources.

3. Find the subsequent career activities of these congressmen through the 1978 election. Those still in the House after the 1978 election and whose vote totals have improved by 10 percentage points or more since 1970 will be classified as "more successful than average." Those who have been defeated for any reelection attempt, whose vote totals in 1978 have declined since 1970, or whose vote totals in 1978 have increased by less than 10% since 1970 will be deemed "less successful than average."

The data relevant to the operational definition above can be found in Appendix 2 to this paper. Let's go on to measure political ambition. (Data relevant to this term can also be found in Appendix 2.) The simplest way to determine a man's ambition is to watch what he does. Conceptually, we can say that ambition involves striving to obtain a social position higher than the one currently being held. For a politician we could measure ambition operationally in the following way.

Operational definition of political ambition:
1. Take all congressmen who have been classified as either program or status types.

2. Follow their career patterns between 1970 and 1979, through the use of the sources mentioned in the preceding operational definition and through the reading of newspaper stories (the use of the New York Times Index is particularly relevant here).

3. All those congressmen who ran for higher office subsequent to the 1970 election (to 1979) will be classified as "more ambitious than average." Those who did not run for higher office will be classified as "less ambitious than average."

4. For purposes of this study, "higher office" will be defined as the office of Senator, President, Governor, or Mayor of a large city (population greater than that of the congressional dis-

213

trict).

We now move to our final measure: ego-references in material written for a public audience. (Again, relevant data appear in Appendix 2.) Our conceptual definition of "ego-reference" is the use of words or phrases which center on the self or achievements of the self. "Material written for a public audience" could include a number of items. In this case the term will refer to the congressman's constituency newsletter—material aimed by each congressman at the broadest public possible.

Operational definition of ego-references in material written for a public audience:
1. Take all congressmen who have been classified as either program or status types and who still remain as congressmen in March, 1979.

2. Obtain from each of these individuals the latest copy of their newsletter to constituents.*

3. From these newsletters two different measures of ego-reference will be obtained. The first will be known as the "ego word score." To obtain this score, do the following:
    a. Find the total number of words used in the news-letter. (An estimation rather than an exact word count will suffice.)
    b. Count the number of ego words. An ego word is defined as any use of the word "I," "me," "my," "mine," or "myself," or the words "us," "ours," "he," and "she," when they clearly refer to the congressman, or the actual name of the congressman.
    c. Find the number of ego words used per 1000 words in each congressman's newsletter. This is the "ego word score."

4. A second ego-reference measure will be known as the "ego accomplishment score." It is obtained in the following way:
    a. Count the total number of times the newsletter makes reference to member-sponsored legislation, mentions an accomplishment of the congressman, shows a photograph of the congressman with a famous individual (such as the President), or mentions an occasion in which the congressman interacted with a famous individual.
    b. Total word count for the newsletter has already been obtained. Find the number of ego accomplishments mentioned per 1000 words of the newsletter.

---

* One could usually obtain this material by writing directly to a congressman's office. In this particular case one of the authors of this book was in Washington in March, 1979, and went from office to office soliciting the newsletters. For one reason or another newsletters could not be obtained from three of the congressmen: Mitchell, Harsha, and Roe.

c. This figure will be considered the "ego accomplishment score."

5. As one measure of ego-reference, congressmen who score above the median on the ego word score (15.83) will be considered "higher than average in ego-reference behavior."

6. As another measure of ego-reference, congressmen who score above the mean (2.84) on the ego accomplishment score will be considered "higher than average in ego-reference behavior."

We now have operationalized all our key terms. We know which congressmen are program and which are status types; and we know how to measure their behavior in a variety of ways. We are ready to begin testing the hypotheses.

Our first set of hypotheses dealt with the different success rates we expected to find among program and status types. We adopted the simplest measure of success: electoral performance. Do status or program types do better over time in elections? Naturally, we expect the status type will far outshine the program type in this regard. And our data strongly back up this expectation. Table 1 tells the story. Here we see data on all those congressmen who <u>tried</u> to remain in the House for the 1970-78 period.

Table 1

The relationship between incentive
and electoral effectiveness, 1970-78*

		Performance at polls:		Totals
		Improved (vote totals increased by 10 percentage points or more)	Stayed same or declined (vote totals increased by less than 10 percentage points or declined)	
Incentive	Status	6	1	7
	Program	3	19	22
	TOTALS	9	20	29

Yule's Q = +.95

$\chi^2 = 13.3$; p < .001

---
* Excludes all members of original sample who died, retired, or ran for higher office during this period.

215

We see instantly an astonishing difference between status and program types. Six-sevenths of the status-oriented congressmen (85.7%) who kept running for re-election during this entire period improved their vote-getting abilities significantly between 1970 and 1978. For these six, their share of the vote increased at least ten percentage points. Only three (13.6%) of the program types matched this record. The vast majority of program types either remained relatively constant in vote totals (an increase of less than 10 percentage points) or declined. Indeed, eight of our original program types declined so badly that they were defeated in a subsequent election. None of the original 10 status types lost a reelection bid for the House. (Two of the three who ran for higher office did lose those elections.)

The extraordinary difference between status and program types in electoral effectiveness is highlighted by the near-perfect Yule's Q statistic of +.95. And we are heartened also by the chi-square results which suggest the unlikelihood that this result could have occurred simply by chance.*

To delve a little further into this subject, defeated congressmen were omitted from the sample and only those who won elections every time from 1970 to 1978 were compared. Even with the worst electoral performers removed, however, the strong relationship between incentive and vote-getting ability remained. Table 2 illustrates this finding. We see that 85.7% of status congressmen improved their popularity considerably between 1970 and 1978, while only 21.4% of program congressmen did so. Furthermore, status congressmen averaged an improvement of 15.1 percentage points in their vote totals during this period, while program congressmen averaged a mere 0.6 percentage point improvement. (The median improvement for status types was 16.0; for program types it was minus 0.8.) The Yule's Q of +.91 and the chi-square figure reinforce our finding that status types do decidedly better than program types in impressing the voting public. (See Table 2 on next page.)

We have hypothesized that not only will status participants be more effective at gaining office than program participants, they will also be more anxious than program types to gain higher offices than the ones they currently hold. To test this hypothesis, we shall take the running for higher office as a measure of ambition and see which of the two types was more likely to try moving upward. Of the 10 original status congressmen, three (or 30%) eventually sought higher office between 1970 and 1978. Only one of the

---

* Strictly speaking, chi-square should not be used on these data, which do not derive from a random sample. However, we have thrown it in anyway so students will see what it looks like and how to discuss it in a formal presentation.

Table 2

The relationship between incentive and electoral effectiveness, 1970-78*

		Performance at polls:		Totals
		Improved (vote totals increased by 10 percentage points or more)	Stayed same or declined (vote totals increased by less than 10 percentage points or declined)	
Incentive	Status	6	1	7
	Program	3	11	14
	TOTALS	9	12	21

Yule's Q = +.91

$\chi^2 = 7.88$; p < .01

---

*   Includes only those congressmen in the sample who remained in the House throughout this entire period.

31 program types (3.2%) sought higher office. Table 3 puts this information into perspective. Again, we see a strong and statistically significant relationship between incentive and behavior. Status types are decidedly more ambitious than program types, as we had hypothesized.

Table 3

The relationship between incentive and political ambition

		Sought higher office between 1970 and 1978		TOTALS
		Yes	No	
Incentive	Status	3	7	10
	Program	1	30	31
	TOTALS	4	37	41

Yule's Q = +.86 $\chi^2 = 9.63$; p < .01

217

To get a broader picture of the differences between program and status types, we can combine some of the data we have been using up to this point. If our conceptual notion of these incentives holds, we would expect status types to be both better vote-getters and more ambitious than program types. Let us combine these two measures. We would hypothesize that status types are more likely than program types to have made, or to have attempted, a major improvement in their political career during the 1970-79 period. "Improvement" in this sense would be increasing vote totals in congressional elections by over ten percentage points; "attempt" at improvement would mean running for higher office.

Testing this hypothesis, we get the data in Table 4. Once again we see the familiar pattern forming. Status types appear much more career-oriented than program types. They appear to work

Table 4

The relationship between incentive
and change in political career

| | | Change in political career, 1970-79 | | TOTALS |
		Major improvement or attempt at major improvement*	Remained about same or declin-ed**	
Incentive	Status	9	1	10
	Program	4	19	23
	TOTALS	13	20	33

Yule's Q = +.95 χ^2 = 15.8; p < .001

---

* Includes all congressmen whose electoral performance improved by more than 10 percentage points between 1970 and 1978 and all who ran for a higher office.
** Includes all congressmen whose electoral performance declined or improved by less than 10 percentage points between 1970 and 1978 (includes those defeated for re-election).

harder at enhancing their career opportunities and most of the time are successful at doing so. We can define 90% of them as "career-promoters," while only 17.4% of program types would earn this classification. The significance of this marked behavioral difference will be explored in the conclusion to this paper.

We move on to our last set of hypotheses. These postulated that status types would be more likely than program types to advertise themselves in materials presented to a mass public. We have found two ways of measuring this self-promotion. Both make use of the constituency newsletter, a common method by which congressmen communicate with their electorate. One measure focuses on "ego accomplishment" references. (How often does the congressman promote his achievements in his newsletter?) The second measure centers on ego-oriented language. (How often does the congressman use words that refer to himself in the newsletter?) We shall find that the two types do differ in the expected direction on both measures, but less clearly on the second one.

Table 5 shows how the ego accomplishment score relates to one's incentive.*

Table 5

The relationship between incentive
and reference to ego accomplishments

| | | Ego accomplishment score | | |
		High (> 2.84)	Low (< 2.84)	TOTALS
Incentive	Status	5	1	6
	Program	4	8	12
	TOTALS	9	9	18

Yule's Q = +.82 $\chi^2 = 4$; $p < .05$

The clear difference between status and program types holds. Five-sixths of status-motivated congressmen (83.3%) rate high on the ego accomplishment score. Only one-third (33.3%) of program-motivated congressmen do so. The median score for status types is 3.85; for program types it is 1.38. (Means are, respectively, 3.65 for status types and 2.45 for program types.) The very strong Yule's Q of +.82 again confirms the strong relationship between incentive and ego accomplishment score, and this relationship is unlikely to have occurred by chance, as our chi-square calculations show.

The data are not so supportive of a relationship between ego word score and incentives. The findings are presented in Table 6.

___

* Numbers are small in Tables 5 and 6 because we are dealing only with those members of the original sample who 1) were classified as either status or program types; 2) were reelected continuously from 1970 to 1978; and 3) supplied a constituency newsletter upon request in March, 1979.

219

Table 6

The relationship between incentive and ego words

| | | Ego word usage | | TOTALS |
		High ($>$15.83)	Low ($<$15.83)	
Incentive	Status	4	2	6
	Program	5	7	12
	TOTALS	9	9	18

Yule's Q = +.47 χ^2 = 1 (not significant)

Clearly, there is some tendency for status types to score higher on the ego word measure than program types. Two-thirds (66.7%) of the former score high in ego word usage, as opposed to five-twelths (41.7%) of the latter. Status types average 20.73 on the ego word score, while program types average 14.90. And the Yule's Q of +.47 confirms the moderate relationship we have been seeing in the data. However, the low chi-square of 1 suggests that there is a better than 3 in 10 chance that these results do not reflect the broader universe of all congressional members. We are therefore extremely hesitant to accept the hypothesis as it currently stands. While all other hypotheses have been strongly supported, we cannot, on the basis of this evidence, retain our belief that status types are more prone than program types to use ego words in their pub-licly-distributed materials.

An interesting side-issue is worth exploring before conclud-ing this section. Earlier, we used data on publicity and committee work to classify all congressmen in the two committees under in-vestigation. (Data shown in Appendix 1 of this paper.) We can also use these data to test another hypothesis—that publicity achieved by congressmen correlates negatively with the amount of committee work they do. This proposition follows logically from our previous theorizing. Those who achieve high levels of public-ity are likely to be status types; and status types are less likely than program types to work hard in committees. So we have a cor-relational hypothesis here. Publicity does not cause committee work, nor is the opposite true. Rather, amounts of work done in committee and levels of publicity attained are both caused by one's incentive.

To test for the expected negative correlation between public-ity and work, we divided congressmen into those "high" and "low" on both variables (high equals above average; low equals at or below average). We then constructed Table 7.

Table 7

The relationship between publicity and committee work

| | | Publicity | | TOTALS |
		High ($>$ 23.6)	Low ($<$ 23.6)	
Committee Work	High ($>$ 2591)	2	31	33
	Low ($<$ 2591)	10	28	38
	TOTALS	12	59	71

Yule's Q = $-.69$ $\chi^2 = 5.18$; p $<$ .05

Our data show moderately strong support for the hypothesis. Those who score high in publicity are indeed likely to score low on committee work; those who are less publicized apparently work harder in committee.

For instance, only one-sixth (16.7%) of the high publicity-attainers scored high on the index of committee work, while over half of the low publicity-attainers (52.5%) did so. Those congressmen who gained more than average amounts of publicity in 1972 averaged only 2,053 minutes of committee work in 1971-72, while those who gained less than average amounts of publicity averaged 2,709 minutes of committee work in the same period. The difference between these two groups becomes clearer when one compares medians. The median high-publicity congressmen spent 1,732 minutes on committee work in this two-year period, compared to 2,669 minutes put in by the median low-publicity congressman.

If we look at these figures another way, we see that those who work hard in committee do not get as much publicity as those who work less. The average hard-working congressman obtained 18.2 publicity mentions in 1972, compared to 28.0 mentions for the indifferently-working congressman. When we compare medians, however, this difference disappears, indeed reverses itself slightly. The hard-working congressman earned 7.6 mentions, compared to 5.6 for the congressman working less than average in committee.

Overall, the strong Yule's Q of $-.69$, and the chi-square finding that this difference was unlikely to have occurred by chance, offer good support of our basic hypothesis. A final indicator of the hypothesized negative relationship appears in Scattergram 1 on the next page. Although the relationship is not overwhelmingly clear, there is a definite tendency for the dots to be forming a line with a negative slope. On the whole, it would appear that publicity is indeed negatively correlated with work in committee. Put another way, the harder you work in committee, the less likely

221

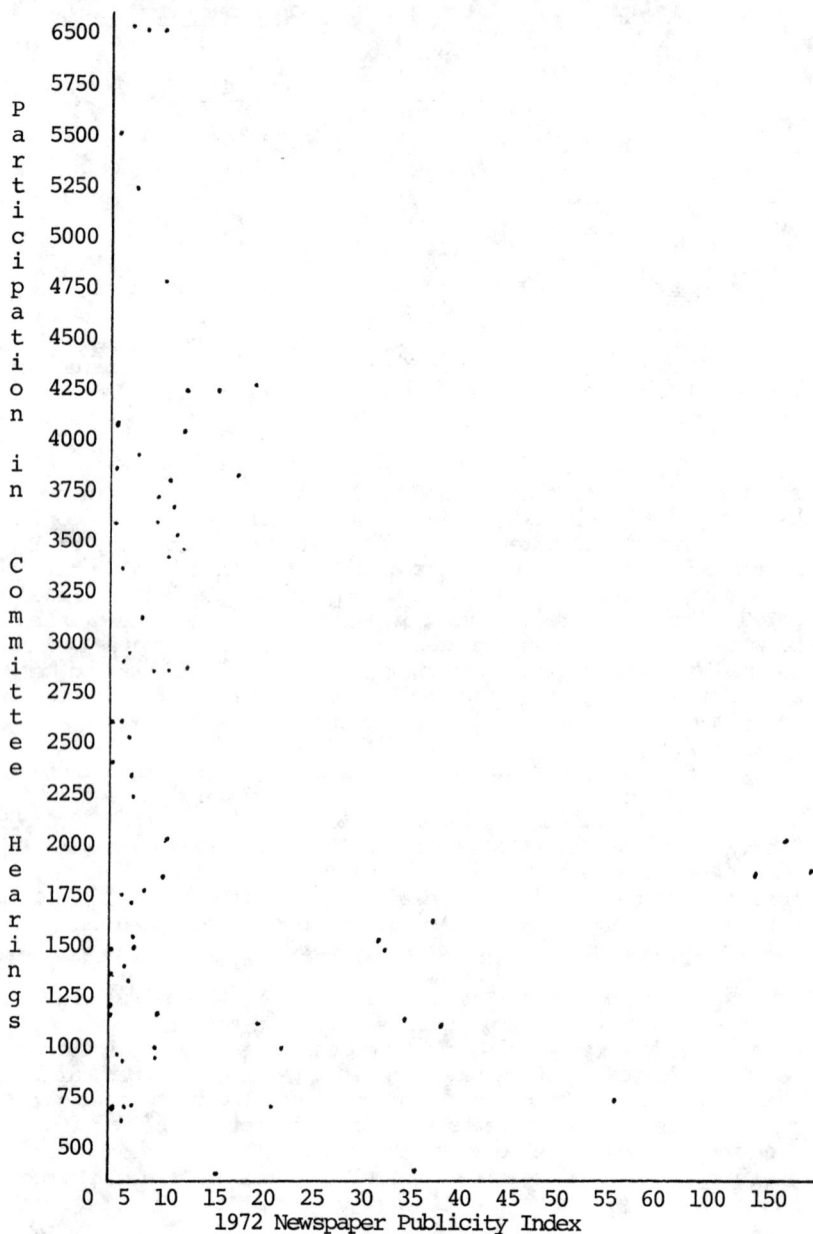

Scattergram 1
The relationship between publicity and committee work

222

it is that you will achieve any recognition as a congressman!

Section 5: Discussion

Some solid and fascinating findings have emerged from our study. First, it appears that the program-status classification itself makes sense. When we divide political participants on the basis of one or the other of these two incentives, we find that they behave in quite different ways from each other. This fact implies that the popularly-held belief that "politicians are all alike" would appear to have no basis in fact. There are actually several types of politician, with the program and status types representing perhaps the most dramatically different pairing.

It follows from this finding that we cannot understand how people will behave in politics until we know what incentive they hold. Therefore, it is important to study and discover incentives among political leaders, so that we can understand (and perhaps predict) their behavior. In short, the first major conclusion of our study is a corroboration of the importance of incentives for explaining politics and a plea for additional study of the subject.

Other key findings of this study focus on specific behavioral differences between the program and the status type. What distinguishes one type from the other? Our data show that status types will be "better" politicians than program types--in the sense of being better able to get elected and reelected to high office. They are also more ambitious than program types--as reflected in their willingness to run for higher office. This greater ambition of the status type compared to the program type is reflected in a statistic we failed to introduce earlier. Program types are much more likely to retire than are status types. During the 1970-79 period 8 program types, but no status types, retired from Congress. Age may have been a factor here, but it still seems dramatic that no status type was willing to withdraw from politics during a period which saw over one-quarter of program types doing so.

A major result of these differing behavior patterns is that status types must be increasing their numbers in Congress, to the detriment of program types--during the last decade at least. It turns out that 70% of the original group of status-oriented congressmen remained in the House 9 years after the 1970 election, when our study began. Only 38.7% of the original program-oriented congressmen remained there in 1979. If this finding has any generalizability, one would expect that the number of status types in Congress, compared to the number of program types, has grown dramatically over the past decade or so.

A final set of findings show another important difference between status and program types. These data help explain why status types are better campaigners than program types. They are advertisers, self-promoters. They are more apt than program types to make positive, shining reference to themselves in materials which they present to their electorate. People reading these handouts get a better image of the status type—who doesn't hesitate to show himself in the best possible light—than they do of the program type—who is perhaps more modest or simply less self-oriented. The hard-sell publicity techniques of the status type make him more than a match for the program type in the art of building a mass constituency.

The potential impact of these different behavior patterns is enormous. From all we have shown, it would appear that status types—more ambitious and more effective campaigners than program types in this day of public relations blitz—will be much more likely to get elected to high office than program types. Our national institutions—specifically Congress—may be undergoing major change. Status types are increasing; program types are decreasing. What does this change imply?

To answer that question, we need to know something about the two types. We already know that status types are not hard workers on nitty-gritty policy matters, and that they are ambitious and exceptionally adept at drawing attention to themselves. Program types, in contrast, work hard in committee and do little to make themselves known. With fewer program types and more status types in Congress, one would expect shallower, weaker laws—or else laws written by people other than the congressmen themselves—their staff, bureaucrats in the executive branch, interest group spokesmen. Many observers believe that developments such as these have already taken place.[3]

One needs to know something else about these two types to grasp the possible type of change the replacement of one by the other might bring about at the national level. We have already shown the startling finding that the more work you do, the less publicity you get. Status types know this very well. They want publicity for themselves, but they know it cannot be derived from compiling a record as a conscientious, hard-working congressman. No, publicity in our age of the electronic media goes to the unusual, the dramatic, the colorful. Congressmen who make outrageously exaggerated accusations, uncover juicy scandals, or make doom-and-gloom forecasts in influential settings (Meet the Press, a Harvard University graduation) will get the headlines or make the CBS evening news. As status-motivated political leaders try to outdo each other in the search for publicity, their negative messages become the primary image filtering through to the mass public. The efforts of any hard-working committee-attender are unreported by the media and unknown by the electorate. Voters become alienated from the political system, surfeited by a deluge of negative and cynical comments about it by that element of the country's political leadership (mostly status types) whose voices and images are picked up by the national media.

It seems entirely possible that the American public's increasing distrust of government springs, in part at least, from the growth of status types at our upper political leadership levels. Where will this trend ultimately take us? One can only conjecture. A change in circumstances could lead to a resurgence of program types, whose hard work and quiet ways do not engender the conflict and alienation brought by the status types. On the other hand, the American people might become so disillusioned with "politics as usual" that they will take some drastic action--perhaps turn to a demagogue who promises to "clean up the mess in Washington." The elections of both Jimmy Carter and Ronald Reagan might both be seen as attempts to move in this direction. One thing seems certain. If status types remain at high levels in our political system, the level of citizen discontent with that system is also likely to remain high for the foreseeable future.

Footnotes to student paper

1. One of the earliest of such studies was Harold D. Lasswell, Psychopathology and Politics (Chicago: University of Chicago Press, 1930). For more recent works which take the same approach, see James D. Barber, The Lawmakers: Recruitment and Adaptation to Legislative Life (New Haven: Yale University Press, 1965); Barber, The Presidential Character: Predicting Performance in the White House (Englewood Cliffs, N.J.: Prentice-Hall, Inc., 1972); and Michael Maccoby, The Gamesman: The New Corporate Leaders (New York: Simon and Schuster, 1976).

2. The major studies of incentives include: James L. Payne, Patterns of Conflict in Colombia (New Haven: Yale University Press, 1968); Payne, Incentive Theory and Political Process: Motivation and Leadership in the Dominican Republic (Lexington, Mass.: D.C. Heath and Company, Lexington Books, 1972); Oliver H. Woshinsky, The French Deputy: Incentives and Behavior in the National Assembly (Lexington, Mass.: D.C. Heath and Company, Lexington Books, 1973); Payne and Woshinsky, "Incentives for Political Participation," World Politics 24 (July, 1972), pp. 518-46; Payne, "Show Horses and Work Horses in the U.S. House of Representatives," Polity 12 (Spring, 1980), 428-56; and Payne, "The Personal Electoral Advantage of House Incumbents, 1936-76," American Politics Quarterly 8 (October, 1980), pp. 465-82. See also Payne, Woshinsky, Eric. P. Veblen, William H. Coogan and Gene E. Bigler, The Motivation of Politicians (Chicago: Nelson-Hall, Inc., forthcoming).

3. For an excellent elucidation of this point of view, see Morris P. Fiorina, Congress: Keystone of the Washington Establishment (New Haven: Yale University Press, 1977).

Appendix 1 (to student paper on congressmen)

Participation and Publicity Rates for Selected U.S. Congressmen*

Congressman	Participation in hearings of congressman's major committee (in minutes), 1971-72	1972 newspaper publicity index	Incentive assigned congressman on basis of these data
Abzug	2,003	206.6	Status
Cotter	660	56.3	Status
Crane	1,409	31.5	Status
Edmondson	1,498	31.7	Status
Koch	1,605	50.8	Status
Lent	1,035	39.6	Status
Mitchell	1,085	34.5	Status
Moorhead	1,860	105.6	Status
Rangel	130	35.4	Status
Reuss	1,920	304.7	Status
Ashley	3,800	10.5	Program
Baker	2,925	3.7	Program
Barrett	5,801	10.1	Program
Blackburn	3,698	8.8	Program
Blatnik	4,788	9.9	Program
Brown	5,483	1.0	Program
Clausen	5,206	5.5	Program
Cleveland	3,606	6.3	Program
Dorn	6,275	4.7	Program
Gettys	2,655	2.0	Program
Gonzalez	3,109	7.1	Program

* The congressmen for whom data was gathered in this table were all members of either the Committee on Banking and Currency or the Committee on Public Works of the U.S. House of Representatives during the 1971-72 session of Congress.

227

Appendix 1 to student paper (p. 2)

Congressman	Participation in hearings of congressman's major committee (in minutes), 1971-72	1972 newspaper publicity index	Incentive assigned congressman on basis of these data
Gray	3,856	21.3	Program
Hammerschmidt	3,953	1.0	Program
Harsha	5,907	7.0	Program
Heckler	2,819	12.1	Program
Howard	3,400	8.8	Program
Jones	3,566	8.3	Program
Kee	4,089	10.3	Program
Kluczynski	2,896	3.8	Program
Miller	3,611	0.0	Program
Mizell	3,402	3.3	Program
Roberts	2,669	0.0	Program
Roe	4,127	0.8	Program
Rousselot	2,810	7.6	Program
St. Germain	3,002	8.6	Program
Schwengel	7,314	5.2	Program
Stephens	3,433	10.5	Program
Terry	3,881	0.0	Program
Widnall	2,795	10.6	Program
Williams	4,224	10.7	Program
Wright	4,231	16.6	Program
Anderson	1,356	4.1	No incentive assigned
Annunzio	662	21.5	No incentive assigned
Archer	1,751	3.0	No incentive assigned
Brasco	557	2.5	No incentive assigned
Caffery	1,585	4.1	No incentive assigned
Chappell	1,122	8.1	No incentive assigned
Clark	660	0.6	No incentive assigned

228

Appendix 1 to student paper (p. 3)

Congressman	Participation in hearings of congressman's major committee (in minutes), 1971-72	1972 newspaper publicity index	Incentive assigned congressman on basis of these data
Dwyer	860	4.5	No incentive assigned
Frenzel	1,784	6.1	No incentive assigned
Griffin	957	21.5	No incentive assigned
Grover	1,493	0.0	No incentive assigned
Hanley	940	7.6	No incentive assigned
Hanna	1,388	3.8	No incentive assigned
Henderson	655	4.2	No incentive assigned
Johnson, A.	2,418	0.0	No incentive assigned
Johnson, H.	2,233	3.0	No incentive assigned
McCormack	932	3.0	No incentive assigned
McDonald	125	14.9	No incentive assigned
McKinney	1,828	7.6	No incentive assigned
Minish	1,394	0.0	No incentive assigned
Patman	7,174	371.1	No incentive assigned
Rees	1,065	22.8	No incentive assigned
Roncalio	1,475	5.0	No incentive assigned
Snyder	1,719	4.0	No incentive assigned
Stanton, J. V.	647	3.6	No incentive assigned
Stanton, J. W.	2,506	3.0	No incentive assigned
Sullivan	4,262	24.3	No incentive assigned
Thone	1,213	0.0	No incentive assigned
Wylie	1,164	0.0	No incentive assigned
Zion	2,030	10.4	No incentive assigned

Appendix 2 (to student paper on congressmen)

Ego Scores and Political Career Data for Selected U.S. Congressmen*

Congressman	Incentive	Ego word score	Ego accomplish-ment score	Change in political career, 1970-79
Abzug	Status	——	——	Ran for higher office
Cotter	Status	14.18	0.75	Remained in House; increase in % of votes received: + 11.6 % pts.
Crane	Status	14.29	4.76	Remained in House; increase in % of votes received: +21.5 % pts.
Edmondson	Status	——	——	Ran for higher office
Koch	Status	——	——	Ran for higher office
Lent	Status	23.77	3.14	Remained in House; increase in % of votes received: + 16.0 % pts.
Mitchell	Status	——	——	Remained in House; increase in % of votes received: + 41.3 % pts.
Moorhead	Status	25.16	4.40	Remained in House; increase in % of votes received: − 19.0 % pts.
Rangel	Status	17.36	3.30	Remained in House; increase in % of votes received: + 10.4 % pts.
Reuss	Status	29.63	5.56	Remained in House; increase in % of votes received: + 24.1 % pts.
Ashley	Program	8.31	1.33	Remained in House; increase in % of votes received: − 3.0 % pts.
Baker	Program	——	——	Defeated (1974)
Barrett	Program	——	——	Died
Blackburn	Program	——	——	Defeated (1974)

* Congressmen in this table include all those who were given an incentive assignment based on data in the previous table (Appendix 1 to student paper).

230

Congressman	Incentive	Appendix 2 to student paper (p. 2) Ego word score	Ego accomplishment score	Change in political career, 1970–79
Blatnik	Program	—	—	Retired
Brown	Program	—	—	Defeated (1978)
Clausen	Program	11.97	8.88	Remained in House; increase in % of votes received: − 10.4 % pts.
Cleveland	Program	20.40	0.68	Remained in House; increase in % of votes received: − 1.5 % pts.
Dorn	Program	—	—	Ran for higher office
Gettys	Program	—	—	Retired
Gonzalez	Program	13.11	0.72	Remained in House; increase in % of votes received: 0.0 % pts.
Gray	Program	—	—	Retired
Hammerschmidt	Program	8.20	0.63	Remained in House; increase in % of votes received: + 11.8 % pts.
Harsha	Program	—	—	Remained in House; increase in % of votes received: − 2.9 % pts.
Heckler	Program	13.48	3.37	Remained in House; increase in % of votes received: + 3.7 % pts.
Howard	Program	21.95	5.57	Remained in House; increase in % of votes received: + 1.2 % pts.
Jones	Program	—	—	Retired
Kee	Program	—	—	Defeated (1972)
Kluczynski	Program	—	—	Died (1975)
Miller	Program	12.20	0.00	Remained in House; increase in % of votes received: + 7.4 % pts.
Mizell	Program	—	—	Defeated (1974)
Roberts	Program	32.14	2.38	Remained in House; increase in % of votes received: − 37.5 % pts.
Roe	Program	—	—	Remained in House; increase in % of votes received: + 13.5 % pts.

Appendix 2 to student paper (p. 3)

Congressman	Incentive	Ego word score	Ego accomplishment score	Change in political career, 1970-79
Rousselot	Program	8.54	1.42	Remained in House; increase in % of votes received: + 34.9 % pts.
St. Germain	Program	21.31	4.37	Remained in House; increase in % of votes received: + 2.2 % pts.
Schwengel	Program	---	---	Defeated (1972)
Stephens	Program	---	---	Retired
Terry	Program	---	---	Retired
Widnall	Program	---	---	Defeated (1974)
Williams	Program	---	---	Defeated (1974)
Wright	Program	19.23	0.00	Remained in House; increase in % of votes received: - 31.2 % pts.

Note: No newsletter could be obtained (and therefore no Ego word score nor Ego accomplishment score) for three congressmen who remained in the House in 1979: Mitchell, Harsha, and Roe.

232